RESISTING MEDICAL TYRANNY

RESISTING MEDICAL TYRANNY

WHY THE COVID-19 MANDATES ARE CRIMINAL

Professor Francis A. Boyle

Waterside Productions

Printed in the United States of America

First Printing, 2022

ISBN-13: 978-1-957807-44-7 (hardcover edition)
ISBN-13: 978-1-957807-12-6 (paperback edition)
ISBN-13: 978-1-957807-13-3 (ebook edition)

Waterside Productions

2055 Oxford Avenue
Cardiff-by-the-Sea, CA 92007
www.waterside.com

Professor Francis A. Boyle is the author of the United States implementing legislation for the 1972 Biological Weapons Convention known as the Biological Weapons Anti-Terrorism Act of 1989 that was approved unanimously by both Houses of the United States Congress and signed into law by President George H. W. Bush with the approval of the U.S. Department of Justice.

IN MEMORY OF RICHARD C. LEWONTIN: TEACHER, MENTOR, FRIEND R.I.P.

July 8, 2021

I write with a most heavy heart and a great deal of personal sadness about the death of my longtime teacher, mentor, and friend Richard (Dick) C. Lewontin, the Alexander Agassiz Research Professor of Biology and Zoology at Harvard. I started studying Population Biology with Dick at the University of Chicago on Monday, January 5, 1970, because of his well-known and strident opposition to the Vietnam War, which I had already opposed as a teenager. I figured that Dick would have something to teach me. He certainly did—for the rest of my life. Dick's courage, integrity, and principles have always inspired and guided me from the very beginning of my career in higher education. I shall always regret, with fondness, that I could not continue working with him.

The last time I spoke with Dick was to wish him a happy 85th birthday. He was still working away in his lab at the Museum of Comparative Zoology. The picture in today's *New York Times* is exactly the way Dick looked when he started teaching me at the age of 19. It brings back so many fine and fond memories of his life and his career, so well spent in making the world a better place. Humanity and science have been impoverished by Dick's death. I also note with sadness the recent passing of his beautiful wife and the love of his life, Mary Jane.

R.I.P.s.

Francis A. Boyle (FAB)
Professor of Law

PEDDLING

Pandemic
Pool closed
Too dangerous

Bike riding
Son's old mountain bike
'Round the hood
35 minutes
Exercise
Daily

After work
Teaching, researching, writing, interviewing
Remote from home

Fresh air
Sunshine
Trees
Grass
Flowers
Gardens
Streams
Lakes

Birds chirping
Crows cawing
Geese honking
And waddling
Dogs barking

Cats

Squirrels

Rabbits

Snakes

Otters

Hawks

Cranes

Possums

Foxes

Eagles

Fishing Ponds

With three sons

Memories fond

Lived here since 7/15/88

Idyllic

Peace

Tranquility

Happiness

Smiles

Great way

To end day

After sturm und drang

Fighting COVID

And its Frankenshots

All day long

Since 1/24/20

'Til when?

Can't say

But I'll be Peddling

Every day

'Til the end

COVID or me

— FAB

CONTENTS

Introduction: U.S. Biowarfare Programs Have 13,000 Death Scientists Hard at Work xiii

Chapter 1: COVID-19 Is an Offensive Biological Warfare Weapon That Leaked Out of the Wuhan BSL-4 in China 1
Chapter 2: My Smoking-Gun Interview 20
Chapter 3: Bioweapons Expert Speaks Out about Novel Coronavirus. . . . 39
Chapter 4: The Israeli Human-Rights Lawsuit against China for the COVID-19 Pandemic. 50
Chapter 5: The Indian Lecture (June 26, 2020). 60
Chapter 6: Recognizing and Pushing Back in the Post-9/11 Police State. 68
Chapter 7: My Advice to African Americans (December 22, 2020) 75
Chapter 8: My Nuremberg Code on Medical Experimentation *Notice!* against the Nazi COVID-19 Frankenshots 89
Chapter 9: The Worldwide Associated Press Hit/Smear Job against Me over COVID-19 103
Chapter 10: The Nazi COVID-19 Frankenshots (May 12, 2021) 106
Chapter 11: My Advice to the People of the Caribbean on Dealing with the COVID-19 Pandemic (June 27, 2021). 119
Chapter 12: Indicting Those Responsible for the COVID-19 Pandemic and the Nazi Frankenshots (August 20, 2021) 135
Chapter 13: Prosecuting Fauci, Slaoui et al., for the COVID-19 Pandemic and Frankenshots 158
Chapter 14: My Advice to the British People (September 16, 2021) 167
Chapter 15: My Advice to the Israeli People (October 15, 2021). 180
Chapter 16: Professor Boyle Says the U.S. Government Is Up to Their Eyeballs in COVID-19 Crimes (October 21, 2021) 191

Chapter 17: Criminal Sabotage by the U.S. Spooks Establishment and the U.S. Scientific/Medical Establishments over the COVID-19 Pandemic. 224
Chapter 18: The Frankenshot: Using the Law to Chase Those Responsible for Harming the American People: A Special Interview with Francis A. Boyle (November 28, 2021). 238

Conclusion 269
Acknowledgment 273
About the Author 275

[**Author's note:** All material in this book—including Q&As, transcripts, emails, and reprinted articles—have been edited for spelling/grammar/punctuation/clarity.]

INTRODUCTION

U.S. BIOWARFARE PROGRAMS HAVE 13,000 DEATH SCIENTISTS HARD AT WORK

(This essay was written by Sherwood Ross, who formerly reported for the *Chicago Daily News* and was a columnist for UPI [*Magazines In Review*] and Reuters [*Workplace*]). He gave me—FAB—permission to reprint it so long as I credited him for it, which I have done. I personally drafted the answers to his questions.)

America's $100 Billion Germ Warfare Industry a "Criminal Enterprise," Author of U.S. Biowarfare Act Says

by Sherwood Ross

The American legal authority who in 1989 drafted the law Congress enacted to comply with the 1972 Biological Weapons Convention says the U.S. today [October 11, 2015] is in flagrant violation of that Convention.

"Since Sept. 11, 2001, we have spent somewhere in the area of $100 billion" on offensive biological warfare, charges Professor Francis Boyle of the University of Illinois [at Urbana-Champaign].

Boyle said an estimated 13,000 "death scientists" in 400 laboratories in the U.S. and abroad are employed making new strains of offensive killer germs that will be resistant to vaccines.

For example, Dr. Yoshihiro Kawaoka's group at the University of Wisconsin has found a way to increase the toxicity of the flu virus by 200 times! Boyle says Kawaoka is "the same death scientist who resurrected the genocidal Spanish flu virus for the Pentagon for offensive biowarfare purposes."

As for fighting flu, the National Institutes of Health [NIH] in 2006, a typical year, got only $120 million from Congress to fight flu, which kills an estimated 36,000 Americans annually. By contrast, Congress gave the NIH $1.76 billion for "biodefense," even though the anthrax outbreak in 2001 killed just five persons.

"These distorted budgetary allocations" (spending 15 times as much for germ warfare as for fighting flu) demonstrate that the priority here is not the promotion of the public health of American citizens but rather to further develop the U.S. Offensive Biowarfare Industry that will someday 'blow back' upon the American people with a catastrophic pandemic," Boyle said.

He went on to say that the Pentagon and CIA are "ready, willing, and able to launch biowarfare when it suits their interests... They have a super-weapons-grade anthrax that they already used against us in October 2001."

Boyle here was referring to the anthrax pathogens mailed to two U.S. senators (Tom Daschle of South Dakota, and Patrick Leahy of Vermont) and others after 9/11 that were traced back to the government's biowarfare lab at Fort Detrick, Maryland.

Boyle's remarks came in response to written questions from Sherwood Ross, a Miami, Florida–based columnist. Asked if the recent outbreaks of Ebola in Sierra Leone and Liberia could be from U.S. government–backed facilities, Boyle replied, "These Ebola vaccines were experimental U.S. bio-warfare vaccines that were being tested out in West Africa. It was a result of testing out of the U.S. biowarfare vaccines at our lab in Kenema, Sierra Leone, that created the West African Ebola pandemic in the first place."

Boyle warned that the Galveston National Laboratory in Texas, a high-containment research lab, has been seeking potential biowarfare agents in the wild in other parts of the world "in order to turn them into biological weapons."

He said, "They should shut down Galveston as an ongoing criminal enterprise along the lines of the SS and the Gestapo—except that Galveston is far more dangerous to humanity than Hitler's death squads ever were."

Boyle added, "American universities have a long history of willingly permitting their research agenda, researchers, institutes, and laboratories to be co-opted, corrupted, and perverted by the Pentagon and the CIA into death science. These include Wisconsin, North Carolina, Boston U, Harvard, MIT, Tulane, the University of Chicago, and my own University of Illinois, as well as many others."

BOYLE CHARGES U.S. GERM WARFARE PROGRAM IS "CRIMINAL ENTERPRISE"

Q&A with Francis A. Boyle on Biowarfare

Francis A. Boyle is a leading American professor, practitioner, and advocate of international law. He was responsible for drafting the Biological Weapons Anti-Terrorism Act of 1989 (BWATA), the American implementing legislation for the 1972 Biological Weapons Convention. His BWATA was passed unanimously by both Houses of the United States Congress and signed into law by President George Bush Sr.. The story is told in his book *Biowarfare and Terrorism* [Clarity Press: 2005]. He served on the Board of Directors of Amnesty International USA (1988–1992) and represented Bosnia-Herzegovina at the World Court. Professor Boyle teaches international law at the University of Illinois College of Law at Urbana-Champaign. He holds a doctor of law, magna cum laude, as well as a PhD in political science—both from Harvard University.

Q: To get some idea of the magnitude of U.S. biological warfare research involving deadly diseases now going forward, the federal government is said to be funding 400 laboratories globally. These labs purportedly are concocting new strains of lethal microbes for which there is no cure. Right off the bat, I'd like to ask you: "Is this a criminal enterprise whose dimensions are being concealed from the American public?"

A: Of course it is! Since September 11, 2001, we have spent somewhere in the area approaching $100 billion on biological warfare. Effectively, we now have an Offensive Biological Warfare Industry in this country that violates the Biological Weapons Convention and my Biological Weapons Anti-Terrorism Act of 1989. We have reconstructed the Offensive Biological Warfare Industry that we had deployed in this country before its prohibition by the Biological Weapons Convention of 1972 that was described by Sy Hersh in his groundbreaking exposé in his book *Chemical & Biological Warfare: America's Hidden Arsenal* [Bobbs-Merrill: 1968].

Our putative adversaries around the world, such as Russia and China, have undoubtedly reached the same conclusions I have derived from the same open and public sources, and have responded in kind. So what the world now witnesses is an all-out offensive biological warfare arms race among the major military powers of the world: the United States, Russia, Britain, France, China, Israel, inter alia. The Biological Weapons Convention has become the proverbial "mere scrap of paper," but my BWATA still remains the law of the land in the United States with a penalty of life in prison for violators. That is why the self-styled "synthetic biologists" proposed to repeal my BWATA so that they can use synthetic biology to manufacture new classes of biological weapons more efficiently.

Q: Exactly what is biowarfare?

A: Biological warfare involves the use of living organisms for military purposes. Such weapons can be viral, bacterial, and fungal, among other forms; and can be spread over a large geographic terrain by wind, water, insects, animals, or human transmission. Toxins—living organisms such as fungi—are also used.

Q: Which are the most dangerous?

A: Today, several U.S. government [USG] labs are at work on anthrax, tularemia, plague, Ebola, botulism, and the genocidal Spanish flu virus.

Q: What do they do with these pathogens?

A: Using DNA genetic engineering, U.S. death scientists are concocting new strains of lethal microbes for which there are no cures. Bacteria, for example, can be made resistant to vaccines, made more virulent, made easier to spread, and made harder to eradicate. Right now, U.S. death scientists are scouring the biosphere around the world to locate any bioagent in nature that they can exploit and pervert into offensive biowarfare purposes.

Q: *USA Today* has done some fine reporting on this subject. Among other things, their reporters have exposed massive incidents of lax security conditions at USG labs and university labs funded by the USG. What might the consequences be of this disregard for safety?

A: This is a bio-catastrophe waiting to happen here in the United States. In fact, it has already happened in West Africa with the Ebola pandemic there. It is only a matter of time before we have a similar pandemic at home caused by U.S. biowarfare programs. In this regard, you should watch the excellent award-winning documentary by Coen and Nadler titled *Anthrax-War* [Transformer Films: 2009] in which I appear and served as a consultant on.

Q: Recently, 13 cases of plague were reported in Arizona, California, Colorado, Georgia, New Mexico, Oregon, and Utah, resulting in three deaths. Could these deadly plague pathogens (infectious agents) have come from the USG's germ-warfare labs?

A: I suspect they might have. But proving it is another matter. Anytime you see some mysterious and widespread outbreak of an exotic disease around the country, you have to factor in to the analytical explanatory equation that it could be the result of some illegal U.S. biowarfare program.

Q: Is it a fact, as alleged, that the anthrax pathogens mailed to two U.S. senators and others after 9/11 trace back to the USG biowarfare lab at Fort Detrick, Maryland? You have written that Senators Daschle and Leahy, both Democrats, had opposed the Patriot Act, which gives the USG unprecedented powers and abolishes Americans' traditional personal liberties. If the anthrax was sent by the Pentagon, was it to intimidate the senators?

A: Yes! I have written about this in my book *Biowarfare and Terrorism* [Clarity Press: 2005]. More recently, my friend and colleague Professor Graeme MacQueen from McMaster University in Canada has also written about this in his book *The 2001 Anthrax Deception* [Clarity Press: 2014]. You are free to read these two books, draw your own conclusions, and see if you agree with us. Over the years, there are numerous interviews I have given on this matter that you can obtain by Googling my name and adding the word *anthrax* in the search engine. The twin purposes of these October 2001 anthrax attacks were (1) to scaremonger the American people and Congress into adopting the totalitarian and Orwellian USA Patriot Act, and (2) to wage an offensive war of aggression against Iraq. As President George Bush Jr. proudly boasted, "Mission accomplished!"—on both counts.

Q: Recently, there have been outbreaks of Ebola in Sierra Leone and Liberia. You have raised the possibility that the USG may be illegally experimenting with these diseases on citizens of those African nations. Could you please elaborate?

A: These Ebola vaccines were experimental U.S. biowarfare vaccines that were being tested out in West Africa. It was a result of testing out of the U.S. biowarfare vaccines at our lab in Kenema, Sierra Leone, that created the West African Ebola pandemic in the first place. I have given numerous interviews to support my conclusions here in more detail. These can be located by Googling my name and adding the word *Ebola* in the search engine.

Q: Is such germ-warfare development work illegal under the BWC Treaty of 1972? (Dr. Boyle was the American attorney who wrote the implementing legislation for the U.S. that passed Congress without a single negative vote.)

A: Yes. The U.S. is a party to the 1972 Biological and Toxic Weapons Convention, which bans the "development, production, stockpiling, and use of microbes or their poisonous products except in amounts necessary for protective and peaceful research…" Colonel David Huxsoll, commander of the Army's Medical Institute of Infectious Diseases, has admitted that offensive research is indistinguishable from defensive research.

Q: Although Russia said it scrapped its germ-warfare program after the Communists lost power in 1991, the U.S. budget for this purpose has increased. Are there any countries or terrorist groups that might realistically attack the U.S. with such weapons? One critic has said that USG's biowarfare push resembles "a dog chasing its own tail."

A: The truth of the matter is that the United States government has been pursuing the development of an Offensive Biowarfare Program and Industry since the Reagan administration and his neoconservatives came to power in 1981. I set forth this earlier biowarfare documentation on Reagan and his neocons in my previous book, *The Future of International Law and American Foreign Policy* [Transnational Publishers Inc.: 1989, chapter 8, "The Legal Distortions Behind the Reagan Administration's Chemical and Biological Warfare Buildup"]. Interestingly enough, the Department of Defense itself reprinted my study as *Current News: Special Edition: CHEMICAL WEAPONS, NO. 1586 (28 May 1987)* and distributed it to thousands of high-level Department of Defense civilian and military officials all over the world.

Q: It sounds fantastic, I know, but scientists once paid by the USG to cure cancer are now being paid to develop deadlier strains of anthrax, dengue, Japanese encephalitis, tularemia, Q fever, and other dread diseases. Comment?

A: On the relationship between cancer research and bioweapons, you should have a look at the book by Dr. Len Horowitz, *Emerging Viruses: AIDS and Ebola – Nature, Accident, or Intentional?* [Tetrahedron Inc. 1996].

Q: You have written that Dr. Yoshihiro Kawaoka's group at the University of Wisconsin [UW] has found a way to increase the toxicity of the flu virus by 200 times. What is the purpose of this horrible-sounding research, and why should UW support it?

A: This is the same U.S. death scientist who resurrected the genocidal Spanish flu virus for the Pentagon for offensive biowarfare purposes. Like all U.S. universities, Bucky Badger U. gets a cut of all research funds brought in from the outside. Here at Chief Illiniwak University, they publicly admitted that they take 51 cents out of every research $1 Buck brought in from the outside and charge it off to "overhead." At most American universities today, money talks and principles walk. My dis-alma mater Harvard is no better, no worse, and no different.

Q: During the 1980–1988 Iraq–Iran war, the Reagan White House okayed the Pentagon's sale of weapons-specific biological agents and poison gas to

Iraq that Saddam Hussein used against Iran and his own Kurdish minority. At least 5,000 Kurds were gassed. And, according to the *Time* magazine of January 20, 2014, the CIA reckoned Iran suffered 50,000 deaths. Doesn't this prove that the White House has used biological agents offensively?

A: Certainly, chemical weapons were used illegally. In addition, the Reagan administration shipped weapons-specific biowarfare agents to Saddam Hussein in Iraq in the hope and expectation that he would weaponize them and use them against Iran. He *did* weaponize them. So far, I have not seen evidence that he used bioweapons against Iran or the Kurds. But these biowarfare weapons that Saddam Hussein produced, thanks to Reagan and his neocons, did "blow back" upon U.S. armed forces when they invaded Iraq in 1991. This "blowback" played a causative role in the Gulf War Syndrome that afflicted U.S. soldiers who participated in Gulf War I under President Bush Sr. I discuss this in my book *Destroying World Order* [Clarity Press: 2004] and in the British TV documentary *The Dirty War* (1993), produced by and shown on Britain's Independent Television Network TV4 that I consulted on and appeared in.

Q: You have pointed out that the Galveston National Laboratory in Texas, a high-containment research lab, admits to seeking potential biowarfare agents in the wild in other parts of the world "in order to turn them into biological weapons."

A: Right! They should shut down Galveston as an ongoing criminal enterprise along the lines of the SS and the Gestapo—except that Galveston is far more dangerous to humanity than Hitler's death squads ever were. They say that their work with Ebola is for a vaccine, but the same technology can also be weaponized. Galveston is working to aerosolize Ebola, just as Fort Detrick worked to aerosolize anthrax. Aerosolization of a biowarfare agent is always the tip-off to the development of a weapon to be delivered by air to human beings who will breathe it in. Fort Detrick should be shut down as well, because it, too, is an ongoing criminal enterprise.

Q: Besides Fort Detrick and Galveston, are there any other biowarfare laboratories you believe should be closed?

A: All of them. Since 1981, the Pentagon has been gearing up to fight and "win" biological warfare without prior public knowledge and review. What's more, American universities have a long history of willingly permitting their research agenda, researchers, institutes, and laboratories to be co-opted, corrupted, and perverted by the Pentagon and the CIA into death science. These include Wisconsin, North Carolina, Boston U, Harvard, MIT, Tulane, the University of Chicago, and my own University of Illinois, as well as many others.

Q: Biological warfare development requires highly sophisticated technology and safe laboratories. No so-called terrorist group is known to possess anything like the requisite facilities. Besides America, what countries have operative biowarfare labs?

A: The U.S., U.K., Russia, France, China, and Israel, for sure. There are several other countries that the U.S. has established satellite biowarfare labs in.

Q: Is there any published data on the USG's expenditures for biowarfare since 9/11? I assume it has taken off like other Pentagon outlays.

A: Yes, there are published figures on this in the open record. The last time I did a calculation from them, the sum was approaching $100 billion. By comparison, in 2012 dollars we spent $30 billion on the Manhattan Project to develop the atom bombs that were then used to destroy Hiroshima and Nagasaki. You can see my book *The Criminality of Nuclear Deterrence* [Clarity Press: 2002, chapter 2, "The Lessons of Hiroshima and Nagasaki"]. So that historical precedent and analogy is a pretty good indication that the U.S. Offensive Biowarfare Industry is intended for use on human beings somewhere. The momentum behind the money propels inexorably toward use of the weapons.

Q: Does the recent Pentagon mail-out of live anthrax virus to 86 laboratories here and to seven nations abroad, bear out your prior criticism of the USG's careless handling of these pathogens?

A: Of course. But I don't believe there was anything "careless" or "accidental" about any of this. The Pentagon knows exactly what they are doing. They are not "incompetent" at the Pentagon. This was deliberate. Just like the anthrax attacks of October 2001 were deliberate.

Q: You contend that the American pharmaceutical industry and the World Health Organization [WHO] are dumping dangerous vaccines in West Africa, where the public is already suffering from Ebola. Why would WHO get involved in this? Can you elaborate?

A: First, to make money. WHO is a front organization for Big Pharma. Second, to reduce the numbers of Black West Africans—genocide.

Q: It's been estimated that 36,000 Americans are dying every year from flu. By contrast, only five Americans died from an anthrax attack, and that was back in 2001. Yet, the National Institutes of Health [NIH] in 2006, a typical fiscal year, received only $120 million from Congress to fight flu but $1.76 billion for "biodefense"?

A: Right! These distorted budgetary allocations demonstrate that the priority here is not the promotion of the public health of American citizens but rather to further develop the U.S. Offensive Biowarfare Industry that will someday "blow back" upon the American people with a catastrophic pandemic.

Q: Scientists who oppose the Pentagon's activity insist that germ-warfare defense is clearly impractical—that every person would have to be vaccinated against every harmful biological agent. Since that is clearly impossible, isn't the only application of a defensive development in conjunction with offensive use?

A: We are currently stockpiling vaccines to immunize our civilian and military leadership elites if and when they decide to wage offensive biowarfare. Per the Constitution, "We the People of the United States" will have to fend for ourselves as best we can with our grossly underfunded and inadequate public health services that have been deliberately starved of money in order to feed the U.S. Offensive Biowarfare Industry Beast.

Q: Recently, Defense Secretary Ashton Carter told a St. Louis audience of government employees, "You're some of the nation's most innovative and inventive physicists, chemists, and geneticists ... molecular biologists," etc. Yes, indeed. How many employees does the Pentagon now have in germ warfare work, and how much is it costing the American people?

A: Overall, I have read a figure that there are about 13,000 death scientists in America today doing dirty biowarfare work who perversely call themselves "life scientists." Dr. Mengele would be proud of them all! As Dr. Strangelove said: "Mein Führer, I can walk!" Seventy years after World War II ended, the Nazis have won.

Q: Given all of the above, does it appear conceivable to you that the Pentagon is developing a massive germ-warfare weapon as a means of intimidating the world? After all, it has positioned itself in about 900 bases around the globe from which it can, and does, strike using conventional weapons, and it has used illegal radioactive ammunition in its war against Iraq.

A: Of course. But not just intimidation. The Pentagon and the CIA are ready, willing, and able to launch biowarfare when it suits their interests. They already attacked the American people and Congress and disabled our republic with super-weapons-grade anthrax in October 2001. A fortiori, they will do so again to foreign states and peoples when deemed convenient. Us too! They have a stockpile of that super-weapons-grade anthrax that they already used against us in October 2001.

Q: Thank you, Professor Francis Boyle.

A: Thanks so much for doing this interview.

Postscript

As you, the reader, can see from the above interview with my friend Sherwood Ross, I predicted in 2015 that there would be a catastrophic biological warfare "blowback" pandemic against the American people as a result of the Offensive U.S. Biological Warfare Industry. Indeed, as far back as the Coen and Nadler award-winning documentary *Anthrax War* (2009) exposing the existential dangers of BSL-4 and BSL-3 biological warfare labs and programs, I predicted: "This is a catastrophe waiting to happen!" It has now happened with the worldwide COVID-19 pandemic that already has and will continue to kill millions of people around the globe and disable tens of millions more.

I have done my best to prevent this universal bio-catastrophe going all the way back to the U.S. congressional briefing I conducted on Capitol Hill in Washington, D.C., at the request and under the sponsorship of the then-Committee—later Council—for Responsible Genetics (CRG) on September 13, 1985.[1] There, I publicly denounced the existential dangers created by the abuse of DNA genetic engineering by the neoconservative Reagan administration to research, develop, test, and manufacture biological-warfare weapons. In order to stop this Nazi Death Science, there I publicly called for U.S. domestic implementing legislation for the Biological Weapons Convention (BWC) and also, in particular, for that implementing legislation to expressly by name to criminalize the abuse of DNA genetic engineering for biowarfare purposes.

The CRG then asked me to draft that U.S. BWC implementing legislation, which became the Biological Weapons Anti-Terrorism Act (BWATA) of 1989 that was approved unanimously by both Houses of the United States Congress and signed into law by President George Bush Sr. with the approval of the United States Department of Justice. Anticipatorily, my BWATA also criminalized by name the abuse of synthetic biology for biowarfare purposes, which is now being conducted. I have been fighting against biological warfare weapons and programs all over the world since then in order to prevent a biowarfare global pandemic against the human race itself. I failed!

Humanity is now involved in the fight of our lives against the COVID-19 pandemic. And it is a two-front war just like World War II was—both against COVID-19, and now against the Nazi COVID-19 "vaccines" that I publicly argued about as early as May 2020, which will be more dangerous than useless. Hence, the title/subtitle of this book: *Resisting Medical Tyranny: Why the COVID-19 Mandates Are Criminal.*

...

1 See Francis A. Boyle, *The Legal Distortions Behind the Reagan Administration's Chemical and Biological Warfare Buildup*, in my **The Future of International Law and American Foreign Policy**, 277–317 (1989). My **Biowarfare and Terrorism** (2005) picks up the story from there.

This book is based upon my extensive and real-world experience actively fighting against biological warfare weapons and programs all over the world since shortly after the founding of the CRG in 1983, when they asked me to get involved in their anti-biological weapons campaign. It is not the purpose of this book to write a history of biological warfare weapons and programs by the major military powers in the world before and after the Biological Weapons Convention of 1972 that continue apace as of today and are still also existentially dangerous—the real sources of the proverbial "next pandemic." Rather, this book is intended to research, document, and analyze the outbreak of the COVID-19 pandemic in the fall of 2019 and its subsequent developments, including the so-called COVID vaccines that I have denominated "Frankenshots."

To its great credit, the CRG was also conducting a second campaign against the use of genetically modified organisms (GMOs) to produce food for human consumption that were generally known as "Frankenfoods." I was not involved in that second CRG campaign, since I had my hands full combating biological warfare weapons and programs for them. But I did follow that second CRG campaign against Frankenfoods in our publication *Genewatch*. So it is only appropriate that I baptized the COVID "vaccines" with the name Frankenshots. Both Frankenfoods and Frankenshots involve the abuse of DNA genetic engineering, and now synthetic biology, to the grave detriment of the human race. But I leave the arguments against Frankenfoods to the extensive publications by the CRG and its members.

Humanity cannot possibly come to grips with, and combat and defeat, the COVID-19 pandemic unless we understand what happened, why it happened, and what was *wrong* with what happened. Only then can the human race win World War III against the COVID-19 pandemic. Toward that end, I have written this book.

— FAB

CHAPTER 1

COVID-19 IS AN OFFENSIVE BIOLOGICAL WARFARE WEAPON THAT LEAKED OUT OF THE WUHAN BSL-4 IN CHINA

CALL FOR A BAN ON THE GENETIC ALTERATION OF PATHOGENS FOR DESTRUCTIVE PURPOSES

3 November 2001
Harvard Divinity School
Cambridge, MA 02138

The recent use of the US Postal Service to disseminate anthrax-contaminated mail underscores a more general threat to people worldwide brought about by the perversion of the biological sciences to cause harm through the deliberate spread of disease. This is the moment to outlaw all destructive applications of genetic engineering. We call on the United States to immediately halt all projects designed to genetically modify naturally occurring organisms for military purposes. We call on the States Parties to the 1972 Biological Weapons Convention to extend the Convention's ban to cover all genetic modification of biological agents for military purposes. Since the line between offense and defense in this context is thin to nonexistent, there should be no loopholes for "defense." Genetic modification of pathogens for development of vaccines or other medical purposes should be carried out in civilian laboratories and under strict international controls. Finally, we call on the United States to support a Protocol to the Biological Weapons Convention to assure strict compliance with the terms of the Convention both by states and by individuals and sub-state organizations.*

Signed,

Francis A. Boyle, Professor of International Law at University of Illinois College of Law, author of U.S. implementing legislation for 1972 Biological Weapons Convention, the Biological Weapons Anti-Terrorism Act of 1989

Jonathan King, PhD, Professor of Molecular Biology at the Massachusetts Institute of Technology and Director of the Biology Electron Microscope Facility

Martin Teitel, PhD, President of the Council for Responsible Genetics

Susan Wright, PhD, Associate Research Scientist at the University of Michigan

**Several developed countries, including the United States, have initiated projects aimed at genetically engineering pathogenic and other microbes for military purposes. Military-sponsored projects include:*

(1) developing "superbugs" capable of digesting materials such as plastics, fuel, rubber, and asphalt;
(2) developing a strain of anthrax that overcomes the protection provided by vaccines in the name of "defense" against such genetically altered strains. These projects are being justified under the terms of the Biological Weapons Convention as necessary for "defense." Far from providing defense, these projects open up the possibility of more dangerous forms of biological warfare against which there is no defense. They also undermine the Convention both because the actual motives for these projects are highly ambiguous (if a country were to withdraw from the Biological Weapons Convention, their projects would have direct offensive applications) and because they will stimulate similar projects elsewhere in the world.

. . .

Starting in August of 2019, I went on a fall semester–long sabbatical to finish up writing my next book. For that reason, I did not engage in my usual due-diligence research to monitor outbreaks of mysterious diseases all over the world in order to determine whether they were natural in origin, or a biological warfare weapon at work, or unknown and inconclusive, which I have routinely done for many years. It was not until Friday, January 17, 2020, that I returned to my office in order to prepare to teach my spring-semester courses starting on Tuesday, January 21, when I began once again to pay systematic attention to the outbreak of strange and exotic diseases around the world. So on January 17, 2020, there came a report on my computer from NBC News titled *Outbreak of Never-Before-Seen Respiratory Virus Prompts CDC to Screen Passengers from Chinese City at 3 U.S. Airports*. The precis for this report read as follows:

NBC News
January 17, 2020

> The CDC has dispatched officials to airports in New York, San Francisco, and Los Angeles to screen passengers from Wuhan, China, the center of a growing outbreak of a never-before-seen respiratory virus.
>
> At least 45 cases of the newly discovered coronavirus 2019 nCoV have been reported in China. Most of the cases are linked to a large market in Wuhan with live animals, but there is some evidence the virus can spread from person to person. Two deaths have been reported.

I then sent this article out to the members of a private biowarfare list that I maintain with a group of people who have an interest in biological warfare weapons and programs, and I asked them the following question: "So the question I have: Is there a Chinese BSL-4 facility near Wuhan from which this might have leaked?" But since I was gearing up to teach two different courses on International Law and International Human Rights Law to large numbers of American law students and foreign lawyers, I did not have the time immediately to research and answer that question.

On Thursday, January 23, I was asked by a journalist working for the publication *Geopolitics & Empire* if I was willing to give them a video-recorded interview on the outbreak of the mysterious disease in Wuhan, China, which was by then rapidly emerging into the widespread attention of all international news media sources. From a previous interview I had given to this journalist on biological weapons, he knew that I had personally called for and drafted the U.S. domestic implementing legislation for the 1972 Biological

Weapons Convention that was named the Biological Weapons Anti-Terrorism Act of 1989 (BWATA), which was passed unanimously by both Houses of the United States Congress and signed into law by President George Bush Sr.

My BWATA was prompted by and specifically intended to counteract in material, but not exclusive, part the abuse of DNA genetic engineering by the neoconservative Reagan administration to research, develop, test, and stockpile biological weapons in violation of the Biological Weapons Convention by criminalizing it all. That is precisely why the Reagan administration so vigorously lobbied against my BWATA in the U.S. Congress. I also anticipated and expressly criminalized by name the similar abuse of synthetic biology for biowarfare purposes.

My 1989 BWATA provided for up to life imprisonment for violators and is still in the U.S. Criminal Code today. I adamantly resisted heavy pressure from the U.S. Department of Justice to advocate for the death penalty for BWATA violators because of my lifelong opposition to such punishment. I could not in good faith and conscience be responsible for getting anyone sentenced to death, no matter how reprehensible and homicidal their biowarfare crimes might be.

I told the *Geopolitics & Empire* journalist that I had not yet had the opportunity to research the matter because I was just starting my first week of classes, but that I would get back to him when I had a chance to look into it. So on the morning of Friday, January 24, 2020, I came into my office and proceeded to research the matter. Sure enough, after just a little bit of research on the internet, I found out that Wuhan did indeed have a BSL-4, as I had originally surmised on January 17, and also that the Wuhan BSL-4 was the only lab in China qualified to do such advanced and dangerous research work on coronaviruses. *Bingo!* It was obvious to me then that the Wuhan coronavirus had leaked out of this BSL-4 and that it was an extremely dangerous biological warfare weapon with gain-of-function properties, based upon the by then-published accounts of its spread in China. For that reason, I then prepared a *Notice* to put out to several hundred news media sources all over the world, and also widely on the internet, about the existential dangers presented by the Wuhan coronavirus that was later renamed COVID-19. My January 24 worldwide *Notice* alert read as follows:

From: Boyle, Francis A.
Sent: Friday, January 24, 2020 11:11 AM
To: Killeacle <fboyle@uiuc.edu>
Subject: Only one lab in China can safely handle the new coronavirus | Live Science

Applying Occam's Razor, this Wuhan [Biosafety Level 4] BSL-4 lab is the source of the Wuhan coronavirus.
I suspect they were developing it as a dual-use biowarfare weapons agent that was GMO'd with gain-of-function properties, which is why it is so lethal and contagious. That is why the PRC originally tried to cover it up, and that is why they are now taking such drastic measures to contain it. They know how dangerous it is.
And this PRC coronavirus pandemic calls into question the safety of all BSL-3 and BSL-4 labs around the world, including and especially here in the United States.
Professor Francis A. Boyle is the author of the US domestic implementing legislation for the Biological Weapons Convention called the Biological Weapons Anti-Terrorism Act of 1989 that was approved unanimously by both Houses of the United States Congress and signed into law by President George H. W. Bush.

From: Boyle, Francis A. <fboyle@illinois.edu>
Sent: Friday, January 24, 2020 10:57 AM
To: Killeacle <fboyle@uiuc.edu>
Subject: Only one lab in China can safely handle the new coronavirus | Live Science

As an escalating viral outbreak unfolds in China, only one lab in the country meets the required biosafety standards needed to study the new disease.

https://www.livescience.com/china-lab-meets-biosafety-levels-new-coronavirus.html

In a malicious and deliberately ordered hit-and-smear job against me that was published all over the world in two related articles by the Associated Press

[AP] on February 15, 2021, which included my picture, AP reported that I was the first person to publicly declare that the Wuhan coronavirus was an offensive biological warfare weapon that had leaked out of the Wuhan BSL-4. I will return to analyzing that February 2001 AP worldwide hit-and-smear job on me later on in this book.

I then contacted the reporter at *Geopolitics & Empire*, sent him my *Notice*, and told him that I was now prepared to give him an interview, which I did later that afternoon on January 24, 2020. During the course of that January 24, 2020, interview, I stated quite emphatically that the Wuhan coronavirus was an offensive biological warfare weapon involving DNA genetic engineering that included gain-of-function properties to make it more lethal and more infectious, and which had leaked out of the BSL-4 located in the city of Wuhan, China. I then proceeded to explain in detail the reasons for my conclusions.

I also stated that every BSL-4 and BSL-3 in the world must be immediately shut down because they all presented existential threats to the entire human race. This is an injunction I had publicly issued in the award-winning documentary *Anthrax War* (2009) by Coen and Nadler about the existential dangers presented by BSL-4s and BSL-3s, in which I appeared and served as a consultant: "This is a catastrophe waiting to happen!"

I also repeated this injunction in that October 2015 interview with my friend Sherwood Ross, published in the introduction to this book: "This is a bio-catastrophe waiting to happen here in the United States." My long-standing prediction finally came true with the outbreak of the worldwide COVID-19 pandemic at the Wuhan BSL-4 despite my best efforts to prevent it ever since I first joined the Council for Responsible Genetics shortly after they were founded in 1983 in order to work on their campaign against biological weapons.

That interview I gave to *Geopolitics & Empire* was then distributed by them all over the internet on Thursday, January 30, 2020, and quickly went viral all over the world. After giving that interview, I was immediately inundated by requests from news media sources all over the globe to explain the reasons for my conclusions, and my recommendations for dealing with the worldwide COVID-19 pandemic.

This deluge of interviews continued relentlessly until about July 1, 2020, when they gradually and mercifully began to taper off. By then, everyone in the world knew exactly where I stood on the origins of the COVID-19 pandemic from the Wuhan BSL-4 as a biological warfare weapon, and what must be done about it, as well the need to shut down all BSL-4s and BSL-3s immediately in order to prevent another global pandemic by some other existentially dangerous biowarfare weapons—the real sources of the proverbial and predicted "next pandemic." The edited transcript from my viral January 24, 2020, videotaped interview with *Geopolitics & Empire* reads as follows:

TRANSCRIPT: Bioweapons Expert Dr. Francis Boyle on Coronavirus

Geopolitics & Empire: *Geopolitics & Empire* is joined by Dr. Francis Boyle, who is an international law professor at the University of Illinois. We'll be discussing the Wuhan coronavirus and biological warfare. He's served as counsel to numerous governments such as Bosnia and Herzegovina and the Palestinian Authority. He's represented numerous national international bodies in the areas of human rights, war crimes and genocide, nuclear policy, and biowarfare. He's written numerous books, one of my favorites being *Destroying Libya and World Order*, which I assigned as mandatory reading material for my own students when I taught at the Monterrey Institute of Technology [in Mexico].

But most important for this interview, he's written a book called *Biowarfare and Terrorism*, and drafted the U.S. domestic implementing legislation for the Biological Weapons Convention, known as the Biological Weapons Anti-Terrorism Act of 1989, which was approved unanimously by both Houses of the U.S. Congress and signed into law by President Bush Sr. Thanks for joining us, Dr. Boyle.

FAB: Wow. Thank you so much for having me on, and thanks for that kind introduction.

Geopolitics & Empire: Now let's get to what's been on the news recently—this coronavirus in Wuhan. There have been some reports recently—there's a really interesting website called GreatGameIndia that has been reporting on this. They've been talking about China, which they say has been complying with the Biological Weapons Convention in recent years. But then there are some people in the U.S. and experts who have been saying that, in reality,

China isn't complying with the weapons convention. And I think neither, perhaps the U.S. as well. I'm wondering if China is developing its own Biosafety Level 4 lab in Wuhan and elsewhere, as you know, as a type of deterrence. Is it a type of a biological arms race that we have going on?

You told me in an email that you suspect China was developing the coronavirus as a dual-use biowarfare weapons agent. Also, what do you make of reports that Chinese scientists have been stealing research and viruses, including the coronavirus, from a Canadian bio-lab this past December? And as well, Chinese nationals have been charged with smuggling vials of biological research to China from the U.S. with the aid of Charles Lieber, who was the chair of Harvard's Chemistry Department. And he also happened to be, in 2011, a strategic scientist at Wuhan University. So, can you tell us what's going on with this recent outbreak in Wuhan?

FAB: Well, those are a lot of questions. I guess we can take them one at a time, but if you just do a very simple Google search on "Does China have a BSL-4 laboratory?" Wuhan comes up right away. It's at the top of the list. So a BSL-4 is the most serious type. And basically, BSL-4 labs—we have many of them here in the United States—are used to develop offensive biological warfare weapons with DNA genetic engineering.

So it does seem to me that the Wuhan BSL-4 is the source of the coronavirus. My guess is that they were researching SARS, and they weaponized it further by giving it gain-of-function properties, which means it could be more lethal.

Indeed, the latest report now is that it's a 15% fatality rate, which is more than SARS, and an 83% infection rate. A typical gain of function travels in the air, so it could reach out maybe six feet or more from someone emitting a sneeze or a cough. Likewise, this is a specially designated WHO research lab. The WHO was in on it, and they knew full well what was going on there.

It's also been reported that Chinese scientists stole coronavirus materials from the Canadian lab at Winnipeg, which is Canada's formal center for researching, developing, and testing biological warfare weapons. It's along the lines of Fort Detrick here in the United States of America. I have three degrees from Harvard. It would not surprise me if something was being stolen out of Harvard to turn over to China. I read that report. I don't know what was in those vials one way or the other.

But the bottom line is, I drafted the U.S. domestic implementing legislation for the Biological Weapons Convention that was approved unanimously by both Houses in the United States Congress and signed into law by President Bush Sr. It appears that **the coronavirus that we're dealing with here is an offensive biological warfare weapon that leaked out of Wuhan BSL-4.** I'm not saying it was done deliberately. But there had been previous reports of problems with that lab and things leaking out of it. I'm afraid that is what we are dealing with today.

Geopolitics & Empire: We'll be talking about Wuhan and the coronavirus and China, but can you give us a bigger context? I know that previously, in interviews, you've said that since 9/11, you think that **the U.S. has spent $100 billion on biological warfare research.** We know that the Soviet Union, if I'm not mistaken, developed anthrax as a bioweapon. And you've also mentioned that the U.K., France, Israel, and China are all involved in biological warfare weapons research.

And something interesting: I believe one or two years ago a Bulgarian journalist and the Russian government shared their concern about the discovery of a U.S. bioweapons lab in the country of Georgia. You've commented how in Africa, U.S. has set up bioweapons labs to work on Ebola, which I think is illegal under international law. But they were allowed somehow to put those in Africa. Can you give us a bigger picture? What's going on with these different countries, and what's the purpose of this research?

FAB: All these BSL-4 labs in the United States, Europe, Russia, China, and Israel are all there to research, develop, and test biological warfare agents. There's really no legitimate scientific reason to have BSL-4 labs. That figure I gave of $100 billion, that was about 2015, I believe. I had crunched the numbers and had come up with that figure for the United States since 9/11/2001.

To give you an idea, that's more in constant dollars than the US spent to develop the Manhattan Project and the atom bomb. So it's clearly all weapons related. **We have well over 13,000 alleged life science scientists involved in the research, development, and testing of biological weapons here in the United States.** Actually, this goes back to and even precedes 9/11/2001.

I have another book, *The Future of International Law and American Foreign Policy,* tracing that all the way back to the Reagan administration under the influence of the neocons, and they got very heavily involved in the research, development, and testing of biological weapons with DNA genetic engineering. It was because of that that I issued my plea in 1985 in a congressional briefing sponsored by the Council for Responsible Genetics—I was a lawyer for them, and they're headquartered in Cambridge, Massachusetts. All the MIT and Harvard people are involved in that, the principal ones. And then they asked me to draft the implementing legislation.

The implementing legislation that I drafted was originally designed to stop this type of work, "death science work," I call it, by the United States government. After 9/11/2001, it just completely accelerated. My current figure, that last figure, is $100 billion. I haven't had a chance to re-crunch the numbers because I just started classes. But you have to add in about another $5 billion per year.

Basically, this is an offensive biological weapons race by the United States government, and with its assistance, Canada and Britain. And so other states in the world have responded accordingly, including Russia and China. They {the PRC} were going to set up a whole series of BSL-4 facilities as well. And you know Wuhan was the first. It backfired on them.

Geopolitics & Empire: Would you basically consider what happened in Wuhan just ineptitude or incompetence on the Chinese part?

FAB: Well, it's criminality. It does appear that they stole something there from Winnipeg. This activity that they engaged in clearly violates the Biological Weapons Convention. Research and development of biological weapons these days is an international crime—the use of it would be. That was criminal.

I'm not saying they deliberately inflicted this on their own people, but it leaked out of there, and all these BSL-4 facilities leak. Everyone knows that who studies this. So this was a catastrophe waiting to happen. Unfortunately, it happened. **The Chinese government under Xi and his comrades there have been covering this up from the get-go. The first reported case was December 1 {later research determined about mid-November}, so they'd been sitting on this until they couldn't anymore. And everything they're telling you is a lie. It's propaganda.**

The WHO still refuses to declare a global health emergency. It said Tedros [Director-General of the WHO] was over there shaking hands with Xi and smiling and yacking it up. The WHO was in on it. They've approved many of these BSL-4 labs. They know exactly what's going on, and that is a WHO research-approved laboratory. They know what's going on too. **You can't really believe anything the WHO is telling you about this either; they're up to their eyeballs in it, in my opinion.**

Geopolitics & Empire: I'd probably agree with you that this outbreak in Wuhan was an accidental leak from the laboratory. But just your thoughts—it's happening at quite an opportune time because, namely, we're smack in the middle of a new US–China cold war, which is currently characterized by economic warfare such as the trade war among other forms of hybrid and technological warfare. And it seems that the Wuhan outbreak will likely hit the Chinese economy hard. The Chinese are flat out dismissing any idea that the U.S. is involved. Like I said, it's probable that they made the mistakes in the Wuhan lab. What are your thoughts on how, seemingly, this would benefit the U.S.?

FAB: When the outbreak occurred, of course, I considered that alternative [U.S. sabotage] too. When you have an outbreak, you're never quite sure who or what is behind it. **It certainly isn't bats, that's ridiculous.** They made the same argument about Ebola in West Africa. I demolished that online. You can check it out. So I kept competing theories about this.

But right now, when you originally contacted me, I said I wasn't prepared to comment because I was weighing the evidence. I'm a law professor and a lawyer. I try to do the best I can to weigh the evidence. But right now, the Wuhan BSL-4, in my opinion, is the most likely source—apply Occam's razor—the simplest explanation. I'm not ruling out some type of sabotage. But right now, I believe that is the source here.

Geopolitics & Empire: And you mentioned the WHO. I'd like to just get your thoughts on the WHO and Big Pharma. There are also some analysts who are downplaying this news-media hype about the coronavirus. You've just said that it seems to be lethal, but if we go back a decade to the 2009 swine flu, I believe it didn't have too many casualties, but I think it greatly profited the pharmaceutical companies. If I recall that back in 2009, **many countries purchased great stocks of the vaccines, and they ended up not using anywhere from 50% to 80% of the vaccines that they purchased.**

You've previously stated in an interview that the World Health Organization is a front for Big Pharma, if I'm not mistaken. Robert F. Kennedy Jr. also agrees, and he says, you know, 50% of WHO funding comes from pharmaceutical companies. And that the CDC itself is also severely compromised. What are your thoughts on the WHO? The CDC?

FAB: You can't trust anything the WHO says because they're all bought and paid for by Big Pharma, and when they work in cahoots with the CDC, which is the United States government, they work in cahoots with Fort Detrick, so you can't trust any of it.

However, the swine flu, and yes, I agree, Pharma, made a lot of money, but that swine flu that I looked at, **it did seem to me to be a genetically modified biological warfare weapon.** It was a chimera of three different types of genetic strains that someone put together in a cocktail. Fortunately, it was not as lethal as all of us feared. So, fine. But as I said, this figure I just gave you was Saturday from the *Lancet*, which is a medical publication, saying it has a 15% fatality rate and an 83% infection rate. So it's quite serious, I think, far more serious than the swine flu.

As for Big Pharma, sure they're all trying to profit off this today, as we speak. There was a big article yesterday in the *Wall Street Journal* that all Big Pharma is trying to peddle whatever they can over there in China, even if it's worthless and won't help. We do know, if you read the mainstream news media, they say there isn't a vaccine.

Well, there *is*. **It's by the Pirbright Institute in Britain that's tied into their biological warfare program over there.** They were behind the hoof-and-mouth disease outbreak over there that wiped out their cattle herd, and it leaked out of there. So it's clear they're working on a hoof-and-mouth biological warfare weapon, but the vaccine is there. I have the patent for it here. I haven't had a chance to read the patent, as it's about 25 pages long, and my classes just resumed. So eventually I'll get some free time and read the patent.

You can't patent a vaccine with the United States patent office unless the science is there. So there *is* a vaccine. Everyone's lying about that, no one's pointing this out—there's a vaccine—but instead, Big Pharma wants to make money, and the researchers say, well, it'll take three months and we're racing forward, you know. Everyone's going to make a buck off of this, that's for sure. But there *is* a vaccine, I have the patent here. It's been patented by the United States government.

So obviously, I don't know exactly how workable it is, but it's a vaccine. I don't know why it isn't out there now. Why isn't someone saying there's a vaccine? Perhaps political leaders have already been vaccinated, for all I know. I really don't know. **But there *is* a vaccine. Pirbright is well known there in Britain, and it's tied into Fort Detrick, and the CDC is tied into Fort Detrick too. So they all know there's a patented vaccine.**

Geopolitics & Empire: And just to get your comment on something to related to this, which was my next question. So I'm not sure if it's that same institute that you just mentioned that has the patent. I read somewhere that the Bill & Melinda Gates Foundation maybe funds or has some connection to that institute that has the patent.

FAB: I think they do. **The Bill & Melinda Gates Foundation, they fund this type of DNA genetically engineered biological warfare work. That's correct. So you can't trust anything they're telling you—that somehow they're out there trying to make the world a better place. I mean, we have Bill Gates publicly admitting that the world would be a better place if there were a lot less people. So the Bill & Melinda Gates Foundation, they are wolves in sheep's clothing, and they are funding this type of stuff, sure.**

Geopolitics & Empire: And just your comment. There was also a report that a consortium of companies that included the Gates Foundation just two or three months ago in October of 2019 held a pandemic exercise simulating an outbreak. I mean, what are the chances specifically of a coronavirus, and it was called *Events 201*. People can find this online, and they gave a list of seven recommendations for governments and international organizations to take. I also find that kind of interesting, how they had this simulation.

FAB: That's correct. It raises that question, the origins of what happened here. But right now I'm just looking at the evidence I have and applying Occam's razor, and we know that Wuhan BSL-4 was researching, developing, and testing SARS as a biological warfare agent. So it could have been that they gave it DNA genetic engineering–enhanced gain-of-function properties, which we do here in the West, in the United States, all the time. **We have all sorts of research that is clearly biowarfare research that has been approved by the National Institutes of Health—it's a joke. They know full well that they are approving all kinds of biological warfare research, and it gets funded by the United States government.**

Geopolitics & Empire: And you've also mentioned in the email to me that what happened in the Biosafety Level 4 lab in Wuhan calls into question the safety of all of these Level 3 and 4 labs around the world.

FAB: They're complete unsafe. BSL-3 and BSL-4 labs are only designed for the research, development, and testing of offensive biological warfare agents. In my opinion, they serve no legitimate purpose at all. They should all be shut down, every one of them. They're simply too dangerous. If you want, there's an excellent documentary called *Anthrax War* by Nadler and Coen, and I'm in it. Repeatedly, at the end, I say with respect to these labs, 3 and 4, this is a catastrophe waiting to happen. Well, I'm afraid the catastrophe has now happened. So there it is.

Geopolitics & Empire: Yeah, I was just watching that documentary before we connected, and I recommend that listeners go and check it out. Do you see, in the future, any countries, if we come to a conflict between the U.S., the EU, Israel, Saudi Arabia, Iran, China, and Russia, I mean, you name it. Do you see any of these countries actually utilizing these biological weapons? I mean, it's illegal under international law, but we know that in the past, international law hasn't been followed. Do you think that there's a real danger of this escalating?

FAB: For sure. That's the only reason they develop these biological weapons—to eventually be used, sure. I mean, it's like the Manhattan Project—we put all that money into developing an atom bomb, and even though it was not needed to end World War II, they still used them at Hiroshima and Nagasaki. So, yes, I think that's correct. **And also, these can be used covertly. Anytime you see an unexplained sudden outbreak of a disease like this anywhere in the world, both for human beings and/or animals, I always suspect that there's a biowarfare agent at work.** I monitor the situations like I did at Wuhan until I can reach a conclusion. Yes, they can be used by the United States government; today they are fully prepared, armed, equipped, and supplied to wage a biological warfare with anthrax.

These other more exotic things I don't know, but they have the weapons, there are stockpiles. We have to understand if you read Seymour Martin Hersh's book published about 1968—he won the Pulitzer Prize—that he had the whole offensive U.S. Biological Warfare Industry in there back before it was illegal and criminal. **Basically after 9/11/2001, that entire industry—the Offensive Biological Warfare Industry—has been reconstituted here in the United States with all these BSL-4 and BSL-3 labs, well over 13,000 alleged scientists sort of like Dr. Mengele working on these things.** Other countries have responded in kind, like Russia and China. France is involved, and Britain's involved. Sure.

Geopolitics & Empire: I just wanted to get your thoughts on this—over the last few years there was the Russian double-agent spy Sergei Skripal, who had allegedly been poisoned with Novichok out in Britain, and I thought it was funny. It just so happened where he was allegedly poisoned, he was right near Porton Down, the British bioweapons lab, I guess the world's first bioweapons lab that was created in 1916. I mean, I don't know if you have thoughts on that whole incident.

FAB: Yeah, it was right down the street from Porton Down, so applying Occam's razor, who do you think might've been behind this, and it was not a nerve agent? A nerve agent would have killed him immediately. This is Novichok. It was something else like BX or something like that. So, fine. But I would just say that I don't think that was a coincidence, but, you know, there you go. Obviously there's a lot of speculation on that.

Geopolitics & Empire: Something else that's kind of interesting. You've written in your book *Biowarfare and Terrorism* that there's also Graeme MacQueen, your colleague who wrote *The Anthrax Deception: The Case for Domestic Conspiracy*—

FAB: Everything he said in there, that's correct.

Geopolitics & Empire: I'm wondering, also, if this new war for biotechnological dominance, whatever you want to call it, if it can also be used as a pretext for the centralization of political power and the initiation of wars, like I guess it did in the 2003 Iraq war. I mean, is this another danger that we get events like this coronavirus, and then governments will call for a centralization of greater power and taking away some of our civil liberties?

FAB: Sure. **If you look at the October 2001 anthrax attacks here in the United States, clearly elements of the United States government were behind that. That was a super-weapons-grade anthrax with a trillion spores per gram, and it floated in the air. Only a very sophisticated biological weapons lab like Fort Detrick could produce that. And they used that anthrax attack, including on Congress, to ram through the USA Patriot Act, which basically turned the United States into a police state, which is what we have now.** You have to understand that the Pentagon, Fort Detrick, made it. The Dugway Proving Ground still has a stockpile of that super-weapons-grade anthrax that we saw in October of 2001 that they can use the next time they want to do something like that to further develop the American police state. Right.

Geopolitics & Empire: Is there anything else you feel it's important to mention regarding this Wuhan coronavirus outbreak or biological warfare, or any other thoughts you'd like to leave us with?

FAB: Well, you just can't believe anything the Chinese government, the WHO, or the CDC are telling you. They're all lies because they know what's going on here, and so you're going to have to figure it out as best you can. But in my opinion, as of this time—and I'm fully prepared to consider further evidence on this—it does seem to me that this was a DNA genetically engineered biological warfare agent leaking out of Wuhan that has gain-of-function properties that can make it more lethal. I think they were probably doing something with SARS to make it a lot more lethal and more infectious. And so for that reason, you have to take extreme precautions, and they're now finally admitting that anyone within six feet can be infected, whereas with SARS, that was about two feet. Well, that's gain of function right there, and that should be a tip-off.

So I guess you're going to have to protect yourself. Laurie Garrett had a pretty good essay in *Foreign Policy* yesterday, and she was over there covering SARS, and she has very good advice in there, except that she took the SARS figure out two to three feet and said, well, you've got to stay two to three feet away. I think you've got to stay at least six feet away because this is gain of function. It can float through the air and infect, and it can get you in the eyes. Any orifice—the mouth, maybe the ears—we're not sure at this point.

Geopolitics & Empire: I'm here on the border of China in Kazakhstan, and I was just reading today that they're no longer allowing Chinese citizens into Kazakhstan without a medical paper, a medical check, to get their visas to enter Kazakhstan.

FAB: Those medical checks are worthless, because this is just public relations by all the governments involved because there's a 14-day incubation period where people can still be infected. **So someone could walk right through a medical inspection and pass through a gate into your country, and then they come down with the coronavirus.** So that's all public relations, in my opinion, by governments, and they know it, and they're just sending people out there to take temperatures and things like that.

It's not like SARS; this is more dangerous than SARS. As I said, I think that Wuhan lab—we know they had SARS in there that they were dealing with, and I think they enhanced it, and I'm afraid that's what we're dealing with. But you know, I'm keeping an open mind as to what other sources there may be, and I wasn't prepared to say anything until that Wuhan lab was right there and dealing with coronavirus. So again, apply Occam's razor. It seems to me that's the simplest explanation here.

Geopolitics & Empire: I guess one of my final questions would be, in the months ahead, apart from what you say—staying six feet away from people—I've read that taking high doses of vitamin C and other things like this can help you. But if the situation develops and gets worse, and they come out with a coronavirus vaccine, should people take it or not? What are your thoughts?

FAB: Well, what I would say is this. Right now, if you look at the article in the *Wall Street Journal*, Big Pharma is trying to sell all sorts of stuff—they're taking all their drugs off the shelf and saying, well, let's see if it works, which is preposterous. The scientists are saying, well, we can get you a vaccine in maybe two to three months, but they're not tested. So what we do know, however, is that the Pirbright vaccine has been patented. So all I can assume is that that might work. But I don't think I'd be taking any of these other vaccines. No, you have no idea what's in there. **You'll be the guinea pig for Big Pharma, and everyone figures they're going to make a lot of money here.** So I'll keep my eyes open on this and how it develops, but I wouldn't trust anything they're trying to sell right now. They're just pulling these things off the shelf.

If they do come up with something in two to three months, even that's not going to be tested in accordance with normal scientific protocol. So it's going to be a crapshoot. **If it's going to help you, indeed it might *not* help you, because for these [DNA genetic engineered vaccines], they'll be using live coronavirus probably and sticking it in there and giving you some live coronavirus on the theory that you'll develop an immunity. That's the way a lot of these vaccines worked out—that's what happened with the Ebola vaccine that created the Ebola pandemic there in West Africa. They were testing out a vaccine on poor Black Africans, as usual, and this vaccine had live Ebola in it, so it gave them Ebola.** So again, I'd be very careful even if they do come up with these vaccines two to three months from now, very careful. Why would you want to inject the live coronavirus in you?

Geopolitics & Empire: All right. I don't believe you have a strong online presence. How can people best follow your work? I suppose to search for interviews as well as get your books.

FAB: Well, basically, I'm blackballed and blacklisted off of all the mainstream news media here on purpose. As far as I can figure out, the U.S. government gave an order that I should not be interviewed

by anyone, so I'm not. I guess you could just put my name in there under Google, Google alert, and some interviews might come up. What happened was that right after the anthrax attacks of 9/11/2001, I was giving a lecture out at Harvard, my alma mater. I was running a panel on biological warfare for the Council for Responsible Genetics, and it was at Harvard Divinity School, and as I was going in, there was a Fox camera crew there from Boston, and I said it looks to me like this has come out of the U.S. government lab. We know they do research and testing on anthrax. Then I said the same thing there at Harvard. Then I gave an interview to a radio station in Washington, D.C. Then I gave an interview on that to the BBC. So the whole world heard it, and at that point I was completely cut off, and I've been cut off ever since. So you're probably not going to hear too many interviews from me here. As for my book *Biowarfare and Terrorism*, you can get it at amazon.com. That picks up the story pretty much from 9/11/2001 until it went to press, and then there are interviews I'd given to an investigative reporter, Sherwood Ross [see the introduction to this book], and a big one I just sent you, and you might want to put that on your webpage. That was pretty comprehensive.

Geopolitics & Empire: Yeah, I read that as well, and I'll include the link in the description of this interview so that people can go check that out. You're not the only academic I know, and I've heard others say that similar things have happened, and I guess that's just the price we pay for telling the truth. Again, for listeners, if people want to have a broader context and deeper understanding of what's happening today, especially with biological warfare as well as foreign policy and international affairs, I urge you to get Dr. Francis Boyle's books and listen to his interviews, as well as his colleague Graeme MacQueen's book called *The Anthrax Deception: The Case For Domestic Conspiracy*. Thank you for being with us, Dr. Boyle.

FAB: Well, thank you, and again, please understand that these are my current opinions. I could change my opinions here based on more evidence. So I'm just looking at the evidence out there as I see it; and you have to understand that there is so much disinformation, lies, and propaganda that it's kind of difficult to distinguish truth from fact. I'm doing the best job I can here.

. . .

CHAPTER 2
MY SMOKING-GUN INTERVIEW

In order to give a plethora of interviews after I blew the whistle on the Wuhan BSL-4 coronavirus on January 24, 2020, I had to work full-time researching, reading, and analyzing all of the information that emerged into the public record about the Wuhan coronavirus, the Wuhan BSL-4, and the worldwide COVID-19 pandemic. In the process of doing so, I also had to read, analyze, and refute my numerous critics who arose to object to my conclusions and recommendations by regurgitating the simplistic propaganda originally generated by the Chinese Communist Dictatorship on Steroids under President Xi as a cover-up campaign, saying that the worldwide COVID-19 pandemic had somehow magically "jumped" from animals to human beings at the so-called wet market located in Wuhan, China. Completely preposterous!

It turns out that my many critics were directly, personally, and financially involved in the U.S. Offensive Biological Warfare Industry discussed in the introduction to this book. These death scientists had vested economic, professional, organizational, and personal interests in attacking my conclusions, and in particular, my clarion call for shutting down every BSL-4 and BSL-3 in the world for creating existential threats to all humanity, as COVID-19 has already done. *They would all be out of a job!* More seriously, some of them who are American citizens could also be prosecuted for violating my Biological Weapons Anti-Terrorism Act of 1989 and subjected to life imprisonment. It was pretty easy for me in subsequent responsive interviews to discredit my critics and their attacks upon me, my conclusions, and my recommendations by performing due-diligence research on their professional backgrounds. You, the reader, can easily do so as well if you want to, by means of a simple internet search.

I am not going to review, summarize, or list all of my many news media interviews here, since you can easily read them or watch them or both by doing a Google search under my name, after January 24, 2020, if you so desire. To be sure, for obvious reasons, many of my interviews and comments have been censored off of Google and its subsidiary, YouTube; as well as Facebook, Twitter, and other social media platforms. So you might have to do some internet digging to find them somewhere if you wish to.

The global mainstream news media and the world's scientific establishment spent well over 14 months almost unanimously repeating in unison this PRC [People's Republic of China] propaganda campaign and cover-up, to the grave detriment of humanity. There was no way we human beings could come to grips with, confront, stop, and defeat COVID-19 if everyone believed and repeated the fairy tale and mantra that it had jumped out of the Wuhan wet market because Chinese people liked to eat bat soup. *Ludicrous!* So I dutifully trudged on with my interviews despite my many death-scientist critics. Too much was at stake for humanity to give up!

The global mainstream news media and the world scientific establishment completely discredited and debunked themselves permanently for knowingly serving as the house organ for this COVID-19 Chinese Communist dictatorship propaganda campaign cover-up. We must never trust and believe any of them ever again! Ditto on the COVID-19 Frankenshots!

Finally, on Wednesday, February 19, 2020, Alex Jones from Infowars.com interviewed me live via Skype from his TV studio at great length. Others have called it my "Smoking-Gun Interview." It is set forth below. You are free to draw your own conclusions from my analysis:

Full Transcript of "Smoking-Gun" Bombshell Interview: Professor Francis Boyle Exposes the Bioweapons Origins of the COVID-19 Coronavirus

Thursday, February 20, 2020 by: Mike Adams
Tags: Alex Jones, biological weapons, bioweapons, coronavirus, Francis Boyle, interview, NIH, outbreak, pandemic, transcript, virus, Wuhan

(*Natural News*) What follows is one of the most important interviews of the year. Biological warfare expert Prof. Francis Boyle appeared as a guest with Alex Jones on the *Alex Jones Show*, sharing his "smoking-gun" findings about the coronavirus being engineered as a weapon that's designed "for efficient spreading in the human population," according to one of the science papers he references.

We confirmed Prof. Boyle's findings by purchasing the full PDF of that paper and reviewing it in a detailed article we posted yesterday at this link.

That paper describes the COVID-19 novel coronavirus as possessing unique "gain-of-function" properties that make it the perfect bioweapon, while confirming these new properties were from artificial origins, not natural viral evolution. (In other words, it was engineered.)

Below, we print the full transcript of the Francis Boyle/Alex Jones interview, along with the video of the full exchange below, via Brighteon.com. (The full show is also posted on Banned.video.)

If you hope to understand anything about what's happening right now with the coronavirus pandemic, the global cover-up, and how **the taxpayer-funded NIH is behind these biological weapons**, you need to hear and share this interview. You have permission to copy this full transcript and full video and post it on your own site. Please give us credit, since our team carried out the transcription task.

Also, note that we are launching Pandemic.news as a new hub for all podcasts, downloadable MP3s, videos, articles, and science-study links related to this coronavirus outbreak. Check it all out at Pandemic.news, which we are just launching today.

Full transcript . . . SHARE this everywhere, re-post, tweet, and cover:

{From FAB: As noted earlier, all transcripts have been slightly edited for clarity, but please excuse any minor errors, as this was transcribed in a bit of a hurry due to the urgency of the message . . . ***bolding*** *emphasis added; please pay special attention to the* ***bolded*** *sentences.}*

Alex Jones: All right. I have not touched the coronavirus today because I was waiting for Professor Francis A. Boyle to come on, a leading American expert in international law responsible for drafting the Biological Weapons Anti-Terrorism Act of 1989, the American implementing legislation for the Biological Weapons Convention. He served on the Board of Directors of Amnesty International and represented Bosnia and Herzegovina in the World Court. He served as a legal adviser to the Palestinian delegation at the Middle

East peace negotiations. In 2007, he delivered the Bertrand Russell peace lectures.

Professor Boyle teaches international law at the University of Illinois and is the author of *Biowarfare and Terrorism*. He holds a doctor of law, magna cum laude, and holds a PhD in political science from Harvard University. His latest book is *Poems Against the Empire*, which is a collection of poetry reflections on his experiences fighting for peace, justice, human rights, international law, social welfare, and the United States Constitution.

And he joins us now. I would call him a classical liberal. A liberal today or leftist is a fascist. It's like a neocon as a fascist. And so the terms don't mean anything. And he's got big, breaking, exclusive news here. And he sent me notes, but I think the best way to do this is for at least the next three segments, he pretty much hosts, so that he can walk you through this. But this is serious news. This is very important news everybody should pay attention to. The Wuhan coronavirus came out of the biowarfare lab. That's even being said by the White House now. Dr. Boyle and others were saying it three weeks ago. The UNC [University of North Carolina] labs should be shut down—everyone investigated for violating the Biological Weapons Anti-Terrorism Act. He's got major studies that have just come out. So he's an expert on bioweapons and the law. We've got eight minutes to break here, then a nine-minute segment, then a ten-minute segment. I'll take us into break, Dr. Boyle. But you go ahead and host. You've got the floor here. Thanks for joining us.

FAB: Well, Alex, thank you very much for having me on. My best to your viewing audience. Yes, I sent your assistant an email on Monday that I had revised my opinion on certain matters, and also, I had come up with what I concluded was the smoking gun that the Wuhan coronavirus came out of that BSL-4 facility. And you'll note now that Senator Cotton is saying the same thing. He was behind me at Harvard Law School, and despite that, the *New York Times* slammed him. And as you know, Senator Cotton is a decorated combat veteran. No surprise there for the *New York Times*. So, yes, I have these scientific studies now.

Basically, I read these things over the weekend, which is why I changed my mind and said I had new information and alerted your assistant on Monday. And today is the first day I could give you an extensive interview. I want to go through these scientific studies so that you and the viewing audience understand their implications. I believe they are the smoking gun of what happened here. The first is by some life scientists: three from Marseilles, France, and one from Montreal clinical research laboratories there. It was published in *Antiviral Research* on February 10, 2020. And I had a chance to read it over the weekend. You know, I read these types of things over the weekend. Now I'm not going to go through this whole study, but they did a genetic analysis of the Wuhan coronavirus. **And let me just conclude, the critical part here is where it says, "And may provide a gain of function to the 2019 nCoV for efficient spreading in the human population compared to other beta coronaviruses." Let me repeat that: "And may provide a gain of function to the 2019 nCoV for efficient spreading in the human population compared to other beta coronaviruses."** And so, Alex, you recall in the first interview I gave to your colleague Mr. Shroyer, and then the follow-up interviews I gave to you, I stated that this was clearly a gain-of-function, offensive biological warfare agent.

Alex Jones: You said that three weeks ago, you said that two weeks ago, and now it's not just big at the Indian Institute. Now more live scientists have scanned it. They're saying exactly what you were saying.

FAB: Right! Well, this article here is the smoking gun.

Alex Jones: Tell people again the article and how they can find it.

FAB: I got it on a Science Direct *Antiviral Research*, February 10, 2020.

Alex Jones: *Antiviral Research*—

FAB: February 10, 2020. And it's a long title, but it starts out, "The spike glycoprotein coronavirus contains a furin-like cleavage site absent in CoV of the same clade."

Alex Jones: So that's exactly what the prestigious Indian Institute said, is that it has the points where the artificial RNA was injected. I mean, they can see right where it happened.

FAB: Right. But this was a genetic—as you know, that was withdrawn under political pressure. But now we have four very distinguished life scientists here. Yes, that's it right there. **And the smoking gun here is on page 11, near the bottom, the last full paragraph from the bottom, where it says, "May provide a gain of function to coronavirus for efficient spreading in the human population—**

Alex Jones: Explain what that gain of function means, because not all of us are experts on this like you, Doctor.

FAB: Right. Well gain of function... Oh, so let me repeat, Alex, as I told you before, **gain-of-function technology is DNA genetic engineering of dangerous biological warfare substances to begin with—**

Alex Jones: It's a souping up of already bad pathogens.

FAB: Right. It's a turbo-charging, and gain-of-function work can only be done safely in a BSL-4 or a BSL-3 facility. So, I think clearly, **this is the smoking gun that the Wuhan coronavirus came out of that BSL-4 facility.**

Alex Jones: So does this mirror what the Indian Institute said, or is this different?

FAB: Well, I think it goes beyond what the Indian study said, but we'll get to that in a minute, the Indian study. I think I've now provided the smoking gun here. **This is clearly a weaponized biological warfare agent, and there is no legitimate scientific or medical use for gain-of-function technology,** DNA technology on biowarfare—

Alex Jones: So there's no excuse that it's a vaccine test that got out.

FAB: That's baloney. **This is clearly an offensive biological warfare agent, and it has no legitimate medical or other—**

Alex Jones: This is beyond sensational. Is that why we're seeing the very serious response to it?

FAB: Well, you know, Alex, we first discussed this over three weeks ago, and they're still attacking me for being a conspiracy theorist and fake news and I'm a nutcase and a nutjob and everything else. So there's been a massive fight back in all the mainstream news media against this. And indeed, as I told you before, I'd been completely censored out of all the mainstream news media here in the United States.

Alex: But everything you said has been confirmed, and now major scientific groups have come out and confirmed it. Let's get back to that smoking gun and recap that and get to all the other documentation straight ahead.

{program break}

Alex Jones: Well, we have a leading expert in international law, an expert in biological weapons and anti-terrorism responsible for drafting the U.S. Biological Weapons Anti-Terrorism Act. Dr. Francis Boyle here. And I'm reading the same studies he's reading. More scientists come out and look at it and say this thing is man-made, and they show how, and they say it's conclusive.

You know, these major Indian institutes came out and said the same thing three weeks ago. And so we're going to walk through more of these studies in this segment, but just as a father, as a citizen, as a human, as a citizen of planet Earth, I'm going to ask Dr. Boyle what he really thinks the end game is here. Was this accidentally released, as we were hoping, and that's bad enough, or is it something even more sinister? Are they using this as an excuse to invade Taiwan, as they're now doing? Dr. Boyle, please continue with the studies; then we'll have the whole breakdown here with the study.

FAB: All right, well, let me get to the second study, which is another smoking gun and a bombshell, Alex. There's no other word for it. You remember in our previous interview, you asked me if this had come out of the BSL-4 facility in Winnipeg, Canada—if it was stolen out of there. I said that that could have happened. Winnipeg is the equivalent of Fort Detrick. They do every type of hideous, offensive Nazi-type biological warfare work up there you can possibly imagine. But again, on the basis of materials, scientific materials, I had a chance to read over the weekend. I have changed my opinion on that. **I think I have the definitive evidence where this came from, and it came from**

the BSL-3 biowarfare lab at the University of North Carolina. Now I have condemned them before because they have done gain-of-function work, DNA genetic engineering on every hideous biological warfare agent you can imagine, including MERS at that time, Middle East Respiratory Syndrome agent, which again, is a biowarfared coronavirus. Now it just came to my mind—

Alex Jones: Say that again because we're going to pull this up as you speak. You said the other study—we pulled it up.

FAB: The study was their gain-of-function DNA genetic engineering on MERS, which is Middle East Respiratory—

Alex Jones: —and that was the University of?

FAB: North Carolina. They have a BSL-3 biowarfare lab there.

Alex Jones: Oh, that's something I keep reading that they do, Level 4 stuff at Level 3s, right?

FAB: I think they are, but they're doing it with a Level 3. The last I saw, that's all they had. But let me go through this study. It's titled "A SARS-like cluster of circulating bat coronaviruses shows potential for human emergence."

Alex Jones: Say it again, because we have radio listeners, hundreds of stations. The name of the paper—"A SARS-like cluster . . .

FAB: "A SARS-like cluster of circulating bat coronaviruses shows potential for human emergence."

Alex Jones: That's 2015, December 21. We have it on-screen.

FAB: That is correct. *Nat Med*, that's it. Now if you look through this carefully, **first notice who was involved in this DNA genetic engineering of SARS, which is already a biological warfare agent to give it gain-of-function activities. And it has all these people there from**

the University of North Carolina at Chapel Hill. It has someone from the Food and Drug Administration, so you can't trust the Food and Drug Administration. And then at the very bottom of the list, who is involved? Zhengli-Li Shi, Key Laboratory of Special Pathogens and Biosafety, Wuhan Institute of Virology, Chinese Academy of Sciences, Wuhan, China. So it's very clear to me that this scientist from the Wuhan Institute of Virology got this gain-of-function technology for SARS from this University of North Carolina lab. And she didn't steal it. What happened was, if you read carefully to the end of the article, the acknowledgments, they acknowledged a National Natural Science Foundation of China Award. In other words, **the Chinese government paid them to have one of their top biological warfare experts involved** in this type of—

Alex: By the way, Dr. Boyle, stay right there.

FAB: Sure.

Alex Jones: I'm reading the paper. I mean, I know you had big news, you sent us links, but I'm just now reading it. And you talk about a smoking gun—this is the Chinese government paying for the exact same thing with a U.S. lab. How did you discover this? This is a smoking gun. How the hell did you find this?

FAB: Well, Alex, I told you that it's part of my professional responsibilities to stay on top of biological warfare, so I came across it in my research. That's just part of the job I do.

Alex Jones: You're explaining it very well, sir, but just dumb it down.... This is too big, and now you've got time, so dumb it down for everybody. Why these two papers are so smoking gun, because I'm sitting there looking at this. This is incredible. This is unbelievable.

FAB: I have more than that.

Alex Jones: Oh, I know.

FAB: I noticed they acknowledged the National Natural Science Foundation of China Award. In other words, **the best scientists at the University of North Carolina took dirty money from China to allow one of their top biowarfare experts from this Wuhan Institute of Virology and Wuhan, which has the BSL-4 facility—they knew exactly what they were doing, and they permitted this Chinese scientist to work with them to give gain-of-function biowarfare DNA genetic capability to SARS**, which is dangerous enough to begin with. And let me just go through some of the language here. It is truly a smoking gun; clearly that laboratory must be shut down immediately, and all those scientists investigated by the United States government for this and their responsibility here, and for violating my Biological Weapons Anti-Terrorism Act of 1989. But let me continue. This is what they said: "We built a chimeric virus that encodes a novel zoonotic spike protein in the context of viable SARS. This approach characterized the threat posed by SARS coronavirus spike—

Alex Jones: Dr. Boyle, stay there. We've got to go to break. This is your bombshell. I'm reading the paper right here. They are admitting that they built the very virus that China paid the U.S. to build, and now that's been released. And why did they release it? So Xi Jinping could grab power and invade Taiwan. Wow. This is unbelievable. No matter what you've ever heard on this show, this is the craziest and the most documented. This is over the top, and we've caught them red-handed. Unbelievable. We'll be right back. Tell everybody you know to tune in right now. This is unbelievable.

[program break]

Alex Jones: But the point is, this is real. Something big is going on. And now I'm looking at all these prestigious reports going back five years ago, how they engineered this, and Dr. Francis Boyle wrote the U.S. biological weapons law, and he's here laying this out, and I can read the reports. It's ridiculous how obvious this is that the Chinese paid a U.S. university—that's all over the news. Yale and Harvard are in trouble for 300-something million, but turns out it's billions total. That's *Wall Street Journal*, *New York Times*, for Chinese Communist funding. So for whatever reason, we're better at science than they are, and they're getting us to finance and build their surveillance grid—all of it.

Dr. Boyle, please go back to where you were before we went to break, and tell how big this is and what's breaking here and the double smoking guns here. And even more, you've got where this came from, because that'll give us the answer hopefully of where it's going.

FAB: Right. Well, to continue, then, it says this approach characterized the threat posed by a spike in primary human airways. In other words, they're designing this to infect human beings by their airways, and then it says, in vivo. In other words, they are using live animals—

Alex Jones: Slow down and start over. Again, give them the paper's name again. This is so huge. They're making it to infect people. You're right. They should be arrested.

FAB: Of course, they should be prosecuted. No question at all about it. I think that's the one you already had up there. But in any case—

Alex Jones: I'm going to stop interrupting. Just recap what you just said. Walk through this again.

FAB: Right. "We built a chimeric virus," so they joined these different biological warfare agents together into a chimera. As I told you, swine flu was—

Alex Jones: And you said three weeks ago it was a chimera.

FAB: Chimera, right. And here they are doing it to have a "spike in primary human airway cells in vivo." That's surrogates for us, OK. Now if you continue here, they took mice, and with their technique here found robust replication comparable to SARS.

Alex Jones: Wonderful.

FAB: So they're using the gain-of-function technology—

Alex Jones: They're testing it to make sure it spreads quickly.

FAB: That's right. And it's not just SARS, it's gain of function. "Together the data confirmed the ability to infect human airway cells," et cetera. They know exactly what they are doing here.

Alex Jones: I mean, just like Ford makes F-150 trucks, you just found out who made this, and they're openly bragging about it.

FAB: Right. Let me continue. Together the data indicate that viruses utilizing what they put together are capable of inducing considerable disease in mice in the context of basically SARS.

Alex Jones: Wow. And again, SARS is the same coronavirus family.

FAB: Right. **It's weaponized coronavirus. They also conclude that they really couldn't find an antibody against it.**

Alex Jones: Wow.

FAB: So it's extremely dangerous.

Alex Jones: Total jerks.

FAB: Let me continue, then—

Alex Jones: I'm just starting to ask, you know, these people better be arrested really quick.

FAB: Right. Now, let me continue here where they say **their new DNA genetically engineered virus constitutes a gain in pathogenesis. That's a gain of function right there; they admit it. Pathogenesis means lethality and infectiousness, and we know that even *Lancet* has said lethality is about 15%. If you disaggregate numbers even put out by the Chinese government, it's about 17%.** So together, these data represent a crossroads of gain-of-function research concerns, and they just make it clear they're going to continue anyway. They also point out that they involved HIV-based pseudovirus, prepared as previously described—

Alex Jones: —which is what the Indians found. Oh my God.

FAB: That's why I was going to get to that. HIV is–

Alex Jones: This is ridiculous.

FAB: No, no. This is the type of Nazi biowarfare work these scientists do, Alex.

Alex Jones: Oh, no, I agree. But they're publishing. They're admitting they did it.

FAB: Let me continue, Alex. In a footnote it says, **"Cells were originally obtained from Fort Detrick."**

Alex Jones: Oh my God.

FAB: That's a biowarfare–

Alex Jones: So that means a U.S. government biowarfare lab was running this.

FAB: They were involved in it too. Yes.

Alex Jones: Jesus. Let me ask you this. When you learned this, this weekend, what was it like? Was your heart beating faster?

FAB: No, I decided to, well, notify your assistant there Monday morning, and then later that morning, CNN in India did an interview with me on this, but that was only for about 20 minutes. And then I had to go back to my teaching. But you know, this is what I do professionally—

Alex Jones: No, I know, but this is unbelievable. I'm reading the report right here from five years ago. Obviously, I don't think the university knew that this would be used for this, but what did they think they were doing when they were giving a foreign authoritarian government a bioweapon? I mean—

FAB: Well, it's all greed. They were paid for—

Alex Jones: It's like you said, they just take the money, like you said, three weeks ago . . .

FAB: —from Communist China and their top biowarfare expert.

Alex Jones: Well, here's an example. I own 50-caliber rifles. If a known criminal came to me and said, "I want to buy them," I'd say, "Hell, no." You don't give criminals 50-caliber rifles. Well, 50-caliber rifles are dangerous, but nothing compared to this. What the hell is going on? How are you as weapons research laboratories under the guise of safety research allowed to give the Chi Comms stuff like this? You're right. I've been on here 25 years. I've never seen a scandal this big. It's all right here. They admit it.

FAB: It's even worse than that because **all this work, this biological weapons work involving the Wuhan virology, was approved and funded by the National Institutes of Health**—

Alex Jones: Wow.

FAB: —which I've discussed with you before, **and the National Institute of Allergy and Infectious Diseases.** I told you before, **these agencies were up to their eyeballs in research development and testing offensive biological warfare weapons.**

Alex Jones: Dr. Boyle, stay there. You're a great professor and amazing. When we come back, you've got to recap it all and boil it down for the average viewer, because I'm smart, the viewers are smart, but I've been on air—I'm not just being dramatic—I've been on air 25 years. I've never been this shell-shocked. I'm reading these mainline reports; we pulled these up from the internet. This is it. This is the very virus five years ago, cooked up, sold to the Chinese government. I know you don't speculate, but when you come back, why is it out now? What's the end game? How bad is it going to get?

[program break]

Alex Jones: This is big, front and center. What we're covering right now with Professor Francis Boyle and the admissions that a U.S. university engineered the exact virus now spreading across the world. So, finishing up with its provenance, the fact that these are the smoking guns, sir, in synopsis, I know that limits the time we have, and I really appreciate it. Come back tomorrow if you can, and then get into the big picture—the response, how you think it got out, why it was released. I mean, I know that's speculation, but we know it's engineered; we know the U.S. government knows it's engineered. We know this happened before Trump five years ago, but still, just how the hell could this happen?

FAB: Well, let me go back here to this second study to point out. It says at the end, "The current manuscript has been reviewed by the funding agency, the National Institutes of Health. Continuation of these studies have been requested and approved by the National Institutes of Health." **Notice the National Institutes of Health under Fauci is funding this Nazi biological warfare work, and they have approved and requested further development of it, which obviously, this study was 2015, and the NIH wanted it to become an even more deadly pathogenetic virus. And you can also then see here the money from the National Institute of Allergy and Infectious Diseases.** This woman is out there now in public, or she's up to her eyeballs in this too, as is Fauci.

And finally, I originally condemned this North Carolina lab because they're doing gain-of-function work on MERS, as I said. Today in *USA Today*, Tony Fauci admits that the lethality rate of MERS is about 36%, whereas SARS is 10%. This Wuhan is 15% to 17%. So, notice Tony Fauci and the National Institutes of Health—

Alex Jones: —are backtracking.

FAB: No, they know full well that **they were paying this North Carolina lab in cooperation with the Wuhan BSL-4 lab and program to develop biological warfare weapons.**

Alex Jones: Is that why Senator Cotton and even the White House were like, "Hey, China, we don't buy the provenance of this," because they know that China paid a U.S. university to do this? Let me ask you this, then: How bad is it going to be? Why did China do this? I know that's speculation, but just as a citizen, not just a lawyer and an expert on this, what the hell—what do you think the end game is? Why is this out now? Will they use it against Taiwan? We know China bought it as a bioweapon.

FAB: Well, let me just discuss one more scientific article with you. *Archives of Virology* 2010, 155. And here, **Wuhan was working with an institute in Australia to DNA genetically engineer a super bioweapon involving SARS and HIV.** That's right in here; you can read it. And apparently it was successful. So as far as I can tell, Alex, what happened was, the Wuhan Institute of Virology took the—and this was the Australian government that knew all about this. And it says this work was jointly funded by the State Key Program for Basic Research Grants from the Chinese Ministry of Science, Technology, and Knowledge; and the other writer here, the Australian Animal Health Laboratory in Australia. So as far as I can figure out here, what happened, Alex, is that **the Wuhan scientists took the North Carolina SARS with gain of function, which is already a biological warfare weapon, and they took the technology here behind this well-developed SARS HIV weapon; and they brought it all back to the Wuhan BSL-4 and tried to DNA genetically engineer it into a chimera, into a biological warfare weapon involving the coronavirus, the HIV virus, and gain of function.**

Alex Jones: It's all clear in the papers. They admit they did this. You've reverse-engineered it: an incredible job. Do you think it was done on purpose, then? Who stands to gain? As a law professor, who would do this? Who stands to gain?

FAB: Well, clearly, China has an expensive biological warfare program, not as expensive as ours. I mean, we have 12 BSL-4 facilities here in the United States all doing this Nazi biowarfare work. They should all be shut down tomorrow.

Alex Jones: Oh, I totally agree. And then giving China the fruits of it. The Chi Comms can come buy bioweapons from us?

FAB: They bought it. What is interesting here, Alex, is that **they didn't steal it; they bought it. And we sold it to them, and we sold them access to it. They brought it back to that Wuhan BSL-4.**

Alex Jones: Is there any race specificness to it?

FAB: Well, as I said before, we have seen one Black African victim reported that I've seen. So right now, I am withholding judgment on that, but you know, the Chinese put all this together for themselves. And, of course, they were planning to use it as biological warfare against us. There's no—I mean, who else . . .

Alex Jones: Do you think that it got out on an accident, or what do you think?

FAB: As of now, Alex, I think it was an accident. Their BSL facilities had leaks of SARS at least twice before, and I believe it was an accident, and that is now confirmed by Chinese scientists themselves. And this is the fourth study I want to put before you.

Alex Jones: Stay there. We'll do five more minutes before Paul Watson takes over. With Dr. Francis Boyle, the author of the U.S. Biological Weapons Anti-Terrorism Act, and all the rest of it. I've been on air 25 years, folks, and this just tops it all. I mean, we're talking about our children, the whole future, everything else. I had this premonition this morning, and now we're just laying this out. This is just end-of-days stuff. If not this, it'll be something else. I mean, what are these labs doing? Why are they selling it to foreign governments? It needs to stop. It's mad-scientist behavior. They want to reduce world population. They want to distribute it out so they can deny who did it. They just want plausible deniability for bioweapons releases and mass population reduction. That's really what's happening.

{program break}

Alex Jones: We've seen the panicked response of governments in action, but their propaganda is that everything's fine. Dr. Francis Boyle is our guest here for another five minutes. Paul Joseph Watson is set to take back over. Our guest authored the U.S. bioweapons law. In the four minutes we've got left, Doctor, we really appreciate you synopsizing or boiling it all down into what you really think is happening in the bombshells. And this new study you were trying to get into on top of all the other studies you just talked about.

FAB: Right. This is the latest study. It just came out this week. Possible origins of 2019 nCoV coronavirus. What is significant here—you can get it at ResearchGate. **What is significant here is that it is by two professors at the South China University of Technology—they're all professors. And their conclusion on this study is that the Wuhan coronavirus leaked out of that BSL-4 facility. Let me repeat—even Chinese scientists are saying now, independently of me, it leaked out. And I believe it was probably an accident, that one of these death scientists there at the Wuhan BSL-4 facility was trying to DNA genetically engineer the North Carolina technology, the Australian technology, HIV, SARS, gain of function, together into the super biological warfare weapon, and somehow got infected.**

There's been speculation by these authors that there was animal residue, or they breathed it in or something like that. That person then got infected, but since it's asymptomatic, they weren't aware of it. And now, even though they're saying it's 14 days, a British health-care expert estimates it could be 24 days. Whoever this expert was, this death scientist went around and did his normal life activities for the next 14 to 24 days, and it spread all around Wuhan.

Alex Jones: Oh, they were playing with fire, and they got burned.

FAB: Right. They shot themselves in the foot, Alex. That's my assessment at this time, yes. I think they were developing it for use against either us or the Russians and/or the Russians. They have a huge border up there.

Alex Jones: Yes, the whole Russian–Sino split.

FAB: Right. That's no longer the case today, but still, Russia has a lot of land there and not very many people.

Alex Jones: Sure, they can wipe out the Russians, that's their target.

FAB: And China has a lot of people, and they need more land, so I'm not ruling out that it would have been directed—

Alex Jones: Sure. China's always been eyeing Russia greedily. All right. All-powerful. If you can come back tomorrow, the next day—we need updates. This is the biggest news ever. And I would just say that this is unbelievable. The reports, the scientific journals, Dr. Boyle—incredible. What do we call this interview? We're still alive. I mean, I don't know what to call this once we post it on Infowars.

FAB: Well, Alex, let me also say **we can't trust the FBI to do the right thing here. They lied, they covered up, and they sabotaged the Amerithrax coming out of Fort Detrick.** We are going to have to get some other federal law investigative agencies in here to deal with that North Carolina—

Alex Jones: And you authored the U.S. law on bioweapons, so I think you're quite the authority on that. So, again, please join us tomorrow or whenever you can, Dr. Boyle. Very powerful information and just amazing. Thank you so much.

FAB: Well, thank you, Alex, and I do hope you can get this out around the world because the mainstream news media in the United States and Europe have been blackballing me and blacklisting—

Alex Jones: Well, sure. I don't even know what to call this. Smoking Gun, Wuhan Virus, Manmade Spreading Worldwide, Cover-up. I mean, China bought weaponized Wuhan virus from us. Thank you, Dr. Boyle.

...

CHAPTER 3

BIOWEAPONS EXPERT SPEAKS OUT ABOUT NOVEL CORONAVIRUS

Analysis by Dr. Joseph Mercola, an American alternative-medicine proponent, osteopathic physician, and internet business personality

Story at-a-Glance

> Francis Boyle, who for decades has advocated against the development and use of bioweapons, suspects COVID-19 is a weaponized pathogen that escaped from Wuhan City's Biosafety Level 4 facility, which was specifically set up to research coronaviruses and SARS.

> According to Boyle, the COVID-19 virus is a chimera. It includes SARS, an already weaponized coronavirus, along with HIV genetic material and possibly flu virus. It also has gain-of-function properties that allow it to spread a greater distance than normal.

> The incubation period for the COVID-19 infection is still unknown, but estimates range from 14 days to 30 days.

> The U.S. government spent $100 billion on biological warfare programs since September 11, 2001, up until October 2015.

> While there have so far only been a limited number of reported cases of COVID-19 infection in the U.S., the U.S. military has designated several detention sites around the country to quarantine Americans, should the situation take a turn for the worse.

As you know, a novel coronavirus (initially labeled 2019-nCOV before being renamed COVID-19 by the World Health Organization) originating in Wuhan City, Hubei Province, in China, is rapidly spreading across the world.

The first case was reported in Wuhan on December 21, 2019. Symptoms include fever, shortness of breath, severe cough, and pneumonia, which, in more severe cases, can lead to impaired kidney and liver function and kidney failure.

On January 21, 2020, the U.S. Centers for Disease Control and Prevention confirmed the first U.S. case—a patient in Washington state who had recently visited Wuhan. Then, the first U.S. death was reported on February 29, 2020, in Washington state.

Less than a week later, CBS News reported on March 5, 2020, that the number of deaths had quickly risen to 11 nationwide in the U.S.—10 in Washington state and 1 in California. Not only that, but as of that day, "The World Health Organization urged governments around the world to pull out 'all the stops'" to fight the outbreak. On the upside, China "appeared to be over the worst" of it, CBS said.

All told, as of March 5, 2020, there were 98,067 reported cases of novel coronavirus infections affecting 88 countries, 80,430 of which were in China. Worldometer.info provides an easy overview of confirmed cases and deaths that you can check for the latest statistics.

COVID-19—A Weaponized Coronavirus?

In this interview, Francis Boyle — whose background includes an undergraduate degree from the University of Chicago, a juris doctor (lawyer) degree from Harvard, and a PhD in political science—shares his theory of the origin of this novel coronavirus.

For decades, he's advocated against the development and use of bioweapons, which he suspects COVID-19 is. In fact, Boyle was the one who called for biowarfare legislation for the Biological Weapons Convention of 1972, and the one who drafted the Biological Weapons Anti-Terrorism Act of 1989, which was passed unanimously by both Houses of Congress and signed into law by George Bush Sr.

At the time of this recording, February 14, 2020, more than 50,000 people in China had been infected with the virus. Certainly, it does not originate from infected bat soup.

As a result of Boyle's antibiological warfare work, which goes back to the early days of the Reagan administration—a time in which they were using DNA genetic engineering to manufacture biological weapons—Boyle has carefully followed "mysterious outbreaks of disease in both humans and animals around the world" that have appeared since then.

> "My biowarfare antiterrorism act was specifically designed to not only deal with regular biological weapons but also with DNA genetic engineering for biological weapons that was just coming into its infancy when the BWC was being drafted.
>
> "Even though the BWC would cover DNA genetic engineering, I wanted to make it clear by name that it was covered. I also made it clear that it covered synthetic biology as well," Boyle says.
>
> "So, when these unexplained mysterious illnesses break out, I monitor them for a while, and usually I just conclude they can be explained by normal reasons: lack of sanitation, poverty, things of that nature. But in Wuhan it seemed pretty suspicious to me.
>
> "There is this Biosafety Level 4 facility there in Wuhan. It's the first in China, and it was specifically set up to deal with the coronavirus and SARS. SARS is basically a weaponized version of the coronavirus.
>
> "There have been leaks before of SARS out of these facilities, and indeed the only reason for these BSL-4 facilities, based on my experience, is the research, development, testing, and stockpiling of offensive biological weapons.
>
> "For that reason, I stated my opinion: that this Wuhan coronavirus leaked out of that BSL-4 facility . . . maybe mid-November . . . and the Chinese government has been lying about it and covering it up ever since."

Many Unknowns Remain

The first reported case of the COVID-19 infection was on December 1, 2019. Depending on the incubation period, which is still unknown, the initial lead, provided there was one, might have occurred anywhere in November. The official estimate is a 14-day incubation period, but a British health expert believes it's 24 days, and North Korean biological warfare experts believe it's 30 days, Boyle says.

> "As for Wuhan and Hubei Province, they're basically under martial law. There's no other word for it. If you read the statements by President Xi and his assistants, they've made it very clear they're at war here, and that is correct.
>
> "They're at war with their own biological warfare agent.
>
> "President Xi just fired the party apparatchiks in charge of this and has brought in trusted military personnel to handle it, as well as large numbers of PLA [People's Liberation Army] forces saying they're health-care workers. They don't look like health-care workers to me. So, as of now, that's my best reading of the situation."

When asked about rumors that the COVID-19 virus might have been stolen from a high – security laboratory in Winnipeg, Canada, Boyle says:

> "It could have been. I want to make it clear that, in my opinion, they were already working on that at the Wuhan BSL-4 facility. They were working on a biological warfare weapon involving SARS, which is a coronavirus to begin with.
>
> "We do know that Dr. [Yoshihiro] Kawaoka at the University of Wisconsin... resurrected the Spanish flu virus for the Pentagon, obviously for weapons purposes, and he specializes in mating the Spanish flu virus to all sorts of hideous biowarfare instrumentalities. And there was a record of him shipping his products to Winnipeg.
>
> Winnipeg is Canada's equivalent of our own Fort Detrick. It's a BSL-4 facility, and yes, they research, develop, test, manufacture, and stockpile every type of hideous biological warfare weapon that we know of. So some of this technology could have been stolen from Winnipeg. I don't know about that, but as I said, the Wuhan BSL-4 was already working on this to begin with.

"They had already developed SARS. SARS had leaked out two to three times before this, and it seems they were turbocharging SARS, which is what {COVID – 19} looks to be. This is a brand-new generation of biowarfare weapons we haven't seen before. Its lethality goes from 15%, as estimated by *Lancet*, up to 17% to 18% by a British health official and even Chinese statistics. Its infectivity is 83%. It can infect maybe three to four people for every person infected.

"It has gain-of-function properties, which means it travels through air at least six or seven feet, and . . . there are reports that even contaminated human feces give it off, that the human feces radiate off maybe six or seven feet. So we've never seen anything like this before in the history of biological warfare, at least in the public record.

"I want to make it clear: I have never worked for the United States government. I've never had a security clearance. I've never had access to any type of secret information.
I just read what is in the public record and the scientific record and try to draw my own conclusions, and that's what I'm giving you today. I could change my opinion if people can provide me reputable scientific evidence to the contrary.

"Right now, I'm standing by my conclusion that it leaked out of the Wuhan BSL-4, the highest level of the Chinese government has known about it, and they've been covering it up from the get-go, until they informed the WHO at the end of December."

Despite Laws, Biowarfare Experimentation Is Alive and Well

As noted by Boyle, the Wuhan lab is a designated WHO research lab, which may sound odd, considering that these facilities specialize in developing and researching dangerous pathogens that can easily be turned into bioweapons.

According to Boyle, we should not be surprised however, as "WHO is up to its eyeballs in this type of work and has been for quite some time." The U.S. Centers for Disease Control and Prevention and the drug industry also appear to have had their hand in many of the outbreaks of what appear to be weaponized viruses.

> "I won't go through the long history of Big Pharma getting involved in this. There's huge amounts of money here. I believe the West Africa Ebola pandemic originated out of the U.S. BSL-4 facility in Sierra Leone, and that they were testing out a so-called vaccine that contained live Ebola and gave it to these poor people," Boyle says.
>
> "As for the CDC, it has been involved in every... biological warfare death science you could possibly imagine.... It's a matter of public record that during the Reagan administration, the CDC and the American Type Culture Collection sent 40 shipments of weapons-grade biological warfare agents to Saddam Hussein in Iraq, in the hope and expectation that he would weaponize these agents and use them against Iran...
>
> "Of course, the problem is that when that war was over... an order was given to U.S. military forces to blow up Saddam Hussein's biological warfare facilities, and that's not how you deal with biological warfare weapons...
>
> "It contaminated our own troops, and that was a causative factor in the Gulf War Syndrome that... murdered about 11,000 U.S. troops and disabled about 100,000."

According to Boyle, the U.S. government spent $100 billion on biological warfare programs since September 11, 2011, up until October 2015, which is no small sum. To put it into perspective, the U.S. spent $40 billion (assuming a constant dollar value) on the Manhattan Project, which developed the atomic bomb. Boyle also estimates that the U.S. has some 13,000 life scientists working within the biowarfare industry.

> "Clearly, the Reagan administration, under the influence of its neoconservatives who definitely believe in biological weapons and ethnic-specific biological weapons (you can see that in the PNAC report),

were engaged in the use of DNA genetic engineering for the purpose of manufacturing biological weapons.

"That is why I gave a Congressional briefing in Washington, D.C., in 1985. I was asked to do that by the Council for Responsible Genetics that I work with, which involves the leading life scientists in the world from MIT and Harvard.

"I spent seven years at Harvard. I have three degrees, and I knew all these people. They asked me to serve as their lawyer and give this congressional briefing. I blew the whistle, and then they asked me to draft the implementing legislation, which I did . . .

"I want to make it clear, I'm not here to speak in their name, I'm only speaking in *my* name, but if you look at my book *Biowarfare and Terrorism*, Professor Jonathan King wrote the foreword. So I have the leading MIT professor of molecular biology supporting what I'm saying, if you don't think I know enough science about it."

US Prepares for COVID-19 Pandemic

Although there have so far only been a limited number of reported cases of COVID-19 infection in the U.S., the U.S. military has designated several detention sites around the country to quarantine Americans, should the situation take a turn for the worse.

Historically speaking, however, government health officials have been vastly exaggerating the threat of pandemics in the U.S., including the bird flu, the swine flu, anthrax, and Ebola.

For example, as detailed in my 2009 *New York Times* bestseller *The Great Bird Flu Hoax*, then–President George Bush Jr. projected that two million Americans would die from bird flu, the best-case scenario taking only 200,000 lives. The final death count in the U.S. from that pandemic was zero.

It generated massive profits, though, as U.S. taxpayer dollars were used to purchase 20 million doses of Tamiflu. One of the people who was able to line his pockets from that hoax was Defense Secretary Donald Rumsfeld, who was president of Gilead Sciences when the drug was created.

> "[The bird flu] was another DNA, genetically engineered biological warfare weapon," Boyle notes. "It was a chimera. It had three different elements in it, and we were all lucky that somehow they attenuated the lethality and the infectiveness of the bird flu."

Whether or not COVID-19 will be similarly ineffective in its spread and lethality remains to be seen. Judging by the statistics in China, "it doesn't look very good," Boyle says.

Understanding the COVID-19 Virus

According to Boyle, the COVID-19 virus is a chimera, like the avian flu virus before it. It includes SARS, an already weaponized coronavirus, along with HIV genetic material. "That was in a published article by Indian scientists. You could see the pictures right there, but political pressure was brought to bear upon them, so they withdrew [the paper]."

This is why some scientists are now looking into using HIV drugs to treat it, Boyle says. COVID-19 may also have a flu virus mixed in, along with gain-of-function properties that allow it to spread a greater distance than normal.

Pandemics Repeatedly Used to Further Police State

Pandemics have also been used to chip away public freedoms. For example, the anthrax scare of 2001 was used as the impetus for signing the Patriot Act, which was the first step in taking away many of our personal freedoms and rolling out a complete surveillance state. To me, such outcomes are far more concerning than the risk of infection itself. Boyle adds:

> "They used Amerithrax to ram the Patriot Act through, that is correct.... We became a police state.... And as I pointed out in *Biowarfare and Terrorism*, I think the same people who were behind the 9/11 terrorist attack were also behind the Amerithrax, but I'm just connecting dots there....
>
> "What's called Amerithrax came out of a U.S. government biological warfare weapons lab and program, and I publicly blew the whistle on that the first weekend of November 2001. The Council for

> Responsible Genetics was having its convention at Harvard Divinity School, and I was chairing a panel with King and other experts on biological warfare, on U.S. biological warfare programs.
>
> "As I was walking into the Harvard Divinity School, Fox TV had a camera crew there, and I said, 'Obviously, this came out of a U.S. biological weapons program, and probably Fort Detrick.'
>
> "I conducted the session and made the same comment. Then I made a comment to a Washington, D.C., radio station to that effect and to the BBC, so everyone in the world heard me.
>
> "At that point, someone gave an order that I was never to be interviewed again by any mainstream news about biological warfare programs. And that's been the case since the first week of November 2001."

As noted by Boyle, George Orwell's book *1984* has become reality. Boyle has since lectured lawyers at DePaul Law School in Chicago about the totalitarian nature of the Patriot Act.

> "Snowden has correctly pointed out that the federal government is spying on everything we say, all of our electronic communications, you name it," Boyle says.
>
> "And again, the proof is, I've been completely blackballed out of the U.S. media. Indeed, if you go back and look at the Amerithrax attacks, they also hit the mainstream U.S. media to make it clear to them that if they covered this issue, they will be killed too."

Bioweapons Are Developed to Be Used

As noted by Boyle, the U.S. government has a large stockpile of Amerithrax—a super-weapons-grade nanotechnology anthrax with one trillion spores per gram—and that's just the tip of the iceberg of the biological weapons developed. What's more, Boyle has no doubt these weapons will eventually be put to use, as they have in the past. He says:

"There was a tabletop exercise at John Hopkins University last fall ... on coronavirus. Tabletop exercise, that's a euphemism for a war game. Their estimate was that it killed 65 million people ....

"John Hopkins is up to their eyeballs in this Nazi biological warfare dirty work. They have a BSL-3 facility there ... that they proudly announce on their website.

"They justify it by saying they're developing vaccines. OK ... how do they do that?
They go out around the world, and this is a matter of public record; and scour for every type of hideous disease, fungus, virus, and bacteria you can possibly imagine. They then bring it back to these BSL-4 labs and develop an offensive biological agent using DNA genetic engineering and synthetic biology ... set up by the Pentagon under DARPA [Defense Advanced Research Projects Agency].... Once they have this offensive agent, they then proceed to develop a vaccine, because the agent is no good unless you can have a vaccine to protect your own people.

"So, they're developing vaccines to have biological weapons, because a biological weapon consists of two elements: the offensive biological warfare agent in the first place; and then, second, a vaccine to protect your own people, and that is what is being done at all these BSL-4 facilities, and many of the BSL-3s as well.

"John Hopkins has a BSL-3, and they admit they do dual use. That's what dual use means. They first develop the offensive biological warfare agent, and then they develop the supposed vaccine."

Indeed, Johns Hopkins University is the biggest recipient of research grants from federal agencies, including the National Institutes of Health, the National Science Foundation, and the Department of Defense. It has also received millions of dollars in research grants from the Gates Foundation. In 2016, Johns Hopkins spent more than $2 billion on research projects, leading all U.S. universities in research spending for the 38th year in a row.

How Can We Best Prevent or Treat the COVID-19 Infection?

Although it's unclear exactly which treatment is the most effective, my guess is that Dr. Paul Marik's intravenous vitamin C protocol for sepsis would be a good starting point, seeing how sepsis appears to be what kills those who succumb to a serious COVID-19 infection.

Marik's retrospective before/after clinical study showed that giving patients IV vitamin C with hydrocortisone and vitamin B1 for two days reduced mortality from 40% to 8.5%. The precise protocol used was 200 mg of thiamine every 12 hours, 1,500 mg of ascorbic acid every 6 hours, and 50 mg of hydrocortisone every 6 hours. Importantly, the treatment has no side effects and is inexpensive, readily available, and simple to administer.

According to Marik, vitamin C and corticosteroids have a synergistic effect, which is part of why his combo protocol is so effective. Still, simply using high-dose IV vitamin C exclusively has been shown to improve survival in patients with sepsis and acute respiratory failure, reducing mortality from 46% to 30%.

It also reduced the number of days they needed to remain hospitalized. On average, those who received vitamin C had by day 28 spent three fewer days in the intensive care unit than the placebo group (7 days compared to 10). By day 60, the treatment group had also spent 7 fewer days in the hospital overall—15 days compared to 22.

While there are no trials that look at integrating hyperbaric oxygen therapy (HBOT), my suspicion is that this would provide a powerful synergy that could get the fatality rate from sepsis even closer to zero. Sadly, HBOT is not available at many hospitals, and even if it were, it is not approved for sepsis.

You can learn more about Marik's sepsis protocol in "Vitamin C—A Game Changer in Treatment of Deadly Sepsis," along with common-sense recommendations for how to lower your risk of sepsis in the first place.

You can also review Marik's PowerPoint presentation, "Hydrocortisone, Ascorbic Acid, and Thiamine for the Treatment of Severe Sepsis and Septic Shock," presented at the 2020 Critical Care Reviews meeting in Australia. For COVID-19 at-home care advice from the WHO, please see "Novel Coronavirus—The Latest Pandemic Scare."

...

CHAPTER 4

THE ISRAELI HUMAN-RIGHTS LAWSUIT AGAINST CHINA FOR THE COVID-19 PANDEMIC

At the end of April 2020, I was contacted by an Israeli human-rights law firm that had sued China over the COVID-19 pandemic in the Israeli court system.[1] This was one of the very first such domestic lawsuits filed against China in the world. They requested that I intervene in the lawsuit on their behalf and that of their clients, and also to provide them with a *Declaration* of my already publicly expressed expert opinion on COVID-19 being an offensive biological warfare weapon that had leaked out of the Wuhan BSL-4 to be used in the ongoing Israeli litigation against China.

Because of the monumental importance of this litigation for combating, stopping. and defeating the worldwide COVID-19 pandemic, I agreed to do so on June 6, 2020. On August 22, 2020, this Israeli human-rights law firm informed me that the Israeli Foreign Ministry had officially served my Declaration upon the government of China as part of these Israeli legal proceedings against it. I guess I will not be lecturing in China anytime soon.

My Declaration is now a matter of public record. I have published it below so that you, the reader, can understand and evaluate the bases for my conclusion that COVID-19 is an offensive biological warfare weapon that leaked out of that BSL-4 located in Wuhan, China. Everything that has emerged into the public record since then further supports and strengthens my arguments

1 Adam Eliyahu Berkowitz, *Israelis, Americans Join Cause to Sue China over Coronavirus,* Israel365 News, (Aug. 28, 2020, 6:13 p.m.), https://www.israel365news.com/148034/israelis-americans-team-up-to-sue-china-over-coronavirus/.

that COVID-19 is an offensive biological warfare weapon that leaked out of that Wuhan BSL-4.[2]

DECLARATION OF PROFESSOR FRANCIS A. BOYLE

Pursuant to 28 USC 1746, Francis A. Boyle makes the following Declaration under penalty of perjury:

1. My name is Francis A. Boyle.
2. I am legally able to make this Declaration because I am over the age of 18 years old and legally competent in every way to swear to these facts.
3. I make this Declaration from within the territory of the United States of America.
4. I am a former advisory board member for the Council for Responsible Genetics and a professor of International Law at the University of Illinois College of Law.
5. My educational background includes an undergraduate degree from the University of Chicago, a juris doctor (lawyer) magna cum laude degree from Harvard University Law School in 1976, a master's degree in 1978 from Harvard University, and a PhD in 1983 from Harvard University in political science specializing in international relations and international politics, from the Harvard Graduate School of Arts and Sciences Department of Government. I went through the exact same PhD program at Harvard that graduated Henry Kissinger before me, and was also an associate at the Harvard University Center for International Affairs for two years. I was a teaching fellow for Harvard Undergraduates for two years in courses on International Organizations, International Law, and International Human Rights Law before becoming an assistant professor of Law at the University of Illinois College of Law in 1978.

---

2 Joseph Mercola, *More Experts Point to SARS-CoV-2 Being Created in a Lab*, Doctor Mercola Newsletter (Sep. 4, 2020), https://articles.mercola.com/sites/articles/archive/2020/09/04/coronavirus-chimera.aspx.

6. I am the author of *Defending Civil Resistance Under International Law*, *The Future of International Law and American Foreign Policy*, *World Politics and International Law*, and other books, as well as major articles on a range of related international law and human-rights issues.
7. My professional memberships include the American Society of International Law, the American Bar Association, the American Political Science Association, and the Lieber Group on the Laws of War.
8. I have been a consultant to Amnesty International and the American Friends Service Committee.
9. I had represented Bosnia-Herzegovina in the International Court of Justice. http://www.un.org/Overview/Organs/icj.html
10. For decades, I have advocated against the development and use of bioweapons. This experience is relevant here because my experience causes me to believe that the SARS-CoV-2 virus or COVID-19 disease is a bioweapon.
11. I drafted the United States domestic implementing legislation for the Biological Weapons Convention known as the Biological Weapons Anti-Terrorism Act [BWATA] of 1989 that was passed unanimously by both Houses of the United States Congress and signed into law by President George H. W. Bush Sr., which still remains on the U.S. statute books today, as amended. My BWATA was also specifically intended to prevent the use of DNA genetic engineering in order to research, develop, test, and manufacture biological weapons. The story is told in my book *Biowarfare and Terrorism* [Clarity Press: 2005], with a foreword by MIT Professor Jonathan King, a cofounder of the Council for Responsible Genetics.
12. I won the University of Chicago's Sigma Xi certificate of merit and prize in biology for my graduating year in 1971. They gave out one per year, and it went to seniors, but in my case, they had to make a special exception because I was a graduating junior.
13. Based on my knowledge, experience, and expertise, the origins of the novel coronavirus, SARS-CoV-2, is a biological warfare weapon.
14. The term *novel coronavirus* means it is a new virus not previously known to previously infect humans.

15. The currently held conventional view is that SARS-CoV-2 was transmitted through animals (zoonotic transmission), specifically bats.
16. I dismiss this notion categorically.
17. This is indeed a bioengineered synthetic virus that was not transmitted from animals to humans without human intervention.
18. For starters, a *Lancet* paper published on February 15, 2020, by physicians who treated some of the first COVID-19 patients in China, showed that Patient Zero, the one believed to have started the transmission, was nowhere near the Wuhan seafood market.
19. What's more, there were no bats of the type in question sold in, or even close to, the market.
20. At least one-third of the patients reviewed at the start of the outbreak also had no exposure or links to that market.
21. This data supports my counterargument that SARS-CoV-2 was not zoonotically transmitted but is in fact a bioengineered virus.
22. U.S. and foreign politicians and intelligence agencies are starting to say they believe the virus leaked from the Wuhan BSL-4 (Biosafety Level 4 lab), which is China's equivalent to the United States' Fort Detrick, where they research, develop, and test biological weapons.
23. The novel coronavirus is SARS, which is a weaponized version of the coronavirus to begin with, to which was added gain-of-function capabilities that increase its virulence, which makes it more infectious and more lethal. COVID-19 also appears to have been aerosolized by means of nanotechnology at the Wuhan BSL-4, which is China's Fort Detrick that has done the same with biowarfare agents.
24. A scientific article reveals that the Australian Health Board was working with the Wuhan BSL-4 "genetically engineered HIV into SARS." So, that is all verified in scientific papers. In addition, it seems to me that they took that all back to the Wuhan BSL-4 and applied nanotechnology to it. COVID-19 appears to have been aerosolized by means of nanotechnology at the Wuhan BSL-4, which is China's Fort Detrick that has done the same with biowarfare agents for aerial delivery. Aerosolization is a hallmark of a biological weapon so that human beings might breathe it. This is something you need to do in a BSL-4 biological weapons lab. Applying nanotechnology is so dangerous that

people working with it have to wear a moon suit with a portable air supply to breathe.

25. We also know that one of the cooperating institutions to Wuhan BSL-4 was my triple alma mater, Harvard; and that the chairman of the Harvard Chemistry Department, Dr. Charles Lieber, a specialist in nanotechnology, set up an entire laboratory in Wuhan where, according to reports, he specialized in applying nanotechnology to chemistry and biology. Harvard is also listed as a cooperative research institution at the Wuhan BSL-4—China's Fort Detrick.
26. My evaluation, based on what I've read in the literature, is that they tried to weaponize all that together. And that is SARS-CoV-2 that we are dealing with now.
27. So, SARS-CoV-2 is SARS, which is a biowarfare agent to begin with.
28. Second, SARS-CoV-2 has gain-of-function properties, which makes it more lethal and more infectious.
29. It has HIV that was DNA genetically engineered into there. That was *also* confirmed by the Indian scientists. And the French Nobel Prize winner in Medicine who won it for discovering that HIV causes AIDS has also stated that HIV has been genetically engineered into COVID-19.
30. It looks like nanotechnology has been applied to aerosolize and weaponize COVID-19. An MIT scientist who did a study found that SARS-CoV-2 traveled 27 feet through the air. And that, I guess, was in laboratory conditions. That, I think, is why it's so infectious, and that is what I believe we are dealing with here.
31. This is also why the six-foot social distancing recommended by the CDC is preposterous; even doubling that might do you no good. If there is nanotechnology involved, it floats above the air, on the air, in the air, and with the air.
32. I am not saying that China deliberately released this, shooting itself in the foot. But it was clear they were developing an existentially dangerous biological weapon that had never been seen before in humanity, and it leaked out of the lab.
33. And as you see in the *Washington Post,* U.S. State Department officials reported back to Washington that there were inadequate safety

precautions and procedures in that lab to begin with. We also know that SARS has leaked out of other Chinese biological warfare labs. So right now, I believe that is what happened here.

34. I personally believe that until our political leaders come clean with the American people, both at the White House and in Congress and our state governments, and publicly admit that this is an existentially dangerous offensive biological warfare weapon that we are dealing with, I do not see that we will be able to confront it. The same is true for Israel.

The Origin of SARS-CoV-2.

35. One of the primary investigators on the 2015 paper from the University of North Carolina—"A SARS-like Cluster of Circulating Bat Coronaviruses Shows Potential for Human Emergence"—was Dr. Shi Zhengli, a virologist who in 2010 had published a paper discussing the weaponization of the SARS virus.
36. Normally, while the coronavirus found in bats may be SARS, it typically does not infect humans, as it does not target the ACE-2 receptor.
37. The infectious agent causing the current pandemic is called SARS-CoV-2—SARS standing for "serious acute respiratory infection"; and CoV-2, indicating that it's a second type of SARS coronavirus known to infect humans.
38. SARS-CoV-2, of course, contains the genetic modification to attach to ACE2 receptors in human cells, which allows it to infect them. Zhengli's publications show that she engineered this bat coronavirus into one which crosses species and infects humans. She has in fact been working on this for more than 10 years.

"That is why I said SARS was a bioengineered warfare weapon to begin with," Boyle says. "And that is what the University of North Carolina and the Australian lab were trying to make even more dangerous with the gain-of-function and the HIV. So ... SARS was a biological warfare agent to begin with, it leaked, and that is the origin of the COVID-19 epidemic."

39. In addition, an Indian paper that ended up being withdrawn due to intense political pressure shows that a specific envelope protein from the HIV virus called GP41 was integrated in the RNA sequences of SARS-CoV-2.
40. In other words, the implication is that the HIV virus was genetically engineered into SARS.
41. So, in summary, SARS-CoV-2 appears to be a bioengineered bat coronavirus—which was initially benign and nontransmittable to humans without human intervention.
42. Zhengli then genetically modified the virus to integrate spike proteins that allows the virus to enter human cells by attaching to ACE-2 receptors. That was the first modification.
43. The second modification was to integrate an envelope protein from HIV called GP141, which tends to impair the immune system. A third modification appears to involve nanotechnology to make the virus light enough to remain airborne for a long time, apparently giving it a range of up to 27 feet. And then, of course, it was given gain-of-function properties at the University of North Carolina BSL-3.

Nanotech Expert with Wuhan Connection Arrested

44. While the BSL-4 lab in Wuhan may have leaked the virus, its creation does not appear to be limited to the Chinese. The chairman of the Harvard Department of Chemistry, nanoscience expert Dr. Charles Lieber, was arrested earlier this year by federal agencies, suspected of illegal dealings with China. Lieber has denied the allegations.
45. The Wuhan University of Technology (WUT) allegedly paid Lieber $50,000 a month from 2012 to 2017 to help establish and oversee the WUT–Harvard Joint Nano Key Laboratory. Lieber also received another $150,000 a month in living expenses from China's Thousand Talents program. Given the fact that I spent seven years as a student at Harvard, I have three degrees from Harvard, and I spent two years teaching at Harvard, I am confident that Harvard knew what the chair of their Chemistry Department was doing in Wuhan. It has also been reported that Professor Lieber worked for Fort Detrick—undoubtedly to aerosolize biological warfare weapons for them.

Researchers Working on Gain of Function to Spanish Flu

46. If you think SARS-CoV-2 is bad, be glad it's not the weaponized version of Spanish flu, which has also been in the works. As I wrote elsewhere:

"The University of North Carolina's work was existentially dangerous, and they knew it at the time. If you read the UNC scientific article co-written by the Wuhan BSL-4 scientist Shi Zhengli ... it says, 'Experiments with the full-length and chimeric SHC014 recombinant viruses were initiated and performed before the GOF research funding pause and have since been reviewed and approved for continued study by the NIH.'

"It says recombinant ... so, they admit it was gain-of-function research. The research was paused by the National Institutes of Health. Why was it paused by NIH? Because there was a letter put out by large numbers of life scientists at the time saying this type of gain-of-function work ... could be existentially dangerous if it got out in the public. Therefore, it had to be terminated .... But the NIH was funding this in the beginning.

"A footnote here: I read the NIH's pause letter to the University of North Carolina, and UNC was doing two gain-of-function research projects. The other one was with Dr. Yoshihiro Kawaoka from the University of Wisconsin, who had resurrected the Spanish flu virus for the Pentagon.

"According to the pause letter, they were also doing gain-of-function work on the flu virus—one could only conclude it was the Spanish flu virus. It did not say the Spanish flu, but they also put a gain-of-function pause on that type of deadly research .... I mean, the Spanish flu, we all know what that is, so imagine giving the Spanish flu gain-of-function properties, making it even more lethal and more infectious. That's exactly what was going on there at that UNC lab.

"Disturbingly, while the NIH halted funding of this kind of gain-of-function research on lethal pathogens in 2014, it reauthorized it in December 2017, and I suspect Kawaoka's work may have been restarted as well, although I have not found proof of it yet.

"So, this was existentially dangerous work that was going on at that UNC lab. Everyone knew it, NIH funded it, and NIAID under Dr. Fauci funded it as well. They knew exactly how dangerous this was. They paused it and then they resumed it," Boyle says.

47. At the first convention of synthetic biologists, in their final report, one of their key recommendations was the repeal of my Biological Weapons Anti-Terrorism Act, because they fully intended to use synthetic biology to manufacture biological weapons, to which my BWATA applied by name.
48. My BWATA law still applies. It provides for life imprisonment for everyone who has done this: all the scientists involved at the University of North Carolina, and everyone who funded this project, knowing that it was existentially dangerous—and that includes Fauci and people at the NIH, the UNC, the Food and Drug Administration, the Dana Farber Cancer Institute at Harvard, inter alia.
49. So, just how would we get that process of justice going?
50. One of the variants of criminal intent is the demonstration of grave indifference to human life. And that is the criminal intent necessary for homicide.
51. So in my opinion, and my advice would be, if we can't get Attorney General William Pelham Barr to sign off on prosecuting these people, then the district attorney, state's attorney, attorney general out there in North Carolina, institute an investigation and indict everyone involved in this North Carolina work for homicide.
52. And that could include up to and including murder, malice aforethought. Again, one of the elements can be manifestation of grave indifference to human life. And it's clear from the 2015 UNC paper, they knew it was gain of function, they paused it because it was existentially dangerous, and it was then reapproved and they continued it.
53. All BSL-3 and BSL-4 laboratories must be closed down, and all biowarfare work with lethal pathogens ceased. They are all existentially dangerous. This is a catastrophe waiting to happen. And it has now happened. Here we are. It's staring us in the face.

54. Certainly, COVID-19 is nowhere near as devastating as the Black Death or the Spanish flu of 1918, both of which exacted a shocking death toll, all without the aid of synthetic molecules and nanotechnology.
55. The very idea that any of these horrific illnesses might be brought back in turbocharged form should be terrifying enough for the world to unite in saying, "No, thanks, we don't want or need that kind of research going on." What value have these dangerous laboratories provided to date compared to the risk they are exposing all of us to?
56. I believe COVID-19 has the ability to become a serious pandemic killer.
57. Based on my expertise and analysis, I conclude that the known characteristics of SARS-CoV-2 are consistent with a bioengineered virus taking a preexisting natural virus and adjusting or modifying the SARS virus with parts of other viruses.
58. This lawsuit in Israel is of utmost and critical importance for bringing justice to the victims of COVID-19 all over the world.

I declare under penalty of perjury that the foregoing is true and correct to the best of my knowledge and belief.

Professor Francis Anthony Boyle
University of Illinois at Urbana-Champaign
College of Law
204 Law Building
504 East Pennsylvania Avenue
Champaign, IL 61820 USA
voice: 217/333-7954
fax: 217/244-1478
E-mail fboyle@illinois.edu
June 6, 2020

. . .

CHAPTER 5

THE INDIAN LECTURE (JUNE 26, 2020)

During the early stages of the COVID pandemic, I gave live interviews to two Indian TV stations then broadcasting on the air: CNN India, and an indigenous Indian television network. During the course of these interviews, I stated my position that COVID-19 is an offensive biological warfare weapon that had leaked out of the Wuhan BSL-4. I also publicly agreed with the Indian scientists who had discovered that HIV was DNA genetically engineered into COVID-19. Later on, **Luc Montagnier from France who had won the Nobel Prize in Medicine for determining that HIV caused AIDS**, would also publicly agree with them. So much for that debate! I also offered to help the Modi government if they wanted my advice.

Because of these activities, I was asked to give an Honorary Keynote Address on "The COVID-19 Pandemic" by the Maharashtra Institute of Technology School of Government at the World Peace University in Pune, India, on June 26, 2020, before their scholarly conference on "Eradication of Biological and Chemical Weapons" that was convened there over that weekend. I was given 20 minutes to speak. So I had to present a most succinct account of my position:

COVID-19 Is an Offensive Biological Warfare Weapon That Leaked Out of China's Wuhan BSL-4 Lab*

by

Professor Francis A. Boyle

Before the International Conference on "Eradication of Biological and Chemical Weapons,"

Maharashtra Institute of Technology World Peace University (MIT-PUNE)

Pune, India
June 26, 2020

Namaste! Thank you very much for having me here today to speak to this outstanding group of peacemakers, to which cause I have devoted the last five decades of my life. I drafted the United States domestic implementing legislation for the Biological Weapons Convention known as the Biological Weapons Anti-Terrorism Act (BWATA) of 1989 that was approved unanimously by both Houses of the United States Congress and signed into law by President George Bush Sr.. My BWATA was instigated by the fact that the Reagan administration and its neoconservatives had gotten heavily involved in the use of DNA genetic engineering techniques to research, develop, and test illegal biological warfare weapons. I set out to stop this with the assistance of my friends and colleagues at the Council for Responsible Genetics at that time—some of the top life scientists in the world from Harvard, MIT, Sloan-Kettering, et cetera. They were founded in 1983 and soon thereafter asked me to join with them in order to work against biological weapons.

Now, so far I have appeared live on Indian television twice in order to discuss and analyze the coronavirus at the very beginning of this pandemic—once with Indian CNN, and it was a very good session. Then a second time with an indigenous Indian TV station, once again a very good session. Both times I told the Indian people that on the basis of my research, I have concluded that COVID-19 is an offensive biological warfare weapon that leaked out of the Wuhan BSL-4 in China.

You have to understand that this Wuhan BSL-4 is China's first Fort Detrick. Let me repeat that: this is China's first Fort Detrick. We all know what goes on at Fort Detrick. Historically they have researched, developed, tested, stockpiled, and sometimes used offensive biological warfare weapons, including and especially by means of DNA genetic engineering and now by means of synthetic biology. That is precisely what I set out to stop with my Biological Weapons Anti-Terrorism Act of 1989. This is what is confronting us here today.

I am not a China-basher. I am not a neoconservative. I am not a warmonger. But I believe that under the circumstances of this global pandemic, I have to tell the truth about what happened here for all of us citizens of humanity to understand, and then to figure out how to come to grips with this. We are literally fighting World War III here. Not against China, but against COVID-19. It threatens all humanity. As you and I just saw from the statistics as of yesterday, the highest level of infection in the world is the United States, then followed by Brazil, and then followed by your India. So this is a very serious battle that we are engaged in here.

Based on my scientific research, and I won't go through it all here, COVID-19 originated out of that Wuhan BSL-4 as a biological warfare weapon. It basically starts with SARS, and SARS is a weaponized version of coronavirus. Earlier SARS had leaked out of Chinese biological warfare labs before. At the Wuhan BSL-4, they manufactured a synthetic recombinant virus for SARS. Then their notorious Bat Queen [Zhengli-Li Shi] brought it to a laboratory at the University of North Carolina that is a BSL-3 Biosafety Level 3 lab. Indeed, all these Biosafety Level 3 and 4 labs have to be terminated immediately. They all leak. That's exactly what happened at the Wuhan BSL-4. I'm not saying China did this deliberately. It was a leak. Fort Detrick has leaked. All of these BSL-4s leak. They are existentially dangerous, and they must be shut down, and the same is true for the BSL-3s.

So the Wuhan BSL-4 took this synthetic recombinant SARS virus over to the University of North Carolina BSL-3, which is a well-known biological warfare center here in the United States that I have publicly condemned before. BSL-3s do every type of hideous Nazi biological warfare dirty work that you can possibly imagine, as well as the BSL-4s, which are far worse. And they took it to the UNC BSL-3 for the purpose of applying gain-of-function technology to it, which means using DNA genetic engineering and synthetic biology to make it more lethal and more infectious.

Indeed, involved in this Nazi death science dirty work was not only the University of North Carolina but the United States government's own Food and Drug Administration that has a long history of being involved in biological warfare. Likewise, my alma mater Harvard, the Dana-Farber Cancer Institute at the Harvard Medical School, which is supposed to be the number-one-ranked in the country if not the world, and is part of Harvard's world-renowned Massachusetts General Hospital complex was involved in this project. (When I was a student at Harvard, I was treated over at Harvard's Mass Gen on my Harvard student health plan.)

There has long been an overlap between cancer research and biological warfare development. This Nazi biowarfare death science project was approved and paid for by the U.S. National Institutes of Health, part of the U.S. Department of Health and Human Services; and NIAID, under the direction of Dr Tony Fauci. Fauci has been up to his eyeballs in Nazi biowarfare death science dirty work since he became the director of NIAID during the neoconservative Reagan administration, and has been there ever since, approving it and funding it and supervising it. My BWATA was specifically designed to stop Fauci and these other American Nazi biowarfare death scientists. To complete the circle, the UNC BSL-3/Wuhan BSL-4 project also acknowledged receiving cells from Fort Detrick. The notorious PRC Bat Queen personally handled all of this Nazi biowarfare death science dirty work at the Wuhan BSL-4, and then brought it to the UNC BSL-3 for gain-of-function enhancement, and then brought this deadly combined biotechnology back to the Wuhan BSL-4.

In addition, your courageous Indian scientists here pointed out right at the very beginning of this pandemic that there is HIV that has been DNA genetically engineered directly into COVID-19. I read that study. It certainly convinced me. They had the pictures there. Of course, enormous political pressure was applied upon them to withdraw that study. But even the French microbiologist Montagnier who won the Nobel Prize in Medicine for determining that HIV causes AIDS, confirmed that study and said that yes, HIV is DNA genetically engineered right into COVID-19.

How did the Wuhan BSL-4 get that? They sent a scientist down to Australia, and working with the Australian Health Board, they DNA genetically engineered HIV directly into SARS, which I have already explained is a weaponized coronavirus. So they brought that deadly biotechnology back to the Wuhan BSL-4, and that can be confirmed by another scientific research paper that I have cited in my interviews on this matter. Indeed, if you doubt my analysis here, about a month ago there was a report by the well-known Five Eyes Committee of intelligence services from the United States, Canada, Australia, New Zealand, and Britain, that was leaked to the *Australian Daily Telegraph*, completely agreeing with my analysis that COVID-19 came out of the Wuhan BSL-4, courtesy of the University of North Carolina and this Australian Health Board. That was published in the Australian news media, and I appeared live on Sky News in Australia at the next available opportunity for about ten minutes or so to discuss this with the Australian people.

The final piece of the puzzle, at least as I have been able to determine so far—and I'm certainly fully prepared to reevaluate my conclusions on the basis of further evidence—is that the Wuhan BSL-4 bragged on their website that they have successfully applied nanotechnology to viruses. Nanotechnology to viruses! What is nanotechnology good for when it comes to viruses? Aerosolizing them! That's what you do with nanotechnology. You aerosolize viruses and bacteria, et cetera, to be used as weapons to be delivered by air in order to be breathed by human beings. Aerosolization—Fort Detrick does it too. Aerosolization is always the tip-off of a biological warfare weapon. It serves no legitimate scientific or medical purpose at all. That is why at the Wuhan BSL-4 when they work there, they have to wear moon suits and use their own portable air supply. Likewise, that's what they do at the BSL-4 at Fort Detrick. That's what all these Nazi biowarfare death scientists do at all BSL-4s.

This is what they do at the BSL-4 right here in Pune. I've seen the pictures. Whatever nonsense they're telling you about what's going on there, this is India's Fort Detrick. India wants to play with the big boys —the United States and China and Russia—and especially compete with their long-standing adversary, China. So they set up their own Fort Detrick in Pune despite the requirements of the Biological Weapons Convention.

So in my assessment of the situation, this is what we are dealing with. This is SARS on steroids. SARS has a lethality rate of somewhere around 14–15% based upon the scientific literature. This is what we are dealing with in India, in the United States, in Brazil, and around the world. It is extremely infectious, it is highly lethal, and it is existentially dangerous. Basically, humanity is fighting World War III against COVID-19. It will kill millions if somehow we do not figure out collectively how to stop it.

In the meantime, we have to shut down all these BSL-3s and BSL-4s, including India's Pune BSL-4, because they will leak again. They all leak. That is what happened here in China. I believe the leak occurred, as best I can figure out, from the public record sometime around or about the first week in November 2019. It had nothing to do with the so-called wet market. This is just a cover story and propaganda by the Chinese Communist government. They covered up the SARS bioweapon leak the first time, and as you know, maybe 1,200 died. Finally, we were able to contain SARS. But this is gain-of-function SARS on steroids that has been aerosolized and has HIV in it. So it is far more existentially dangerous than the original SARS itself. And that is why I went live on Indian television twice to explain to the Indian people what you are up against here in India. And now I am doing this a third time, at more length at this scholarly conference.

With all due respect to your previous speaker, and I mean that, the main problem here is not so-called terrorist organizations. The main problem here has always been terrorist governments like the United States, the United Kingdom, Russia, China, France, Israel, et cetera, and now I regret to say, India, with your Pune BSL-4. You will note that at your Pune BSL-4, they're running around in there in moon suits with portable air supplies so that they can aerosolize whatever biological warfare weapons they have there for delivery to human beings.

This goes all the way back to the neoconservative Reagan administration and their Tony Fauci getting involved in applying DNA genetic engineering to biological weapons, which I tried to stop with my BWATA legislation. Since that time, there has been an offensive biological warfare weapons arms race that has been going on by the major industrial countries of the world: the United States, Britain, China, Russia, France, and Israel; and now I regret to report that India has joined their ranks too. That is what is going on here. That is what we confront as human beings.

It is a long-term problem. All these BSL-3s and BSL-4s have to be shut down immediately, including the one here at Pune. It will leak. There's no doubt about it. West Nile virus leaked in the United States from the Department of Agriculture Biowarfare lab there on Plum Island. It has infected people all over the country. Lyme disease also leaked from that same USDA biowarfare lab on Plum Island and has infected people all over the country. There is a long history of the USDA doing dirty Nazi biowarfare work on plants and animals.

So COVID-19 leaked from that Wuhan BSL-4 probably around or about the first week in November. The first case was publicly reported about November 16. At that point, at least if not sooner, the Chinese government realized there was a leak there, and they proceeded to lie about it and cover up about it, just like they did on SARS; just like the United States government has done on Fort Detrick and Plum Island and some of its other biowarfare labs. They all cover up on it because they know that what they are doing violates the Biological Weapons Convention and is morbidly and fatally and existentially dangerous to human beings as well as to animals and plants. So I am not singling out China here.

Indeed, there was a U.S. State Department delegation that went out to that Wuhan BSL-4. The PRC had been asking for American help and advice to construct it—the world-renowned experts on biological weapons and warfare are made in the U.S. and U.K. The State Department came back, and you can read their report in the *Washington Post*, saying that there were serious safety and technology problems at the Wuhan BSL-4. So it leaked, China covered it up, and here we are today. If the PRC had acted immediately and effectively to shut down the city of Wuhan and its surrounding area the moment they had notice about it somewhere around or about November 1–16, 2019, instead of covering it up, perhaps we could have avoided this entire calamity and worldwide pandemic.

Let me just repeat that this research was approved and funded by the U.S. National Institutes of Health and the U.S. National Institute of Allergy and Infectious Diseases under Tony Fauci. They all knew all about it. They all funded it. That Wuhan BSL-4 was also a WHO research lab. Imagine that—the WHO being a sponsor of China's first Fort Detrick!

My alma mater Harvard was involved, and they knew all about it and were a Wuhan BSL-4 sponsoring institution as well. Imagine Harvard being a sponsoring institution for China's first Fort Detrick. Their Dana-Farber Cancer Institute at Harvard Medical School/Mass Gen was involved in the manufacture of COVID-19. Harvard's Chemistry Department professor/chair was over there. He is a specialist in nanotechnology applied to chemistry and biology. He worked for Fort Detrick. He had his own nanotechnology laboratory over in Wuhan. Harvard knew exactly what he was doing! So what we are dealing with here is a cabal and a cult of Nazi biological warfare death scientists who do this type of existentially dangerous dirty work in all of the advanced industrialized countries of the world.

Let me conclude, then, with where we stand today. Since as the Indian scientists correctly determined—and that was confirmed by the French Nobel Prize winner in Medicine—HIV is DNA genetically engineered into COVID-19, which I agree is the case, then you are not going to be able to develop a safe and effective vaccine for COVID-19. There is no vaccine today for HIV/

AIDS despite having tried to develop one for the last three decades. Personally, I don't think there will ever be a safe and effective vaccine for COVID-19. And even if Big Pharma says it has developed a vaccine for COVID-19, it will probably be more dangerous than useless.

I think the best we will be left with is therapeutics and drugs. Therapeutics and drugs have significantly reduced the death rate for HIV/AIDS, and they have significantly reduced the death rate for cancer. We've tried to find a vaccine for cancer for the last generation, and it's failed. But the therapeutics and drugs have worked. I respectfully recommend over here in India that you take your top scientists and put them to work on therapeutics and drugs. I believe that any vaccine for COVID-19 will be more dangerous than useless. Therapeutics and drugs are where you should put your money, time, scientific talents, resources, and expertise. Thank you.

. . .

CHAPTER 6

RECOGNIZING AND PUSHING BACK IN THE POST–9/11 POLICE STATE

I gave a lecture before the Lawyers Committee for 9/11 Inquiry and Truth on September 13, 2020, during their weekend-long conference commemorating the 19th anniversary of the 9/11/2001 terrorist attacks, held under the overall theme of "Recognizing and Pushing Back the Post-9/11 Police State" (attorney David Meiswinkle was moderating the event). They asked me to lecture on two topics: (1) the U.S. anthrax attacks of October 2001, otherwise known as Amerithrax; and (2) the COVID-19 pandemic. They gave me 20 minutes for the one lecture on the two topics. Perforce, my lecture had to be even more succinct than the one I had previously given in Pune, India, set forth in the previous chapter:

. . .

Thank you, David, for having me on. I did want to express my condolences to those viewing our program who are next of kin or friends of the victims of the 9/11 attacks, and the first responders. We all want to get to the truth here of what really happened, and that is why I am appearing here today. Nineteen years ago today about 11 a.m., on September 13, 2001, I was contacted by a producer for the *O'Reilly Factor* to appear that night to debate Bill O'Reilly on war versus peace. Him for war and me for peace. Obviously, two days after the attacks, that was like deliberately walking into a buzz saw. But the lot had fallen to me, and I decided I had to debate O'Reilly.

I appeared that evening. I think I did send David a copy of my write-up on that, and I argued quite simply in front of millions of people that the evidence was not there. What the government was saying simply did not add up.

I have been continuously arguing that point ever since then, and as you know, the more the evidence came out, the less the government account made sense, including the *9/11 Commission Report*, which was a cover-up drafted by Condi Rice's buddy. I continued to argue this point in every interview I gave until the anthrax attacks, as David correctly pointed out.

I had called for and drafted the United States domestic implementing legislation for the Biological Weapons Convention, known as the Biological Weapons Anti-Terrorism Act of 1989, that was passed unanimously by both Houses of the United States Congress and signed into law by President George Bush Sr., and is still there on the books providing life imprisonment for violators. And I followed all of this very closely, and finally, as was correctly pointed out by my friend Graeme MacQueen, Senators Daschle and Lahey were holding up the passage of the United States Patriot Act.

Well, as it turned out, the Patriot Act had already been drafted over there in the Department of Injustice under Ashcroft by this Federalist Society lawyer Viet Dinh. It was ready to go, and he just pulled it off the shelf and put it out there. All of a sudden, Daschle and Lahey got hit with anthrax. The *New York Times* printed the technology behind the letters. It was super-weapons-grade anthrax, a trillion spores per gram, with a special silicon coating that enabled it to float in the air. So I immediately realized that this could only have come out of a United States biological weapons program and laboratory, and probably by wearing a moon suit with your own portable oxygen supply because it was just too dangerous.

So I immediately called up a high-level official in the FBI, Marion "Spike" Bowman, who was a top-level lawyer in their counterintelligence division. Bowman and I had both spoken at a conference on international terrorism at the University of Michigan Law School. I gave a speech on the Lockerbie bombing matter that I was heavily involved in. Bowman gave a speech on biological weapons, and afterward, I had a nice talk with him about it. I explained my involvement in drafting the implementing legislation, and in following this matter intently since about 1983 or so when the Council on Responsible Genetics asked me to get involved in the matter for them and handle it.

I still had Bowman's card right there in my office, so I pulled it up. I immediately called Bowman and got through immediately to him. I said, look, now this is the day the anthrax technology was reported in the *New York*

Times. I think that was about October 26. And by the way, I've written this all up in my book *Biowarfare and Terrorism*, if you want to have a look at it with footnotes. And I told Bowman, a high-level lawyer in the FBI headquarters, "Look, this is super-weapons-grade anthrax. It could only have been manufactured in a United States biological weapons program and laboratory, and there is a complete list of these things in the Pentagon's Biological Defense Research Program [BDRP], and it was also revealed in the summer of 2000 in the book *Germs* by Miller and Broad of the *New York Times* that the CIA was also involved in an anthrax biowarfare program." Bowman then said, okay, he was going to forward my information on to the FBI people handling the anthrax investigation. I said fine and hung up the phone.

It then occurred to me that I had a complete list in the public record of all U.S. government biological warfare programs including anthrax, which I got from the BDRP. Back in those days, you could actually get those things. It was listed right there in the Biological Defense Research Program by the Pentagon in an appendix. The Council on Responsible Genetics asked me to do a critique for this BDRP to respond to the United States government. You can read that critique in my book.

So I immediately called back Bowman and said, "I told you this could only have come out of a U.S. biological warfare weapons program by the Pentagon. I have the complete list here for anthrax." I then ran through the entire list right out of the Pentagon's BDRP. By the way, that cover-up was written right here at the University of Illinois in our Computer Engineering Research lab run by the Department of Defense.

So I said, "That's your list. It's a very short little list. And we also know that the CIA is doing this. Obviously you're going to have to go over there to the CIA with warrants and subpoenas and root out exactly what they were doing over there. But these are the people who I'm sure were behind certainly the Daschle and Lahey technology, and probably behind the anthrax attacks themselves."

Bowman then said to me, "Well, we're working with Fort Detrick on this."

I said with all due respect, "Fort Detrick could be the problem here. You could have someone on the reservation who is now off the reservation."

Bowman then said, "OK, I'll send all this information on to the FBI people in charge of the investigation." This was the last week in October 2001. And I gave him the citation for the anthrax list on this matter.

I had assumed that the FBI was handling this diligently. Then what happened as we know, this attack involved Ames-strain anthrax. So the FBI did send people out to the U.S. government lab at Ames, Iowa, where they had the collection of all the Ames-strain anthrax. And the FBI told these people to destroy all of it. That was also reported in the *New York Times.* So at that point I knew full well that the FBI was involved in a cover-up here for either the Department of Defense or the CIA or both. This destruction of the Ames collection was obviously obstruction of justice, and it was a felony. So you could not believe one thing at all from that point in time on what the FBI was saying. The investigation was a joke and a fraud and an obstruction of justice and a felony. I won't go through the rest of the FBI's bogus investigation here.

Now it also turns out that Marion "Spike" Bowman killed the request for the FISA warrant into Moussaoui's computer up there that was asked for by the FBI field office in Minnesota. They requested a FISA warrant to get into Moussaoui's computer, and according to the David Ray Griffin book *The New Pearl Harbor*, it was Spike Bowman who personally killed that Moussaoui FISA warrant. The alleged grounds given were: Well, we never would have passed the FISA requirements.

Well, that's total baloney! As we know, the FISA court is a kangaroo court with a rubber stamp that almost never denied any warrants—certainly not with the evidence being presented up there in the FBI field office in Minnesota. They could have gotten that FISA warrant in August and access to Moussaoui's computer, and maybe the whole thing would have been exposed and stopped, and we never would have had 9/11.

Anyway, I pointed that out in my book *Biowarfare and Terrorism*, and I argued in 2005 that it was my opinion that if we got to whoever was behind the anthrax attacks, that would lead to whoever was behind the 9/11/2001 attacks, because it seemed to me they were coordinating with each other. As I put in my book, this was a one-two blow against the American republic, against the American people, and against the American Constitution.

And by the way, Mueller was the director of the FBI at the time of 9/11. He had just been appointed by Bush Jr. We know Bush Jr. had been briefed in August that a terrorist attack was coming, and he completely ignored it. We know Ashcroft was flying around in a private plane. Obviously, he had been warned. As for Mueller, I had been up against him before in the Lockerbie bombing matter. Mueller was the one who fixed the facts against

Libya and had been lying to the American people about it ever since. I can assure you that the people over in Scotland do not think for one minute that the two Libyans were behind that bombing. Indeed, they sent a camera crew all the way over here to the United States to interview me on that point, and I explained it all to them.

So, yes, as Graeme MacQueen pointed out, all the facts indicate that this was super-weapons-grade anthrax, and it came out of a U.S. biological warfare program run by the Department of Defense and/or the CIA. Indeed, later on, even the *New York Times* reported (I believe in December 2001) that the CIA was involved in developing super-weapons-grade anthrax. And as Graeme and I and others have concluded in this matter, Battelle [Memorial Institute] was involved and working on this anthrax, probably for the CIA. And the danger here is that anthrax lives for decades, so there is still a stockpile of super-weapons-grade anthrax out there that can be used again against the American people, the American Congress, and the American Constitution. My guess is that the stockpile of super-weapons-grade anthrax is still at Dugway [Proving Ground] today.

Now, this then moves into the current COVID-19 pandemic. Right after I spoke with Bowman in the last week in October telling him the anthrax came out of the United States biological warfare weapons program, I then went out to the Harvard Divinity School where I was chairing a workshop for the Council on Responsible Genetics against biological weapons.

On my way into the Harvard Divinity School, there was a camera crew from Fox News in Boston asking me my opinion about the anthrax attacks. I said it's obvious this came out of a United States biological warfare program because they would be the only people capable of producing super-weapons-grade anthrax.

Inside, I said the same thing at the Council on Responsible Genetics workshop; and my colleague there, Professor Jon King, who is founder of the Council on Responsible Genetics, a professor of biology there at MIT, and heads their Electron Microscope Program, said the exact same thing. I then came back here to my office, and starting the first week in November, gave an interview to Pacifica Radio Network in Washington, D.C., which went out nationwide, saying this exact same thing. Then the BBC called me, and I said the exact same thing live on the BBC.

Then an *order* was given by someone never to interview me again by anyone on biological warfare or biological weapons in the mainstream news media, and that order has held up until today with respect to the COVID-19 pandemic. On January 24, 2020, I issued a worldwide *alert* to well over 500 news media sources and all over the internet that the Wuhan coronavirus was an offensive biological warfare weapon based on DNA genetic engineering and with gain-of-function properties, that had leaked out of that Wuhan BSL-4, which was China's Fort Detrick. I felt it was existentially dangerous, and every BSL-3 and BSL-4 in this country and indeed the world, should be shut down.

As a matter of fact, I noted that in the award-winning documentary *Anthrax War* (2009) by Nadler and Coen. I said, "This is a catastrophe waiting to happen!" And it has now happened. I then gave an interview to *Geopolitics and Empire* later that day, January 24, 2020, saying the exact same thing: This is a biological warfare weapon, existentially dangerous, it had leaked out of that Wuhan BSL-4, and every BSL-3 and BSL-4 had to be shut down immediately. That interview went viral all over the world.

I then worked full-time giving interviews starting the next week, until finally they tapered off around July 1. I'm not going to go through all those interviews here. You can Google my name starting January 24 and see all the interviews I have given.

Now we find out from the Woodward tapes for his book *Rage* within the last week that Trump has been lying from the get-go on COVID-19. That it is existentially dangerous. It travels through the air. This is because Wuhan BSL-4 publicly bragged about applying nanotechnology to viruses. Nanotechnology is necessary to aerosolize viruses for delivery by air to human beings. That's the only reason you aerosol a virus like this. Fort Detrick does the exact same thing. We all know Fort Detrick is involved in the research, development, testing, and stockpiling of biological warfare weapons. Anthrax was one of them; COVID-19 is another.

Finally, at the end of April 2020, an Israeli law firm contacted me, and they had sued China in the Israeli court system over the COVID-19 pandemic. They asked me to get involved in the lawsuit and to give them a Declaration of my expert opinion that COVID-19 was an offensive biological warfare weapon that leaked out of the Wuhan BSL-4, which I did do, dated June 6, 2020. I sent a copy of that Declaration to David. He has it there, and if David wants to distribute it to you, that's fine with me. If you want a copy, ask David for it.

I then gave a lecture on June 26 at the Maharashtra Business Program school at the Peace University in Pune, India, saying the exact same thing and going through all the evidence for them. All the arguments I originally made as of January 24 have been routinely confirmed by every source coming out in reputable news media sources since then, up to and including all of the Woodward tapes.

We've been lied to from the get-go by the Trump administration on COVID-19. We've been lied to by the CDC acting under pressure from the Trump administration, by the National Institutes of Health, and by NIAID under Fauci. They've all been lying and spinning about how dangerous COVID-19 really is. It floats through the air. It has a lethality rate maybe in the area of 15% for SARS. This is SARS on steroids. That is what is confronting us today here in the United States, as well over 200,000 Americans who have died already. We have to be aware of this. We cannot trust what the Trump administration is saying, or the CDC, or the National Institutes of Health, or NIAID.

You are going to have to rely upon independent experts who have not taken one penny of this dirty Nazi biological warfare work that the U.S. government has been involved in since after 9/11/2001 under the pretext of Amerithrax that they inflicted upon us. My estimate as of 2015 is that at least 13,000 scientists have been involved in the research, development, and testing of biological warfare weapons. You cannot trust any of these people! You have to get outside independent experts who have not taken this type of money to give you proper advice on how to combat COVID-19, which is staring us in the face right now. It could prove to be just as deadly as the Spanish flu virus if it is not handled and dealt with, and certainly it has not been.

Thank you very much for your attention.

...

CHAPTER 7

MY ADVICE TO AFRICAN AMERICANS (DECEMBER 22, 2020)

(The host is an African American community leader in Chicago.)

Host: Thank you so much for joining me today, Dr. Boyle.... I had asked Dr. Boyle to be my first guest considering the situations going on in the world, and specifically, the Black community.... I'm sure many of you already recognize him. I reached out to him, and he didn't say let my people call your people. He didn't know me from a can of paint. But he said without hesitation that he's definitely interested in talking to us. So I just want to thank you, first of all, for your passion. And before I start to ask you a few questions, I just want to tell the audience who you are. I'm sure that many of you know you've seen him. Some of you have been in touch with me, saying you saw him on interviews at the beginning of this pandemic and other things, so many of you already know him.

Dr. Boyle is a magna cum laude graduate of Harvard Law School and is from the University of Chicago. He is a professor and human-rights activist. He's a homie; he's from Chicago. He's represented victims of human rights and war crimes all over the world and has served as an adviser to numerous international bodies in these areas as well as in the areas of nuclear policy and biowarfare.

As a human-rights activist, Dr. Boyle has also served as a board member of Amnesty International and actually did the U.S. legislation for the Biological Weapons Convention, known as the Biological Weapons Anti-Terrorism Act of 1989 that was approved unanimously by both Houses of the U.S. Congress and signed into law by President George Bush Sr. So it's no small thing for him to make time for us today and particularly have such a passion to address the concerns that we have in our community right now. I wanted to ask you specifically about the COVID vaccination and other vaccinations in the African American community. What do you see in that area that makes you hair-trigger on this issue?

FAB: Well, thank you for having me on, and my best to your viewing audience. The reason I was so enthusiastic is that I grew up on the South Side of Chicago, not the suburbs, but the city itself, west of the Dan Ryan. And then I went to the University of Chicago for college. And, of course, when you said you were with WVON, I used to listen to WVON [Voice of the Negro] as a kid, so I was happy to be on there. I have pointed out that the current vaccines by Pfizer, and now by Moderna, are part of a U.S. biological warfare weapons program. And today I just sent you my analysis of what was in the *New York Times.*

Host: About the placenta?

FAB: Right. The *New York Times* science section confirmed that these two vaccines that I will call Frankenshots, attack the placenta. Let me repeat that. All African American women living in the Chicago metropolitan area, these two Frankenshots—

Host: And let me ask you, not just Chicago right, but period.

FAB: Sure, but I'm appearing here because I'm a Chicagoan.

Host: Yeah, we want the world to know this.

FAB: You're all my brothers and sisters up there. So, yes, I'm speaking to all African American women, but especially my sisters in Chicago and Chicago metro. And on the south side, for sure. That I grew up with.

Host: All right, man.

FAB: The *New York Times* today confirms what I had been saying. These vaccines will attack your placenta. They will give you—I'm the father of three sons; I was there for the delivery of all three of my boys like a modern dad these days. It could give you a miscarriage, a stillborn; it could give genetic disabilities to your children. We don't know. And, indeed, if I remember correctly, they deliberately excluded pregnant women from the first round of guinea pigs.

Host: Wow.

FAB: Because I think they had a pretty good idea this was targeted to get your placenta and your babies.

Host: Wow.

FAB: If you listen to the mainstream news media, they're saying, Oh, well, at the top of the list should be African Americans. Because they're the victims of injustice.

Host: And the majority of African Americans are prisoners as well. Right?

FAB: And so to compensate them for being victims of injustice, we're going to give them these vaccines first. Right. African Americans have been the victims of grave injustice for hundreds of years, but you've got to ask yourself, have they now seen the light? Like St. Paul on the road to Damascus, being struck down by lightning? Of course not. This is designed to go after your babies' placentas. So it's clear. That's why African Americans here are at the top of the list, and as you know, they're going through your communities trying to get you to take these two Frankenshots.

Host: Absolutely.

FAB: And I'm speaking here today in the strongest terms possible, certainly to say to my sisters, African American women there, don't take them. As for the men, we have no idea what they're going to do to you. This is messenger RNA that they are going to inject into you. It is extremely powerful genetically; it could change the entire genetic composition of your bodies, both men and women. And so you don't want to take this. Plus, I have the grant here.

Guess who's funding this brand-new technology, which, by the way, has never been tried out on anyone before? Why are African Americans at the top of the list here? It's pretty simple, you know. Where the Pentagon admits they paid for and sponsored this new type of technology, biotechnology, that is involved in the two types of Frankenshots they're trying to sell to the African American community today, and especially to you, my African American sisters. A very dangerous situation here. Very dangerous.

Host: You mentioned two things there. You mentioned the Pentagon. And there's a particular division of the Pentagon called DARPA that you've referenced before, and DARPA has basically funded all kinds of things—it's for pharmacology, or the robot hybrid police force and soldier force, robotics, et cetera. So could you tell us—

FAB: Yes, that is correct. This was funded by DARPA, the Defense Advanced Research Project Agency of the Pentagon, and this is the Moderna press release from 2013 called "DARPA awards Moderna Therapeutics a grant for up to 25 million to develop messenger RNA therapeutics." That's exactly what the Moderna Frankenshot is. And the Pfizer Frankenshot is the same type of technology. Let me also read it to you; then I won't go through the whole press release. To provide the US population. So everyone, but there are priorities.

Host: Yeah, exactly.

FAB: African Americans, Latinx, American Indians, poor people, homeless people. They're at the top of the list in that, as well as the elderly.

Host: Yeah, what they call the useless eaters. Now, let me ask you—

FAB: That is exactly correct. This is the Nazi useless-eaters philosophy at work that was condemned by the Nuremberg Tribunal in its 1946 Judgment, but let me read the rest of this press release for you. Protection against "emerging infectious diseases." Where is it emerging out of? Their own labs. They are creating them. DARPA, as you correctly point out, is in the business of creating new weapons and new weapons systems, advanced cutting-edge weapons systems. This goes back to at least 2013: "emerging infectious diseases, and engineered biological weapons." Who engineers them? DARPA and these Nazi death scientists, places like Pfizer, and Moderna, who have developed this messenger RNA bomb that they are now trying to get the African American community to take, both men and women, but especially threatening women.

Now, let me say one last quote and then I'll take your question. "Even in cases when the pathogen or infectious agent is unknown." Why is it unknown? Because they are in the process of developing it. The United States government has a program where they send out these Nazi death scientists all over the world to find bacteria, fungi, toxins of whatever type to bring back here, put in their labs, and see if they can weaponize them. Now that basically is what they said they're going to do here. And that is what these two so-called Pfizer, and now Moderna, vaccines are designed to do. It's very simple. They are biological weapons. They are components of a biological weapon, and they are targeting African Americans near the top, Latinx, people of color, the elderly, and the poor. So you're correct. This is the Nazi philosophy of useless eaters. It's going to be like the Tuskegee experiment that they inflicted on your men.

Host: Now, let me ask you about what we can do about it. I'm going to ask you in a little while about that spike protein and its incompatibility with African Americans. But also, before I get to that, while we're on the subject of the Nazi useless-eaters eugenics campaign, you were the author of the legislation for the Nuremberg ruling. Can we use that? Can we cite that as a defense against taking the vaccine for, perhaps, our jobs?

FAB: Right, well, I called for and drafted the United States implementing legislation for the Biological Weapons Convention, known as the Biological Weapons Anti-Terrorism Act of 1989. That was passed unanimously by both Houses of the United States Congress and signed into law by President George Bush Sr. Now I first called for that in 1985. I got involved in opposing biological weapons around 1983 for an organization called the Council for Responsible Genetics, headquartered in Cambridge, Massachusetts, with some of the top life scientists in the world from Harvard and MIT.

Let me say one other thing, and this was provoked by the Reagan administration getting involved in the use of DNA genetic engineering to research, develop, and manufacture biological weapons. As you know, the Reagan administration—you know their attitude toward African Americans. It was populated by these so-called neoconservatives. Well, look at the neoconservative manifesto, *Project for a New American Century.* And this is all in my book *Biowarfare and Terrorism.* You can get it on Amazon.

Host: *Biowarfare and Terrorism?*

FAB: *Biowarfare and Terrorism.* If you look at the neocon manifesto *Project for a New American Century*, they call for the United States government to get into biological weapons, and specifically, ethnic-specific biological weapons that can be used against people because of their ethnicity, such as African Americans, people of color, yes.

Host: And that was under Reagan, right?

FAB: Well, under these same people that worked for Bush Jr.

Host: Absolutely. And I want to make a point there about how it showed up, even in the streets, so to speak. I went to Disneyland in 1983—I think it was 1983. And I went to Epcot Center, and I went to the World of the Future exhibit. And I went in, and all of the little machines and robots and people in the World of the Future were Aryan. Literally, they were all blond, blue-eyed, white. It was like there was no ethnicity in the World of the Future at Epcot Center. And I knew even then that there was a very nefarious agenda in place.

FAB: Well, if you read the PNAC report, and I have it cited in my book, this passage, it calls for ethnic-specific biological weapons and warfare. And we know the CIA worked with the Afrikaner apartheid regime in South Africa to develop the biological weapons to be used against Black people in South Africa. That is a fact. That came out in the Truth and Reconciliation hearings there, conducted by Archbishop Tutu. The CIA was working with them on ethnic-specific biological weapons to be used by white racist Afrikaners against the Black population of South Africa. So the CIA has been involved in this for a long time.

Host: I'm sorry—you were cut off. The CIA is what?

FAB: They've been involved in this for a long time: an ethnic weapon since under the Afrikaner apartheid regime—that all came out in the Archbishop Tutu hearings. You can find that yourself, yes.

Host: So my question regarding this Nuremberg ruling against biological weapons is—the Antiterrorism Act, is that something that we can cite? Take this, this vaccine for your job? Can we cite that as a legitimate defense against taking the vaccine?

FAB: Yes. And also I gave an interview, which I will send to you. I'm invoking the Nuremberg Code on Medical Experimentation. That's directly on point, the Nuremberg Code on Medical Experimentation that requires anyone to be given a brand-new vaccine like this to first get informed and voluntary consent. And you can say no. Indeed, you can use my name if you want, my sisters, and say Professor Boyle has said, under the Nuremberg Code on Medical Experimentation, we don't have to take these vaccines, and we are not going to take these vaccines, period.

Host: Now, I want to specifically ask now—a lot of our sisters today are health-care workers. Everybody's in scrubs today—they're home health-care workers or CNAs, not high-level executives or with a lot of power. And they have strategically placed home-care workers legally under the domestics category. And domestic workers, you know, under the law, which was established many years ago, don't have certain legal rights. There's no salary minimum, you could pay them anything, et cetera. So a lot of them are very, very underpaid, and they're already very exploited. And they're the first people who are being lined up to take this, all the scrub wearers. So how can they object effectively?

FAB: I will send you a video they can use; they can download the relevant parts onto their cell phones where I'm saying this. They have my permission; they don't want to take the whole thing, but the part where I'm saying you have a right to resist on their cell phones, for sure. But second of all, they're going to have to get some lawyers up there in Chicago to make these arguments for them. You've got excellent African American lawyers there in Chicago. Tim Wright, the lawyer for Harold Washington, is a friend of mine. And your lawyers are going to have to fight for them. And I'm happy to work with African American lawyers. I'm Irish American, so the Irish American lawyers in Chicago—there's an organization there called the National Lawyers Guild, and they could help you too.

Host: Called what? You broke up.

FAB: National Lawyers Guild. But in the meantime, they can just take a snippet of my interview, explaining the right to resist, put it on their cell phones, and say, "This is what the world's leading expert says on it, and he's a law professor at the University of Illinois."

Host: Now where is that interview?

FAB: This is the state of Illinois, and I'm a law professor at the leading state law school here. So I think I'm a pretty good authority for them to use, but they're going to have to get lawyers at the end of the day, because the employers, once they're not able to persuade these women to take these Frankenshots, are going to threaten to fire them. So you're going to have to line up lawyers out there in Chicago to defend them, to prevent this from happening. I recommend that you set up a committee of women to try to get this organized, right?

Host: And where is this interview that they can download?

FAB: I'll send it to you after this.

Host: OK, I'll make that available.

FAB: It's a long interview, so you don't want to do the whole interview. You want to do the part where I say you have a right to resist these Frankenshots because of the Nuremberg Code on Medical Experimentation. And I drafted the law, and I am a professor of International Law at the University of Illinois College of Law, which is the premier law school in the entire state of Illinois.

I've been teaching there 42 years. So that's a pretty good authority to start, but eventually, and as soon as you can, you will have to line up lawyers to defend these women. Because they're good women at heart, but they're exploited, and they're going to need some lawyers to get this organized, and stand up for them. But I know you have them up there in Chicago because I've worked with many African American lawyers up there in Chicago.

Host: And everywhere, and this definitely is for everybody.

FAB: This is correct.

Host: Our hearts are in Chicago, but this is for everybody. So do know that.

FAB: That's true. My heart is in Chicago. I grew up there. I lived there the first 21 years of my life, on the South Side, right there cheek by jowl with the African American community. But I'm giving this message, certainly, to all African American women. And I've been completely censored out of the mainstream news media. So I'm going to rely upon you to get this message out to all African American women and men. They can't take these vaccines.

Host: No one can. And the thing that I want to ask you, to use the word *experimentation* is a real key word because it usually is going to take years, maybe even decades, to bring a vaccination to market. And this allegedly is long before we ever heard of coronavirus. Are there, five months, and like, oh, here you go. Here's a vaccine for you.

FAB: Right. And by the way, these are Trump vaccines. Think about that. Even your Senator Kamala Harris, now the vice president–elect, said she was not going to take a vaccine developed by Trump. Think about that.

Host: I don't care who is developing it, because now I want to ask—

FAB: One other point. So far, Trump has refused to take his own vaccine. So think about that. If he isn't gonna take his own vaccine, why should African Americans? It's preposterous.

Host: So let me ask you—I'm Bill Gates, on the subject of him. I read that basically he's got investments in six different vaccines, six different companies, at least... and there is a patent on one affiliated with him that has a very interesting patent number, apparently 060606. And then, also, there's a technology, a patented technology, that is light-based, that's supposed to be able to detect whether or not you have taken the vaccine remotely, called luciferase. So he says we're already set to go with regard to what you need to know about the vaccine, and blah, blah. Can you speak a little bit to Bill Gates and his reputation around the world with vaccinations?

FAB: Gates has said he's a eugenicist. He wants to see fewer people in the world. You know, again, it's like the Nazis. But for our case here, again, we're dealing with two vaccines. I call them Frankenshots, but one by Pfizer, and the other by Moderna. Now, the Pfizer vaccine was co-developed by BioNTech. It's called the Pfizer BioNTech vaccine, but it's the same DARPA technology as Moderna. Well, the Pfizer BioNTech vaccine—guess who has paid for BioNTech? Bill Gates. This is one of his vaccines for sure.

Host: Precisely.

FAB: This fits in with his espousal of eugenics. Right? And we all know, it's like the Nazi attitude toward the Jews, right? We have too many African Americans here, and we need to cull the herd. That's exactly the philosophy here, yes.

Host: For the term *eugenics*, that's basically what that means. That we need to get rid of what they deem as useless eaters, those people who are—

FAB: And the *Untermensch*. The Nazis were the *Übermensch*, the above men. And the others were the Untermensch like Jews, Roma—the name for Gypsies—but they prefer Roma, and Slavic people. They were all deemed to be Untermensch.

Host: And Untermensch means what?

FAB: Under. Under men.

Host: Those people they consider inferior.

FAB: Inferior races of people. The Jews, the Roma, the Slavic people living in Eastern Europe. And, of course, homosexuals. So this is the philosophy here at work, and guess who the Untermensch are here in the United States of America as far as the white-racist plutocrats who run this country?

Host: I guess that would be me.

FAB: What can I say? That's just the nature of the system. The African Americans always have been America's Untermensch, and I regret to say nothing has really changed.

Host: And now we're going to make it up to you by giving you this vaccine first. Like suddenly we've just discovered you've been treated really badly. So prisoners first, the elderly first. All these people ... and he just said they want to reduce the population by 20, 25%. He's stated that. I've put that video out on numerous occasions.

FAB: And they know. You see, I've written about this myself. They know that soon, maybe no later than 2025 or 2030, and they're playing with the census; soon people of color will be the majority in this country, if you look at the demographic statistics.

Host: Around the world.

FAB: That frightens them to death. I'm just telling you about America, where we live. I'm not saying this about anywhere else, but soon, and I would say no later than 2025 or 2030, Trump is playing games with the census. As we know, people of color will be a majority in this country, and that scares them to death. They don't want that to happen. So what do you do? You reduce the numbers.

Host: Well, and this new administration, I don't want to give false hope, because Bill Gates, Hillary Clinton—they're all in the same little cartel, and they are already really promoting this vaccination and a complete lockdown when he gets in office, et cetera. It's all part of planning the same narrative of "You must get this vax or die" kind of situation. So I don't think we're necessarily going to jump out of the frying pan and not jump into the fire as the new year rolls around.

FAB: I don't think Biden's gonna help you here. The rhetoric might be better, but I think the game plan is already in play. I'm a political independent, but Democrats versus Republicans, Tweedledum versus Tweedledee. So maybe Biden and Harris will be the black-velvet glove, but it will still be covering the white-racist iron fist. And, indeed, with all due respect to Senator Harris, that might be why Biden picked Senator Harris in part, to use her to better sell the policies of white-racist plutocrats to African Americans. I mean, she's a woman of great accomplishment—

Host: Let me tell you, you don't have to explain it to me, because I believe, I know, her reputation as a prosecutor is code for "Lock up Negroes."

FAB: You're correct.

Host: She is, in my opinion, a person who follows orders. California had the most draconian laws on the books in regard to three strikes, and she executed it very well and locked up hordes of Black people. But they know if they put a brown face in, or a little beige face in, that we'll all jump in and vote for that person, even if it's to our own detriment. I already know that she's useful for our extermination as well. That's me speaking. You don't have to co-sign that.

FAB: She did go to a very fine law school and everything. But you're right about her mentality. I was originally hired here to teach Criminal Law. I always taught it from the perspective of the defense. But most people who teach Criminal Law in America are former prosecutors, and they all have that former-prosecutor mentality, which is lock them up and throw away the key.

Host: And I was a pretrial investigator for five years, so I saw inside the system. My mother was a probation officer for 25 years. I used to watch trials after school every day throughout high school, so I've had an intimate bird's-eye perspective of looking at the system and the disparities. So I saw that too. I don't want to keep you a whole lot longer. You've been so gracious. I could get into a whole bunch of other things, like the colonization of Mars and how they're trying to set that up so they can leave us here.

FAB: I think we've covered the basic points, and the reason I'm appearing here is to send this message to all African Americans, but especially to African American women: Don't take these vaccines. Period. They could kill your babies in your wombs. And I say that as the father of three sons. I don't want to see this happen. And I'm also saying to African American men, we have no idea what this messenger RNA is going to do to your entire genetic composition and your children, because whatever it does to you, it will do to your children.

Host: Yes. And I will say this. I did hear another scientist say that the particular spike protein in the mRNA vaccine is not in large quantities in African Americans, period. So to front-load that into our system could wreak incredible havoc on our bodies. But then again, if the goal is to exterminate, then why not?

FAB: I think I've discussed with you tonight in all seriousness why I believe those will be the consequences if you African Americans start to take these Frankenshots. Yes, I'm afraid so.

Host: Well, Dr. Boyle, I so appreciate you taking the time to speak with us tonight, I really do. I am very grateful for the time, and if anyone wants to get your book, it's called *Biowarfare and Terrorism*.

FAB: It's on Amazon and is written in plain English. I think any of our brothers and sisters could read that book and understand what's going on here, especially the part about ethnic-specific weapons. It's right there, and who are the top ethnicities the white-racist plutocrats want to reduce?

Host: Yes, for sure.

FAB: It's pretty clear.

Host: It is very clear. And I guess, lastly, I'll reach out to you to get information on that video, the interview.

FAB: I'll send it to you.

Host: OK, and with that, I just thank you very much.

FAB: Thank you, and again my best to all my friends there in Chicago, and especially on the South Side and Hyde Park and South Shore.

Host: Praise God. Okay, God bless you. Thank you.

FAB: Thank you, bye-bye.

...

CHAPTER 8

MY NUREMBERG CODE ON MEDICAL EXPERIMENTATION *NOTICE!* AGAINST THE NAZI COVID-19 FRANKENSHOTS

Thereafter, during the fall semester of the 2020–2021 academic year, I gave numerous interviews about the COVID-19 Frankenshots. I argued that they violated the Nuremberg Code on Medical Experimentation that arose out of the *Medical/Doctors* Case at Nuremberg for the prosecution and conviction and execution of Nazi doctors. The COVID-19 Frankenshots are a Nuremberg Crime and a Nuremberg Crime against Humanity. No good ever came out of the Nazis. So no good will come out of these Nazi COVID-19 Frankenshots.

I also argued that the COVID-19 Frankenshots would be more dangerous than useless. There is no evidence to believe that there was a safe and effective "vaccine" against an offensive biological warfare weapon that had gain-of-function properties and HIV that is DNA genetically engineered right into it, and that had been nano-technologized. These COVID-19 Frankenshots give the victims live COVID-19 cells. Why would anyone in their right mind want to be injected with cells from an offensive biological warfare weapon with gain-of-function properties and HIV that is DNA genetically engineered right into it and that has been nano-technologized? You very well might end up giving yourself COVID-19.

As a result of these numerous and widespread interviews, I began to receive many requests from plaintive people asking me to give them something that they can use to prevent being injected by the COVID-19 Frankenshots. These requests became even more numerous and more desperate after the first Frankenshot was rolled out right after Trump lost his presidential reelection in early November 2020. But there was no way I could respond to them at the time. I was teaching a maximum course load of International Law and The Constitutional Law of U.S. Foreign Affairs to large numbers of American law students and foreign lawyers. In addition, I was finishing up production work on my fall 2019 sabbatical-leave book, *World Politics, Human Rights, and International Law* (Lexington Press: 2021), which I had a professional obligation to complete as expeditiously as possible. My publisher was waiting for my revisions with bated breath. There was no way I could research and write up this requested project in my spare time. I had none. The life of a law professor!

I handed in my final grades on both courses just before Christmas Eve and then spent the holidays with my family. I needed some downtime. I had been continually fighting COVID-19 and its Frankenshots from January 24, 2020, on.

When that period of rejuvenation and refreshment was over, I had some free time to do the necessary research to complete this citizen-requested project before the Martin Luther King Jr. Day holiday, when my classes would resume again the next day. So due to popular demand, I immediately undertook the requisite research and drafting for this citizen project. Eventually I came up with a document that I titled the Nuremberg *Notice!*. It was deliberately intended to be short and succinct and to the point—and shocking at first sight. I wanted people to be able to print it out and show it to anyone who was trying to force them to give or take a COVID-19 Frankenshot. I figured that my blunt Nuremberg *Notice!* would force that perpetrator to think twice and refrain from doing so. That would give the potential victim the opportunity to seek advice, counsel, assistance, and representation from a lawyer in their immediate vicinity before taking or giving the COVID-19 Frankenshots.

I then circulated my Nuremberg *Notice!* to several hundred media sources, and all over the internet. Here is what my Nuremberg *Notice!* had to say:

From: Boyle, Francis Boyle
Sent: Sunday, January 17, 2021 4:33 PM
To: Killeacle <fboyle@uiuc.edu>
Subject: Notice against COVID Vaccinations!
I have drafted a Notice that you can use to resist COVID vaccinations. Please feel free to circulate. FAB

NOTICE!

By authority of the Nuremberg Code on Medical Experimentation, I do hereby exercise my right to refuse to submit to or to administer the COVID-19 vaccine. The United States Government has prosecuted, convicted, and executed Medical Doctors who have violated the Nuremberg Code on Medical Experimentation. Aiders and abettors of Nuremberg Crimes are equally guilty and have also been prosecuted, convicted, and executed.

Serendipitously, journalist Regis Tremblay then contacted me about giving him an interview over the COVID-19 pandemic. I explained to him all about my recently released Nuremberg *Notice!* and suggested he interview me about it. He readily agreed and taped the interview. He then packaged my Nuremberg *Notice!* together with my interview and circulated it all over the internet under the title: "Francis Boyle—Nuremberg Code Is Your Defense." You can find it by Googling my name, as indicated below. Just click on the *Comment*, and you can hear my interview live if you want to. My sincere thanks to Mr. Tremblay for doing such yeoman service on behalf of the people of the world. The edited text of my interview explaining my Nuremberg *Notice!* is set forth below:
From: **YouTube** <noreply@youtube.com>
Date: Thu, Jan 21, 2021 at 12:41 PM
Subject: New comment on "Francis Boyle – Nuremberg Code Is Your Defense"
To: Regis Tremblay <tremregi@gmail.com>
New comment on "Francis Boyle – Nuremberg Code Is Your Defense"

YouTube

Jerry Alatalo commented on your video

Francis Boyle – Nuremberg Code Is Your Defense

Peace.

Jerry Alatalo
NOTICE By authority of the Nuremberg Code on Medical Experimentation, I do hereby exercise my right to refuse

to submit to or to administer the COVID-19 vaccine. The United States Government has prosecuted, convicted and executed Medical Doctors who have violated the Nuremberg Code on Medical Experimentation. Aiders and abettors of Nuremberg Crimes are equally guilty and have also been prosecuted, convicted, and executed. Francis A. Boyle Law Building 504 E. Pennsylvania Ave. Champaign, Illinois 61820 USA fboyle@illinois.edu Phone: 217-333-7954 Fax: 217-244-1478 * Thank you, Francis Boyle and Regis Tremblay

---

Welcome to another edition of *Global Conversations* with Regis Tremblay, coming to you from beautiful and historic Yalta in the Crimea of the Russian Federation. Yalta is a vibrant city that energizes and surprises all who live and come here. Young and old relish this historic and beautiful place located between majestic mountains and the Black Sea. Welcome to another edition of *Global Conversations*. My guest today, returning for the second time, is Francis Boyle. He's a professor of International Law, and he's the authority on COVID-19 as a bioweapon. He recently created a statement that people can use to resist the COVID-19 vaccine, and this statement is based on the Nuremberg Principles. Francis, welcome back to the show.

FAB: Regis, thank you very much for having me on. My best to your viewing audience, and Happy New Year to everyone.

Regis Tremblay: Well, you've published that statement that you gave people permission to republish and to share. Explain to me just exactly what it is.

FAB: Regis, as you know, I've been giving continual interviews on COVID-19 since January 24, 2020, and I won't go through all that here because I gave you a very lengthy interview on that. But starting then in the fall with these so-called vaccines, it's clear that they are existentially dangerous. I won't go through all of that here, but the two we have, Pfizer/BioNTech and Moderna, are DNA genetically engineered, and they were funded by the Pentagon's DARPA: The Defense Advanced Research Projects Agency. So I've been giving interviews against these vaccines—I call them Frankenshots, there's no other word for them— and how dangerous they are.

So what happened was a lot of people in different stations in life contacted me and said, Can you give me something I can use to resist these shots, these Frankenshots, from being forced to take them? I've been contacted by people in the U.S. military about that. We have the previous Gulf War Syndrome—this will be Gulf War Syndrome on Steroids. And I've also been contacted by health-care workers who don't want to give these Frankenshots because they know they're existentially dangerous, and as you know, large numbers of health-care workers are not taking them. All these requests happened in the fall, but I was teaching a full-time course load, with a lot of students and getting a new book out, so I just said, Look, download the segment from one of my interviews onto your cell phone, and use that.

Eventually I was finished for the semester, got my grades in, classes done, spent some holiday time with my family, and then what happened was that President-Elect Joe Biden had given this speech where he said he is going to inject 100 million of these Frankenshots into 100 million Americans in the first 100 days of his administration. Now this will be a total catastrophe! It's already shaping up as a catastrophe even before then, as today, Trump is leaving office—thank heavens for that! And at that point, then, I decided, OK, I had to respond to the requests that all these people had made to me to give them something they could use. So I sat down and drafted this *Notice!* that can be used for people to resist getting the Frankenshots, or doctors, health-care workers, health technicians, pharmacists, others, to resist giving the Frankenshots. So let me just go through it with you to explain it here.

I decided to keep it very short, very succinct but hard-hitting, and to reduce it to its bare-bones minimum. So I entitled it *Notice!* with an exclamation point by authority of the Nuremburg Code on Experimentation. Now this goes back to the *Medical/Doctors* case at Nuremberg where the German doctors were put on trial for all sorts of experimental techniques that they applied on completely innocent human beings, including and especially the

Jews, as we all know. And these medical doctors—some of them were executed. If you read through the entire *Judgment*, it's quite lengthy, but you'll see all the terrible types of experiments that German doctors were doing, and procedures and drugs and everything else to people. And we're all aware of Dr. Mengele and what he did at Auschwitz. Everyone is aware of that. There were many other German doctors involved in this.

And the *Judgment* came up with what was called the Nuremberg Code on Medical Experimentation that set forth requirements for engaging in any type of experimental techniques or procedures or drugs or anything like that on human beings. And this Nuremberg Judgment—in particular, the Nuremberg Code on Medical Experimentation—became part of customary international criminal law.

Now, I had dealt with this once before in the defense of Captain Dr. Yolanda Hewitt-Vaughn, who was the highest-ranking military officer in Gulf War I by Bush Sr. to refuse to give experimental medical vaccines for the biological warfare agents of anthrax and botulin because she correctly believed that these vaccines violated the Nuremberg Code on Medical Experimentation, so she couldn't give them. As well, I think there was a Helsinki Code and her ethical obligation as a doctor she took when she was sworn in—the Hippocratic Oath: "Do no harm!" She was court-martialed for, among other things, desertion. She did not desert.

I helped defend her, and at her court-martial, we argued the Nuremberg Code on Medical Experimentation in her defense, and it was a very tough situation. She was given a kangaroo-courtroom court-martial proceeding down at Fort Leonard Wood in Missouri. And I won't go through it all here; she was facing five years. But at the end of the kangaroo-court proceeding, she got almost three years, and they took her away in chains to Fort Leavenworth, where they stuck her in medium security—a little bitty woman.

At that time, I was on the Board of Directors at Amnesty International USA, and I got her immediately adopted as a Prisoner of Conscience by Amnesty International. And I think due to Amnesty's efforts, we got her sentence cut down to 14 months. And then I got her out of Leavenworth after eight months.

Now in the course of this court-martial, both in the Article 32 hearing and then in the court-martial itself, we went through the culpability of the Nuremberg Code on Medical Experimentation for these biological warfare

Frankenshots for anthrax and botulin. We went through the whole thing, so I was completely familiar with it.

And by the way, these first Frankenshots led to the Gulf War Syndrome for U.S. troops that out of about—and these are just estimates because the Pentagon is still lying and covering it up—out of about 500,000 troops that were inoculated, 100,000 were disabled, and 11,000 were killed. And these were healthy young men and women in the U.S. armed forces. So you can imagine, then, what these new biological warfare agent vaccine Frankenshots are going to do, especially to the elderly, senior citizens, et cetera. And we're seeing that they're being killed right now as we speak. There in Norway there were 23—they died; they were killed.

Now, at the end of the kangaroo court-martial, we had a press conference with actress Margo Kidder introducing me to the media, and we had satellite dishes there, and I said that Bush Sr., Colin Powell, Cheney, and Schwarzkopf had all inflicted a war crime on our troops in violation of the Nuremberg Code on Medical Experimentation. That went out nationwide. I was told by a lawyer who was at the White House at the time that they heard me, and they were all shaken up. Later on, Senator Jay Rockefeller held hearings on these Frankenshots, the first ones, and he came out and said the exact same thing I had said, that Bush and the rest of them had violated the Nuremberg Code on Medical Experimentation and had committed a Nuremberg Crime on our own troops. You can read about that in my book *Biowarfare and Terrorism*, and the write-up of my defense on Captain Hewitt-Vaughn is in my book *Destroying World Order.*

So that all being said with that background, I realized that what we are going to have here was the Gulf War Syndrome on Steroids, especially for the people targeted. This is basically the Nazi philosophy of "useless eaters." So I put this together, this *Notice!*, on the basis of that litigation experience that I'd had previously dealing with these issues.

And understand, Regis, I am not part of any anti-vax movement. I am agnostic on that. They can do what they want on that. I've been attacked and disparaged, saying, "You're an anti-vaxxer." I am not. My specialty is alleged vaccines dealing with biological warfare agents, which COVID *is*, and for anthrax and botulin, *was*. That's how I first got involved here. So I started out by saying that by the authority of the Nuremberg Code on Medical Experimentation.

Now, that's a lot of background just for the beginning of it, but I didn't want to write a scholarly treatise here or a long law-review article. I wanted something that ordinary people could read and understand. And the word *Nuremberg* there, I would think most people would have a general idea that the United States, the Soviet Union, France, and Britain prosecuted Nazis at Nuremberg so people could understand the severity of the situation.

Then I continued: "I do hereby exercise my right under the Nuremberg Code to refuse to submit"—so that people who were contacting me and saying, "I need something to prevent taking these Frankenshots"—they would have it. And large numbers of employers are telling people we have to have these Frankenshots, and I've given them something they can use to say, "No, I'm not taking them." Indeed, I just heard from an active-duty military guy yesterday on this, and I sent it to him, and he said "Thank you!" He's going to use it because they're giving it to people in the military.

And then the second prong, "refuse to submit or to administer"—so that health-care personnel can use it. Doctors, nurses, health-care workers, medical technicians. As you know, here in the United States, they're having pharmacies do this, and they're even hiring other people to do it. We don't even know what their qualifications are.

So I did it two-pronged so that it can be used by health-care workers like Dr. Hewitt-Vaughn to say I'm not going to inject human beings with this Nazi Frankenshot. And I've already heard from health-care workers thanking me, saying this is exactly what I want, I'm going to use it, and I will circulate it to my fellow health-care workers.

Then I wanted to make it clear how serious this was. This isn't a joke, and it isn't a fraud. And I wanted to shake up anyone who is reading this *Notice!* that one of my clients, I guess, would give to their employer. And so I said the United States government has prosecuted, convicted, and executed Medical Doctors who have violated the Nuremberg Code on Medical Experimentation. Yes, that is correct. You can read the *Medical/Doctors Judgment*. You should be able to find it online, and at the end of the *Judgment*, they have the sentences of the convicted, and several of these doctors were sentenced to death.

Now, just recently, I heard from a medical doctor saying, sentenced to death? You must be exaggerating, and that undercuts the significance of everything you're saying. And my response was, obviously you were never required to read the Nuremberg Code on Medical Experimentation in medical school, because if you did, you would know that, in fact, medical doctors were sentenced to death and executed. And this shows, I think, the problems with medical-school education today. And I'm not here to say the legal profession is much better, being a law professor since 1978 and having entered Harvard Law School in 1971, but at least we made a concerted effort to reform teaching ethics to students.

But if you read the news media everywhere in print, on TV, everywhere, you see all these doctors advocating these Nazi Frankenshots. It's astounding! And it's very clear that in medical school they were never required to read the *Nuremberg Medical/Doctors* case, let alone the Nuremberg Code on Medical Experimentation. And it just shows you that medical doctors, certainly here in the United States, have not been properly trained in medical ethics and are not aware of what the standards are. Dr. Hewitt-Vaughn was, but I regret to report at that time that she was the only doctor I personally knew of in the entire U.S. military doctors corps and nurses corps and medical technician corps who refused to give out those Nazi Frankenshots. So we're seeing the abject failure of the medical profession here in the United States certainly to train medical doctors in accordance with appropriate ethical standards.

And I would say the same thing for the so-called life scientists who got their PhDs in the life-science industry. Just look at how many of them have come out and advocated these Nazi Frankenshots in violation of the Nuremberg Code on Medical Experimentation.

I do have firsthand experience. I have three degrees from Harvard, and I had friends and teachers at Harvard, at least three of them, in the Harvard Biology Department, who were three of the most ethical and principled human beings I have ever known in the world. And, of course, they taught their PhD candidates to be ethical. What happened everywhere else? Where are the life scientists saying that the Nuremberg Code on Medical Experimentation prohibits these COVID-19 Nazi Frankenshots?

Then I added a third sentence just to deal with others who are not the potential victims or the health-care workers, but others assisting. For example, I had a person say, Well, what do I say if a police officer comes and forces me to take one of these shots? So I added a third sentence: Aiders and abettors of Nuremberg Crimes are equally guilty and have also been prosecuted, convicted, and executed. And that is a correct statement of law, Regis. That goes back to the *Zyklon B* case where Zyklon B, the trade name for prussic acid, was originally used by the SS in concentration camps to exterminate vermin. And then the SS decided to try it out to exterminate human beings, and as we know, large numbers of Jews, but others as well. And the owner, the chief operating officer and another fellow, were prosecuted at Nuremberg in the *Zyklon B* case, and two of them were found guilty of aiding and abetting Nuremberg war crimes, and they were sentenced to death and executed. So I drafted this little statement for the purpose of being used by people who either did not want to take these shots or did not want to give these shots, and to shake up anyone who would force them to take these shots or to give these shots or any other way aid or abet them.

Now, others have said, What if this doesn't work? At that point what I say is, you've got to get yourself a lawyer, then, in the jurisdiction where you live, and try to use these arguments either to prevent getting the shot or prevent giving the shot, and that all depends on the health laws of the states of the Union in the United States. I am not licensed to practice law in *all* of them; I'm only licensed to practice in *one* of them, and there are a variety of laws. So you'll need to get yourself a lawyer, if push comes to shove, and work out with that lawyer an appropriate defense based upon using my warning, my *Notice!* here under the applicable health-care laws in that state. For example, California has adopted the Nuremberg Code on Medical Experimentation; it's in there.

So I don't have time to research all 50 states of the Union or anything like that. I did take the time to draft this *Notice!* for people to use, and then I tell them, for a follow-up, get a local lawyer, and I'm happy to work with your local lawyer based upon what your health-care law says there. There are a variety of laws in many states, and see if we can use the Nuremberg Code on Medical Experimentation.

Regis Tremblay: Wow, Francis. I was going to ask how effective can this be if an ordinary person or an ordinary health-care person or even a police officer—how effective they can be just knowing about this *Notice!* that you wrote?

FAB: Knowledge is power, Regis, and that's why I circulated this all over the internet for people to use, yes.

Regis Tremblay: Well, I'm going to post it in this particular interview, but I want to know, could I have your permission to post your contact information, your email address, in case lawyers or doctors or anybody wants to contact you for some kind of guidance?

FAB: Sure, I've been giving this guidance all along. But understand, I'm just at the start of this process. For the reasons indicated, I didn't feel compelled to draft this *Notice!* until Joe Biden announced that he was going to inject 100 million of these Frankenshots into 100 million completely innocent Americans in 100 days. We have, I believe, a humanitarian catastrophe on our hands here. This is what motivated me to act, and fortunately to your credit, you're the first person who has given me an interview on this matter. And so I would hope, Regis, that you could take this interview I gave you and circulate it all over the internet, because this *Notice!* is valid anywhere in the world where people are contemplating these Frankenshots. It is drawn up under international criminal law that applies anywhere in the world. These arguments apply if you do not want to give the Frankenshots or take the Frankenshots, yes.

Regis Tremblay: So people all across the planet, all across Europe, thousands are resisting this; they will be able to use this statement as well, obviously.

FAB: I would recommend it be translated. They say English is the universal language, but being of French ancestry, I know the French certainly disagree. So I would recommend it be translated into different languages. I regret to say I used to have conversational French, and I was involved in so many antiwar activities that I couldn't keep it up, so what can I say. I think it definitely needs to be translated into French. Regis, maybe you could do that for me.

Regis Tremblay: We can certainly make an appeal to people to do that. You know, the show we did last month on COVID-19 as a bioweapon has been seen almost 600 times on my YouTube channel. I have no idea where else it spread, but I'm hoping that this show will attract many, many more people. I think it is so important. People are terrified all over the world, and many people unwittingly are just lining up and begging to have this shot.

FAB: Let me say, then, please understand that you are the first person in the media who has had this interview, and so there is a responsibility on your part to get it out as widely as possible. I know you'll do that. That's why I've given it to you. I haven't given this interview to anyone else. Just you.

Regis Tremblay: Well, I appreciate that, Francis.

FAB: My advice would be, don't take these things. But do take this quite seriously. Social distancing, masks, washing your hands, yes. All those things must be done.

Regis Tremblay: Well, Francis, I can't thank you enough for the time you've offered to me, and I'm really kind of happy that I'm the first person you've given this interview to. You can count on me to do everything in my power to get this out as widely and broadly as possible. So thanks again. I very much appreciate the work you've done, the knowledge you've shared, through your books and your articles and your lectures and your interviews, and I think those of us who survive are going to owe you a debt of gratitude. Thank you so much.

FAB: Well, thanks, Regis, and again, thank you so much for taking the time to do this interview and getting the message out.

Stop Mass Medical Experimentation https://vaxnotice.com/

NOTICE!

By authority of the Nuremberg Code on Medical Experimentation, I do hereby exercise my right to refuse to submit to or to administer the COVID-19 vaccine. The United States Government has prosecuted, convicted, and executed Medical Doctors who have violated the Nuremberg Code on Medical Experimentation. Aiders and abettors of Nuremberg Crimes are equally guilty and have also been prosecuted, convicted, and executed.

The Nuremberg Code

1. The voluntary consent of the human subject is absolutely essential. This means that the person involved should have legal capacity to give consent; should be so situated as to be able to exercise free power

of choice, without the intervention of any element of force, fraud, deceit, duress, over-reaching, or other ulterior form of constraint or coercion; and should have sufficient knowledge and comprehension of the elements of the subject matter involved, as to enable him to make an understanding and enlightened decision. This latter element requires that, before the acceptance of an affirmative decision by the experimental subject, there should be made known to him the nature, duration, and purpose of the experiment; the method and means by which it is to be conducted; all inconveniences and hazards reasonably to be expected; and the effects upon his health or person, which may possibly come from his participation in the experiment. The duty and responsibility for ascertaining the quality of the consent rests upon each individual who initiates, directs, or engages in the experiment. It is a personal duty and responsibility which may not be delegated to another with impunity.

2. The experiment should be such as to yield fruitful results for the good of society, unprocurable by other methods or means of study, and not random and unnecessary in nature.
3. The experiment should be so designed and based on the results of animal experimentation and a knowledge of the natural history of the disease or other problem under study, that the anticipated results will justify the performance of the experiment.
4. The experiment should be so conducted as to avoid all unnecessary physical and mental suffering and injury.
5. No experiment should be conducted, where there is an a priori reason to believe that death or disabling injury will occur; except, perhaps, in those experiments where the experimental physicians also serve as subjects.
6. The degree of risk to be taken should never exceed that determined by the humanitarian importance of the problem to be solved by the experiment.
7. Proper preparations should be made and adequate facilities provided to protect the experimental subject against even remote possibilities of injury, disability, or death.
8. The experiment should be conducted only by scientifically qualified persons. The highest degree of skill and care should be required

through all stages of the experiment of those who conduct or engage in the experiment.

9. During the course of the experiment, the human subject should be at liberty to bring the experiment to an end, if he has reached the physical or mental state, where continuation of the experiment seemed to him to be impossible.
10. During the course of the experiment, the scientist in charge must be prepared to terminate the experiment at any stage, if he has probable cause to believe, in the exercise of the good faith, superior skill and careful judgement required of him, that a continuation of the experiment is likely to result in injury, disability, or death to the experimental subject.

["Trials of War Criminals before the Nuremberg Military Tribunals under Control Council Law No. 10," Vol. 2, pp. 181–182. Washington, D.C.: U.S. Government Printing Office, 1949.]

. . .

CHAPTER 9

THE WORLDWIDE ASSOCIATED PRESS HIT/SMEAR JOB AGAINST ME OVER COVID-19

On February 15, 2021, the Associated Press (AP) published all over the world two separate dispatches attacking me for being a super-spreader of disinformation on the COVID-19 pandemic because of my by-then well-known position that COVID-19 was an offensive biological warfare weapon that had leaked out of the Wuhan BSL-4.

According to my legal research assistant, those two AP dispatches produced well over 58,000 news media hits in publications all over the globe. The AP accurately reported that I was the first person to have publicly claimed that COVID-19 was an offensive biological warfare weapon that had leaked out of the Wuhan BSL-4. Here is the backstory to that worldwide AP hit/smear job against me and my analysis of it:

In late May of 2020, I received a request from an AP reporter to give him an interview on my position that COVID-19 is an offensive biological warfare weapon that had leaked out of the Wuhan BSL-4. Over the years, I had given many interviews to the AP on a variety of matters. So I just assumed that even if the AP did not agree with what I had to say, they wanted to get the story straight from the horse's mouth and would at least fairly and accurately report what I had said, together with, of course, opposing opinions by other experts in the dispatch. Fair enough. So I agreed to give the interview in early June 2020.

Then, I was informed that there would be three AP reporters interviewing me at the same time. At that point, I knew this interview was going to be sinister—that someone very powerful had ordered the AP to do a hit/smear job on me that would be published all over the world. But by then I had been arguing my position that COVID-19 was an offensive biological warfare weapon that had leaked out of the Wuhan BSL-4 to all comers of the world since January 24, 2020. Besides, I have been a lawyer since January 10, 1977, and a law professor since August 21, 1978. I am used to arguing my position against all adversaries all over the world, including successfully before the International Court of Justice. So I gave all three of the AP reporters the interview. It was 90 minutes long. Let me repeat that: I gave a 90-minute interview to three reporters for the Associated Press. It was obviously going to be a hit/smear job against me.

I had given the AP the entire story right there on a platter to report if they wanted to. They did not. Instead, they twisted it and perverted it for their own demented purposes. I did the best I could. But I knew right from the very get-go that AP and three of its reporters were up to no good.

During the succeeding eight months right up to publication of the two AP dispatches, I continually supplied the lead reporter from the AP with a constant stream of evolving information, documentation, and analyses backing up my position that COVID-19 was an offensive biological warfare weapon that had leaked out of the Wuhan BSL-4. Instead of taking into account what I had provided to the AP for the story over those many months, it turns out that during all that time, the AP was working in conjunction with the Atlantic Council to research and prepare their hit/smear job against me, knowing full well it would be published all over the world. Someone very powerful had ordered the AP to hit/smear me right from the very get-go. That order stood no matter what. The truth be damned!

When the two AP dispatches finally came out on February 15, 2021, I joked to two of the AP reporters that, as the truism says, "There is no such thing as bad publicity." But again, these two dispatches that the AP had published all over the world were obviously designed from the very get-go to discredit me, smear me, and perform a hit job on me. As I saw it then, I now had proof that someone very powerful had ordered the AP to discredit me and smear me. Of course, this indicated to me that I had been telling the truth all along; otherwise, the AP would not have bothered having three reporters interview me for 90 minutes. Time is money!

I had obviously hit some very powerful people right between their eyes with my position that COVID-19 was an offensive biological warfare weapon that had leaked out of the Wuhan BSL-4. Some very powerful people had decided to fight back against my campaign that I had launched and waged since January 24, 2020, all over the world's news media. They decided to respond in kind. Well, at least the odds were fair: me against the AP.

You, the reader, are free to draw your own conclusions from my account. But as I see it, the AP and whoever ordered them to perform this hit/smear job on me shot themselves in the foot. Tactically, they should have just ignored me. Obviously, they figured they could not—a testimony to the truth of what I was saying. But strategically, they had disseminated my position all over the entire world's news media. As a result of these two AP dispatches, I received many more media requests from all over the world to explain my position since January 24, 2020, that COVID-19 is an offensive biological warfare weapon that had leaked out of the Wuhan BSL-4.

As a matter of fact, it is the AP that is the super-duper super-spreader of fake news, disinformation, propaganda, defamation, and outright character assassination all over the world. The AP can never be relied upon by anyone to provide fair and accurate information on anything ever again. You will have to look elsewhere other than the AP for your news.

In any event, I will not be giving another interview to the AP. The AP and its three reporters can rot in hell with Judas and their 30 pieces of silver each! Whether you trust AP dispatches ever again is up to you, dear reader. I certainly shall not.

Associated Press: *Cum grano salis! Caveat emptor!* [Take this with a grain of salt! Buyer beware!]

...

CHAPTER 10

THE NAZI COVID-19 FRANKENSHOTS (MAY 12, 2021)

Alex Jones: Well, my friends, a lot of explosive, historic things are happening here, and Dr. Francis Boyle has been coming on the show for at least 20 years. He's an author and researcher, and he got a special PhD at Harvard on globalism and how the new world order really operates. He also went to the University of Chicago, where they also do their training, and he's been exposing them for decades. He's been a top war-crimes prosecutor at the UN. He wrote the U.S. Biological Weapons Law in the early 1990s. He contributed heavily to world law, and so he's probably the best guest you can get on, because he's the leading expert on the law on chemical biological weapons, hands down. And also prosecuting people.

So yesterday, I didn't do that for headlines, and I figured it wouldn't get a lot of headlines. It did from Media Matters and others, because they don't want people talking about this, and I said, clearly, now everything Dr. Boyle said 14, 15 months ago here has been proven. You have—and I'll go over some of the names here like I did yesterday—you have Dr. Peter Daszak hiring Ralph S. Baric from North Carolina in 2015 when there was media attention on the gain-of-function illegality. They moved it to Wuhan, where he was with their military and others, but six programs funded by Fauci and by Gates directly to the tune of $3,748,000-plus on gain of function. We have the video of him saying we got five viruses to merge them to build a vaccine, exactly what Boyle said on our show in February of last year, and that they were going to develop the bioweapon to make the vaccine. He says it on the video. This is the director of the program who directly got the waiver from Fauci and the federal agency that he headed up, the National Institute of Allergy and Infectious Diseases.

Then he writes the *Lancet* report that's come out. His colleagues leaked it; he confirms it's real. That he wrote the report that said no connection to Wuhan, and said don't put us in there, they'll know we're covering up. Smoking gun after smoking gun. So what is the penalty for building a biological weapon illegally, and accidentally letting it out versus what has all been proven?

Boyle said a year and three months ago that it's been all vetted and proven. Now, this is beyond Pulitzer Prize stuff, and he doesn't care about that, but that's the level of this stuff—then what does it mean that with all the preparation, the power grab, the Operation Lockstep, the end game we're witnessing with Klaus Schwab and the Great Reset, how they've gotten all this power and all these companies have all doubled, tripled their wealth? I believe they released it on purpose to lock down the world and bring you under control.

Boyle, at least, disagrees with me because it hasn't been proven yet, but that's where I see this going. We'll cover that maybe at the end of the interview, but I want to mention this, go to him now, it's all over the news. Rand Paul is bringing it up. Fauci lies when I have NIH websites saying they funded gain of function under Fauci's direction as late as 2017 in the U.S.

People are charged for lying to Congress, so there is a smorgasbord of importance, and so I'm going to leave it up to Dr. Boyle to think where we should go first in this. But you don't care about vindication; you care about stopping this madness. You also point out that the Frankenshots are illegal, another violation of the Nuremberg Code that is punishable by death. And so, give us your expert take on this full spectrum. What area should we tackle first, Professor?

FAB: Well, thank you for having me on, Alex. My best to your viewing audience. I think Senator Paul did a great job yesterday nailing Fauci to the wall, and I would encourage that you put the entire interchange there on Infowars so people can see it, because the *New York Times* had almost nothing on it, just a little blurb basically making fun of Senator Paul. As we both know, he's an ophthalmologist, which is a high degree of specialty in medical training, and he is obviously a very bright man. As I've said before, we are fighting World War III here. It's a two-front war: first against COVID-19, and second against the Frankenshots. And now as you know, regretfully it's just been reported that they are going to start giving the Frankenshots to 12 – and 15-year-olds.

This is the future of humanity, and here in America these are our children and our grandchildren. The next generation. These kids are going to be poisoned in their system from the get-go.

We have no idea—not just the deaths here, but also the disabilities that are going to afflict them for the rest of their lives. This is Dr. Mengele, Auschwitz-type stuff we are dealing with here. So I'm afraid we're just going to have to do a two-front war here, like World War II that my dad fought in—in Europe and the Pacific. We have COVID-19, and we have the Frankenshots. We have to stop the Frankenshots immediately, especially so they do not start giving them to our children. They're predicting they'll be ready to go soon, no later than the end of the summer. That has to be stopped. Dead in the water. There's no question at all about it for the next generation of humanity.

Now that it's come out that COVID-19 is an offensive biological warfare weapon that has been DNA genetically engineered, it has gain of function, it has synthetic biology. It also has nanotechnology in there, so it can float in the air. Well, of course these Frankenshots aren't going to deal with it. That is why Baric at the UNC when they did put this whole thing together with the Bat Queen from the Wuhan BSL-4—and we have to understand that Wuhan BSL-4 is China's Fort Detrick—they did not move into developing the vaccine because they knew a vaccine was hopeless. There was no way you could possibly have any type of safe and effective vaccine for an offensive biological warfare weapon.

Alex Jones: Well, exactly. It's not just about credit; it's about reality. If people listen to you now, you didn't just call that it was from the lab, you called that you can't have a vaccine for it, But [the scientists] still went ahead with one that instead attacks proteins in the body, and it turns out Fauci did studies at the University of Texas Level 4 lab in 2012, and they told him don't make vaccines, extreme caution, it causes blood clots in the rats. I mean, this is insane.

FAB: I read that study. You're right. They were warned on this from the beginning. I'm sure Fauci knew all about it. And again, not to toot my own horn, but on January 24, 2020, I also said that this undoubtedly involved gain-of-function DNA genetic engineering, which it did.

Alex Jones: You said it before; the scientists even said it. It's about people who are listening to you, because you've been dead-on. I respect you so much. Maybe you're right that it was an accident. I start asking, Why would they do something so crazy? Why would they make a five-stage weapon virus and then release the damn thing?

FAB: Well, Alex, look. I've been opposing DNA genetic engineering for biological warfare purposes since shortly after I joined the Council for Responsible Genetics in 1983 and they asked me to handle their biological warfare weapons work for them. Alex, this is all Nazi-type science. The people who do this, the scientists who do this, they have a Nazi mentality. We must understand that. It's been that way for as long as I've been fighting these people. They do not care. It's that simple, and when I first publicly blew the whistle on this in a briefing on Capitol Hill, it was 1985, after I began working for CRG in 1983, and I said we had to stop this.

Alex Jones: Let's talk about how we stop it and the laws that are in place—national laws, local laws, international laws, the whole situation with the Nuremberg Code.

With Dr. Francis Boyle, this is Alex Jones, and this could not be a more important subject. Tell everyone you know to tune in now. We'll be right back.

{break}

Alex Jones: Welcome back, folks, Alex Jones here. On Monday night, Tucker Carlson went on in a 14-minute piece that took a lot of courage. His contract lets him do whatever he wants. He's the only person at Fox who has a contract like that, and he will not be silenced, and he knocks it out of the park. And I noticed that Fox always posts his full show on YouTube, but they didn't post it that day, and they still haven't as of this morning. They don't want you knowing about this, because if this comes out, it's over for the out-of-control Big Pharma, which is the heart of the global corporate UN system, which isn't the UN. The UN just represents these mega corporations that are extremely authoritarian, who have this attitude of "Oh, the blood out of Arkansas has HIV in it? Let the hemophiliacs have it, they deserve to die." That came out in the Bayer situation. Just like Bayer and Monsanto and Round-Up, they knew that was killing people; they didn't care.

But it's beyond not caring. You mentioned this, Dr. Boyle, and by the way, we do have the full seven-minute exchange between Fauci and Senator Paul, a video of it. I'll play a short segment of it, but you talk about immunization with SARS, coronavirus vaccine leads to pulmonary pathology, the University of Texas federally funded study that Fauci funded out of the same institute of Allergy and Infectious Diseases that he was heading, and it's heavily studied. Wolfgang Woodard, who's on an advisory board to the EU; and Dr. Yeadon. the former chief scientist at Pfizer, they signed a letter in December warning of this protein spike having the body attack itself, and now we're seeing that: record heart attacks, strokes, even in young people who are taking this mRNA shot, but also the others that do a similar thing.

Why would they do that? And I know you're not supposed to ask why evil does what it does, because it's crazy, it wants power. Why did Hitler do what he did? Why did Stalin do what he did? But I don't ever see them getting away with this. Fauci's on record running those gain-of-function projects before all this came out. Now his own people are on video bragging about it. Are they megalomaniacs? Do they think they're invincible? You've been around these people. What's wrong with them?

FAB: Well, Alex, again you pointed out this Nazi mentality. Certainly there at Harvard when I spent seven years there going through the same PhD program that produced Kissinger, Brzezinski, Huntington… McGeorge Bundy, the architect of the Vietnam War for Kennedy and Johnson, taught in the Harvard Government Department before I did. So this goes back at least that far to the Kennedy administration, in my direct personal experience.

Alex Jones: So they just like the power of life and death over people?

FAB: You really have to study the Nazis, Alex. As you said, why did Hitler set out to exterminate the Jews? It made no sense. Even Hannah Arendt pointed this out in her classic work *Origins of Totalitarianism* that militarily it was totally insane for Hitler to be devoting all those resources to exterminating the Jews when he was losing World War II on both fronts. It appears to be insanity to most people, but if you have this Nazi mentality, it makes perfect sense, and you are correct that Klaus Schwab there of Davos said that Kissinger was one of his mentors at Harvard. Kissinger is absolute evil. I went through the exact same PhD program at Harvard. They gave me Kissinger's old office there at Harvard's Center for International Affairs. Harvard trained me to be a Kissinger for my generation. Yes, this is what goes on there.

Alex Jones: How do we believe these people? How do we stop this madness?

FAB: I think, first of all, just looking at the agenda, we have to save our children from these Frankenshots. That's for sure. And we do have time between now and the end of the summer when they say that they're going to start mass inoculation with Frankenshots of our 12 – to 15-year-old children. That's the future. I think we're making progress on convincing adults not to take these Frankenshots. We have to keep doing that.

Alex Jones: I'm going to go to the vaccine centers off-property with huge PA systems. I'm going to read them the news articles about the trials, where as young as two-year-olds are having heart attacks and dying after they take it, and Big Pharma just moves forward. Healthy 2-year-olds have heart attacks and die, 15-year-olds have heart attacks and die, in the studies, and they just keep going forward.

FAB: Just go back and also read the Nazi doctors' *Medical* case at Nuremberg to see what the Nazi doctors were doing, and several of them were convicted, and a few were executed. That was done by us, so I'm afraid I know this is hard for people to accept, but the best precedent for what we're doing here were Hitler and the Nazis, at least in my recent experience. Second Fort Detrick has a manual on how to contain biological warfare agents and how to remediate biological warfare agents. You see these death scientists like Fauci, who've done 95% of this going back to Reagan and his neocons, who wanted to get into using biological warfare with DNA genetic engineering.

Alex Jones: Dick Cheney wrote in April 2000, *Rebuilding America's Defenses for PNAC*, "We need to work through the media to legitimize the use in the near future of race-specific bioweapons."

FAB: Right, that's in the PNAC report, Alex. I cite that in my book *Biowarfare and Terrorism*. The neocons and I think that might have been drafted by Bolton himself; the neocons fully supported biological warfare and race-specific biological warfare as well, sure. Outright genocide. There's no question about it. The problem, Alex, is all this communistic dictatorship propaganda about the Wuhan wet market prevented us right from the get-go to come to grips with COVID-19. This is not natural, or anything at all like that. As I said in my worldwide media alert on January 24, 2020, it's an existentially dangerous offensive biological warfare weapon. Fauci knew that early on. Redfield, the former director of the CDC, in his interview on CNN, said, yes, the leak happened over there at the end of September, early October. And they knew about it.

Alex Jones: And that's what you said in February of last year.

FAB: They knew about it; they knew about the leak. All they had to do was call up the Baric contract and article on the NIH and NIAID Fauci computers. They saw it right there, and instead of acting immediately and effectively to stop it, they just let it move on.

Alex Jones: You're using technical jargon, but we're gonna explain what you mean when we come back. They were running the program, knew exactly what was there, and how deadly it was and what they were up to.

We will be right back with our special guest, Dr. Francis Boyle. Stay with us; this is history happening right now, and as he predicted, they were doing it to test for a future vaccine. So we'll talk about that when we come back.

[break]

Alex Jones: I can tell you right now that the people who funded this, the Bill Gateses and Anthony Faucis, are not pleased, and I wanted to ask Dr. Francis Boyle who predicted all of this or accurately laid it all out and predicted how deadly the vaccine would be and wouldn't help people, to ask him more about how we defeat these people and how we educate the public. Because I'm always asking why they are doing it. The public goes, "There's a reason they do that, that's crazy." Well, you're not crazy, so it's important to answer why they do it:

power, control, corporate domination, UN control, forced inoculation, medical tracking systems, a way to get around your medical records, a way to get big tech involved in your life, the social credit score. But I said this yesterday, and I was very serious, because I wanted to get you on the show, this had just broken, and you've talked about the Nuremberg Code, and you've put this warning out:

NOTICE!

> By authority of the Nuremberg Code on Medical Experimentation, I do hereby exercise my right to refuse to submit to or to administer the COVID-19 vaccine. The United States Government has prosecuted, convicted and executed Medical Doctors who have violated the Nuremberg Code on Medical Experimentation. Aiders and abettors of Nuremberg Crimes are equally guilty and have also been prosecuted, convicted, and executed.

Well, here's Media Matters. I didn't say this to be a shock jock, and I gave more of an expansion here, but I said Bill Gates, Fauci, from my evidence, are all funding this, all involved, and they should be charged; they should be investigated and found guilty of producing an offensive biological weapon. Whether they released it on purpose or whether it leaked, it's a crime. You wrote the U.S. law on biological warfare and put [life imprisonment] in there. As a lawyer, as a father, as an American, what do you think of my statement? Because I'm not saying I want any violence against him, I don't want any vigilantism; I'm saying what they're doing is a war crime. What they're doing is experimental medicine, lying to us and saying it's safe, trying to force people into it, and a lot of people are getting sick and dying. What is the response to this, and what do you make of my statement?

FAB: Everyone involved in the UNC BSL-3, all Americans, and also over at that Wuhan BSL-4, they all must be prosecuted under my Biological Weapons Anti-Terrorism Act of 1989. One point I do disagree with you about, Alex, is the Department of Justice [DOJ] and the negotiations over my legislation, which by the way, was passed exactly the way I wrote it. I originally put life imprisonment in there; the DOJ wanted the death penalty.

I'm a lifelong abolitionist, I guess, going back to my mother. She told me I didn't get it from my father. So I resisted pressure to put the death penalty in here. So as of now, my legislation would only provide for life imprisonment, but you are correct. Fauci and everyone involved in COVID-19—and that would include as we know from the Baric article not only people at UNC but also the FDA—and you'll note that the FDA is the one that gave the emergency authorization used for the COVID Frankenshots, right? And the FDA now has said, Oh well, now we're going to allow you to inject Frankenshots into children.

The FDA is up to its eyeballs in COVID-19, and everyone involved in that—there's just one name here, but I'm sure more were involved. They should all be prosecuted, and the FDA should be taken down for what they've done here. Likewise, Biden just appointed this Dr. Walensky from Harvard Medical School. I don't know her personally. Harvard and the Harvard Medical School are up to their eyeballs in COVID-19. It says that right there on the Baric article. The Dana Farber Cancer Institute, Harvard Medical School—you can't trust anything Walensky or the CDC is telling us.

Alex Jones: And let me just correct myself; I was going from memory. I thought your legislation had a death penalty in it. I must have misunderstood. I was just asking under the Nuremberg Code, what is the punishment for producing a biological weapon that you're intending to infect the public with?

FAB: Let me correct it that you are right, there is another federal statute that I do address in my book *Biowarfare and Terrorism* on the use of weapons of mass destruction that does provide for the death penalty if people die as a result of it. Right now, I'm not saying anyone deliberately used COVID-19. You and I can respectfully disagree, but so far I'm still going along with the leak. But it was a knowing leak. All these BSL-3s and BSL-4s leak. The Nuremberg Code per se has not been put into U.S. criminal law. It is an article of customary international criminal law, but the Supreme Court—and you know this is before Roberts and all the rest—has said it's a requirement of due process of law; you really need to codify these types of requirements.

Alex Jones: There is hope because you got them, with suits and attention, to stop experimental anthrax shots. You were the tip of the spear there that killed tens of thousands of U.S. troops. That's been confirmed. Even the Defense Department now admits those were killing people. So experimental drugs, experimental vaccines, aren't even legal in the military, much less the citizens, and I see this a lot on the news, and I saw it on Twitter: "Alex Jones is a liar. The FDA has approved all these shots and says they're safe." None of that's true. In fact, the inserts on these drugs are blank.

FAB: That's correct, and your viewing audience has to understand that the FDA is up to its eyeballs in an offensive biological warfare weapon, COVID-19, that is existentially dangerous. Their approval of anything is totally worthless. You cannot believe one word the FDA is telling you, and the same for the CDC, and that was true before Walensky. We know full well that the CDC was involved in biological warfare weapons work at least going back to the Reagan administration. I have official government documents on that in my office. (I'm hunkered down at home here.) So you can't believe anything the CDC is telling you. They're just lying and covering it up, as is Fauci—certainly Fauci. Collins, Baric, and the rest of them must be prosecuted under my Biological Weapons Anti-Terrorism Act and face life imprisonment for what they have done here and all the death and destruction and disability that they have inflicted, yes.

As for Gates, he's been very careful to stand behind the scenes and fund all this, so we need to find out what Gates knew. We need to go over there with search warrants from judges and get into Gates's home, his office, and most important, the Gates Foundation; and find out exactly what Gates knew, when did he know it, what was he funding, and what did he know about it. Because we also have, in addition to my Biological Weapons Anti-Terrorism Act, the general federal statutes on conspiracy and aiding and abetting, and that would apply, I believe, to people like Gates.

But we have to get more definite information on precisely what Gates himself was doing. Here, I'm just speaking as a prosecutor trying to nail someone. As for the rest of them, we already have them, like Fauci and the rest of them, we already have them in the documents that were produced. Francis Collins. You know Fauci was lying yesterday.

Alex Jones: We're in the final segment. I want to play a couple minutes of Rand Paul and get your final comment on that. The fact is that a former top world prosecutor for the UN for Milosevic and more, you're saying that it's cut and dried. That's what I see. I see the head of the program admitting they were combining five viruses. I'm getting chills.

We'll be right back in the final segment, and then the war room. Francis Boyle is our guest. We're going to be talking about Mr. Daszak when we return, and the smoking gun.

{break}

Alex Jones: Hit pause and back this up ten seconds, I'm going to play it and get Dr. Boyle's take. For regular listeners, you're missing the TV side of this. We have the NIH website up, and Fauci's name is on the program, and it says that they lifted the pause it started in 2015; it started back in 2017. This was a controversy starting in 2014, running until whatever happened at the lab last year, intentional or leak. So I'm no scientist, but I know how to read the damn newspaper. This has been a big controversy. He's lying about, I don't know, something really obvious. I mean, he sounds like a Bugs Bunny character or something, and he's up there gaslighting us. Let's play the clip and get Dr. Boyle's take on it.

{various clips play}

Alex Jones: The individual who ran the program from the EcoHealth Alliance, Peter Daszak, saying they were getting funding, mentioning the funding, we have the documents, and then we have him admitting they were combining five viruses together into one. Everything you said 16 months ago, or 15 months ago, what do you make of this level of lying? What the hell is going on there, Doctor?

FAB: Well, I think Senator Paul should refer Fauci officially to the Department of Justice [DOJ] for perjury, that's lying under oath to a material matter, that's five years. And I think Senator Paul should make that public, and indeed I would hope that the members of his Committee, at least maybe some of them, maybe Republicans and Democrats alike, could sign on to that letter and refer Fauci to the DOJ for prosecution for perjury. Clearly he perjured himself; there's no question about it. But we've had officials of the U.S. government get up in front of congressional committees and—

Alex Jones: Clapper says the NSA has never spied on one American.

FAB: Right. There's a long history of this, Alex, and they get away with it. That's the problem. But here we now have three million people who've died all over the world of this. So I would encourage Senator Paul to line up some of his colleagues on that Committee and refer Fauci to the DOJ for perjury prosecution and release the letter to the DOJ to the attorney general, definitely.

Alex Jones: I'll say this. I've been watching Fauci's body language for years, even before all this, and he does not look happy now. He finally looks scared. He's not looking too arrogant now, is he, Doctor?

FAB: No, I think Senator Paul did a pretty good job of nailing him. He obviously has to tough it out here as he sees it, because he knows he's violated my Biological Weapons Anti-Terrorism Act and faces life imprisonment if all this collapses around him, yes. That's for sure. He knows what's happening. COVID-19 involves synthetic biology, that's what the Bat Queen brought from China's Fort Detrick to the UNC, synthetic biology, SARS, to then soup it up, as Senator Paul correctly pointed out.

Well, in my BWATA, I anticipated synthetic biology, and I made it clear that in synthetic cells or using synthetic cells likewise, it means a felony, you face life imprisonment. That is why at the first meeting of the so-called synthetic biologists, one of their first recommendations was to repeal my Biological Weapons Anti-Terrorism Act because they knew they were going to get involved in biological warfare. Indeed, I will say here openly, Alex, it's well known that the entire field of synthetic biology was envisioned and financed and started by the Pentagon's DARPA.

Alex Jones: They're all up to their eyeballs in it, so that's why they're protecting each other. Now we've had a disaster of historic proportions.

FAB: That is correct, Alex, that all these officials that the American people have been relying upon, they're lying. They're up to their eyeballs in this, and three million people have died already. We have at least 900,000 American deaths that have now come out because they've been deliberately underestimating it. I don't think Biden's going to bring this under control. His chief of staff, Ron Klain, has been running things. He was behind me at Harvard Law School. Klain was the architect of the cover-up of the fact that the Black West African Ebola pandemic came out of that BSL-4 at Kenema, Sierra Leone, that was set up by the USAID that works closely with the CIA, Fort Detrick, Tulane, et cetera.

Alex Jones: It's literally Tuskegee experiment on steroids. Doctor, thanks for coming on, on short notice, vindicated again. This is the big global story. It's got the system very, very scared. Thank you for coming on.

FAB: Alex, thanks for having me on, and let's stay in touch as developments occur.

Alex Jones: Absolutely, thank you very much.

. . .

CHAPTER 11

MY ADVICE TO THE PEOPLE OF THE CARIBBEAN ON DEALING WITH THE COVID-19 PANDEMIC (JUNE 27, 2021)

(The host is a news director broadcasting to people of color in the Caribbean.)

Host: He's nothing short of a legend in his respective field. Harvard educated, the author of the BWATA legislation, and of course, many books on that very same subject. One of the world's most prominent, and we're certainly very fortunate to have him with us today. We welcome to the Awakening World Truth Summit, Dr. Francis Boyle. Good afternoon.

FAB: Hi. Thank you very much for having me, and my best to your viewing audience.

Host: And certainly we appreciate you. We understand how busy you are and how busy a time this is, so to take some moments to speak to the audience and to us, we appreciate that. And we'll just start by saying that the work you do is incredible. We appreciate it, we have followed it, and certainly a lot of the insights are intangible that you acquired throughout the course of your career that we wish to share with our population. So again, thank you for being here.

FAB: Well, thanks. I've traveled all over the Caribbean, and I'm happy to speak with some of my friends down there.

Host: Fantastic. So as we talked about at the World Truth Summit, Dr. Francis Boyle, you have almost a half century of experience with respect to biowarfare. Specifically today, we'll talk about the vaccines and what's been happening over the last 18 months or so with COVID, but really over the last 18 years or so with the mass rollouts of mass inoculations. Please share with us your background and what you do.

FAB: Sure. Well, I won't go through all of it here, but in 1983, the Council for Responsible Genetics was founded in Cambridge, Massachusetts, where MIT and Harvard are located, and soon thereafter they asked me to get involved in their work against biological weapons. And as part of that in 1985, they organized a briefing on Capitol Hill for members of Congress in Washington, D.C., on this entire matter, and in particular the Reagan administration's abuse of DNA genetic engineering for the purpose of the research, development, and manufacture of biological weapons.

As you know, the Reagan administration were all neoconservatives, and these people believed in biological weapons. They even believed in race-specific biological weapons like the criminal apartheid regime in South Africa was trying to do against its Black people. After conducting the briefing there, at the end I said it was high time for us to have the United States adopt domestic implementing legislation for the Biological Weapons Convention, which we did not have at that time, making the research, development, and testing of biological weapons a U.S. domestic crime. And I also said that even though the Biological Weapons Convention clearly prohibited the use of DNA genetic engineering for biological warfare purposes, we needed to make that crystal clear in the domestic implementing legislation.

So the Council for Responsible Genetics said they supported my proposal, asked me to draft it—the domestic implementing legislation—which I did, and then we proceeded to lobby it through the U.S. Congress, where finally in May of 1989, my legislation (Biological Weapons Anti-Terrorism Act of 1989) was passed unanimously by both Houses of the U.S. Congress and signed into law by President George Bush Sr.

So ever since then, since sometime after 1983, I've been involved in efforts against biological weapons, which I believe COVID-19 is. I expressed my opinion on January 24, 2020, that COVID-19 was, and is, an offensive biological warfare weapon that's existentially dangerous. It has gain-of-function properties, and it leaked out of that Wuhan BSL-4, which is China's Fort Detrick. We all know what Fort Detrick is about, and the Wuhan BSL-4 is China's Fort Detrick. So I've been pointing that out since then, arguing it, giving many interviews, lectures, and things of that nature. I think I sent you a formal lecture I gave at an international conference against biological and chemical weapons at Maharashtra University in Pune, India, basically laying out the case, and where we are today. This COVID-19, in my opinion, is extremely dangerous, and we have to treat it as such.

Now we're into the next stage of these so-called vaccines, and as I pointed out in my first interview against them, which I gave in May of 2020, and then also in that lecture I sent you that I gave at Maharashtra University in India, I don't see how there could be a safe and effective vaccine for COVID-19 because of the way it was researched and developed specifically on purpose as a biological warfare weapon. We don't have any type of successful vaccine against a biological warfare weapon.

I did work in the run-up to Gulf War I by President Bush Sr. to help defend Captain Doctor Yolanda Hewitt-Vaughn, who refused to give experimental vaccines for anthrax and botulin biological warfare weapons. And she was court-martialed for that, and I came to her defense pro bono in February 1991. I won't go through all these details.

Host: Excuse me, Doctor, is that what they refer to when we talk about the Gulf War Syndrome?

FAB: That's right. What happened there, I helped defend her at her court-martial using the Nuremberg Code on Medical Experimentation developed in the prosecution of Nazi doctors after World War II, and some of them were executed by us, the U.S. And to make a long story short, although she was convicted in a kangaroo-court proceeding, I got her adopted as a Prisoner of Conscience by Amnesty International. She was facing five years; she was sentenced to 33 months. I got her out of Fort Leavenworth after eight months.

And during the course of this court-martial, I held a press conference there at Fort Leonard Wood in front of two satellite dishes; and I accused President Bush; the secretary of defense at that time, Cheney; Colin Powell; and Norman Schwarzkopf of inflicting a Nuremberg crime on our own troops. That went out nationwide. I was told by a lawyer at the White House that they heard what I said and were upset. Well, eventually it turned out that what I would call these Frankenshots—DNA genetically engineered like

Frankenfoods—they inoculated 500,000 U.S. troops, and out of the 500,000 inoculated, they killed about 11,000 and disabled about 20%.

Host: Of their own troops.

FAB: Right, of the U.S.'s own troops, that's correct. And so what little track record we have on vaccines, Frankenshots for biological warfare weapons, that's it. And so based on that experience, I said I think that's probably a floor of what's going to happen here because the victims there, they were healthy young men and women in the U.S. armed forces. That's what they suffered. So I'm afraid that we're going to be seeing that, if not worse, with these COVID Frankenshots.

To be honest about it, I did not realize at the time, and certainly I don't think Dr. Hewitt-Vaughn realized at the time, how catastrophic those Frankenshots would be. But she was a real prophet, and eventually within about two years after I came to her defense, I realized that there was a terrible humanitarian catastrophe here known as Gulf War Sickness, in addition to what happened there with the U.S. armed forces. Gulf War Sickness also was conveyed by U.S. veterans of the Gulf War to the health-care workers who treated them and also to family members, indicating that there was a biological warfare agent at work.

Host: Is that like a shedding?

FAB: Not shedding per se, but actual communication, live communication. There was a biological warfare agent at work that was communicated, and eventually a doctor in the private sector—the Veteran Affairs doctors were worthless because they had been instructed to tell the veterans this was all in their head, so they couldn't get proper treatment in VA hospitals. But a private physician did detect a DNA genetically engineered mycoplasm at work. So that probably went back to the Frankenshots, and the keynote, here the proof of the pudding, I was also involved in blowing the whistle on Gulf War Sickness for British/U.K. Gulf War troops.

Host: I was going to ask you exactly that: if there were any other troops other than the American troops. We know it was given to the American troops; it was given to British troops as well?

FAB: That's exactly correct, and when I realized we had this catastrophe was, I would say, about two years after I came to the defense of Captain Doctor Hewitt-Vaughn, and TV Station 4, a private TV station in Britain, contacted me about blowing the whistle on Gulf War Sickness for U.K. troops who were in fact coming down with it because they had taken the exact same Frankenshots our troops did. And so I served as consultant with them on that documentary called *The Dirty War*, and it was released, I believe, in the spring of 1994 with front-page headlines all over the U.K. Finally, the Ministry of Defense admitted that there *was* such a thing as Gulf War Sickness even though the Pentagon was having their VA doctors tell our troops that it was all in their heads. Now the top-off here is this: the French troops who also fought in Gulf War I refused to take those Frankenshots.

Host: Why is that?

FAB: This was because back in their wars in Indochina, they had been given experimental anthrax vaccines that made them all sick. So they refused the Frankenshots, and indeed they did not come down with Gulf War Sickness, except there were a small number of French command troops who served with our command, and they did take the Frankenshots, and a small number of them did come down with Gulf War Sickness. So it's clear the Frankenshots did—

Host: There's a correlation.

FAB: Right.

Host: Let me ask you, because I have a Professor Dr. Quist Haddad, and he talked about the use of what he coined as Frankenshots in Sierra Leone in West Africa, and I was wondering what you may or may not know about that.

FAB: Yes, I blew the whistle on that too. It was clear based on my research. Again, I've been monitoring ever since my involvement here in 1984, so I routinely monitor all mysterious outbreaks of biological illnesses, pandemics, epidemics, to see if it's natural. So it was clear to me very quickly that the Black West African Ebola pandemic came out of the Kenema, Sierra Leone,

Biosafety Level 4 lab that was right there on the scene, and they, it appears, were testing out experimental DNA genetically engineered experimental Ebola vaccines as part of the Pentagon's own biological warfare weapons program without telling these people, and that set off this pandemic. It killed about 12,500 of them. The Kenema BSL-4 was funded, set up, by USAID, which as we know is a front organization for the CIA.

Fort Detrick was over there supervising these experimental Ebola Frankenshots. Tulane University was over there, a well-known center for biological weapons here in the United States, and the Harvard/MIT Broad Institute was over there, a well-known center for synthetic biology. And synthetic biology as a field was funded, sponsored, set up, by the Pentagon's DARPA (Defense Advanced Research Project Agency), so synthetic biology is basically a wholly owned subsidiary of the Pentagon. And as a matter of fact, in the first convention of synthetic biologists, they released an extensive report with recommendations, and near the top of the list of recommendations was the repeal of my Biological Weapon Anti-Terrorism Act. Because I had already anticipated synthetic biology, and I put it into my Act, making it a crime punishable by life imprisonment. It's still on the books today. It's all explained in my book *Biowarfare and Terrorism*. Yes, it's in there.

Host: So we spoke earlier with Dr. Zalinkel, and it speaks to the point of what you just mentioned. He said that our DNA is a center of communication, and that the mRNA interrupts—it's a synthetic interruption of our DNA communication, and so as you talk about synthetic, of course, of medicines and whatnot, it seems eerily reminiscent of what you just described in Sierra Leone.

FAB: Well, as a matter of fact, it turns out that the Pentagon's DARPA paid for the Moderna vaccine and for the technology behind Moderna and also the Pfizer/BioNTech vaccine. I have that documentation. So it goes back to their own biological warfare programs. You see, what happens here is they first develop a biological warfare weapon, and I believe that's what happened at the Wuhan BSL-4 too. That's their Fort Detrick. After they've developed the weapon, then in case of blowback on their own troops or their own people, they then proceed to try to develop a vaccine using reverse engineering. They reverse-engineer the biotechnology they've used to make the weapon. Now what they do then to justify this in public, however, and it's pure propaganda, is to say, Oh, well, we can envision some exotic disease out there that we still don't know about that could infect human beings. And therefore what we are going to do is use DNA genetic engineering and/or synthetic biology to create this disease so that we can then give you a vaccine to protect you from the disease we have already developed. So that's the scam that they use to try to sell these things to the U.S. Congress and the American people.

Host: It's confounding, because it's controlled conflict, it's like a Hegelian Principle. Create the problem, and then of course have the solution waiting and ready to go. I wanted to get your thoughts on both the CDC and the FDA approval process, because apparently none of these vaccines, of course, are approved, and being employed solely on the base of emergency authorization. It seems terribly irresponsible.

FAB: Right. The CDC is pure evil. You cannot trust anything they are saying or have ever said to you. This goes back to my work against the Reagan administration's biological warfare weapons; and during the Reagan administration, the Center for Disease Control and American Type Culture Collection, which is supposed to be a scientific institution keeping copies of all types of biological agents. They sent 40 shipments of weapons-specific biological agents to Saddam Hussein in Iraq in the hope and expectation that Saddam Hussein would weaponize those agents to use them against Iran, against the Iranian people. This is sick and demented, and certainly whatever the public perception is for anyone, any institution in the U.S. government that would do that is sick and demented.

So you can't believe anything the CDC is telling you. Indeed, Biden's current director of the CDC, Walensky, she's from the Harvard Medical School, and the Harvard Medical School was involved in the development of COVID-19 at the University of North Carolina BSL-3 working with the Chinese Bat Queen from the Wuhan BSL-4, which is China's Fort Detrick. And the U.S. Fort Detrick was also involved here. Likewise, Harvard is a sponsoring institution of the Wuhan BSL-4. Think about that—Harvard being a sponsoring institution of Fort Detrick. We all see what's going on there, right?

Harvard also had the chairman of its chemistry department, Lieber, who worked for Fort Detrick, applying nanotechnology to biowarfare weapons. That's his specialty, nanotechnology. Nanotechnology is used to make biological warfare weapons able to be delivered by air. Aerosolization. That's how people are infected with biological weapons—they breathe them. And Lieber, Harvard knew, was working for Fort Detrick applying nanotechnology. And we also know that Lieber had his own lab over at Wuhan, right there at the scene of the crime, specializing in nanotechnology. And the Wuhan BSL-4 bragged on their website that they had applied nanotechnology to viruses, so it appears that that is also a component unit of COVID-19. They've applied nanotechnology to it. They lied from the get-go. They said you could only get it by touching the surface or something like that. No, it is nanotechnology. It travels through the air. They finally admitted that it travels in the air, on the air, above the air. There was one MIT scientist who determined it traveled up to 28 feet in their lab. A Cornell scientist, yes; it traveled 21 feet. So it has nanotechnology involved here, and that's why it's so communicable.

As for the FDA, you can't believe anything they're telling you either. The FDA is clearly listed as being involved in the research, development, and testing of COVID-19 at the University of North Carolina BSL-3 working with the Chinese Bat Queen from the Wuhan BSL-4, which is China's Fort Detrick; and the U.S. Fort Detrick also was involved in this project at the UNC BSL-3. So you can't believe anything the FDA is saying. This emergency use is total baloney. It violates the Nuremberg Code on Medical Experimentation.

In Gulf War I, those Frankenshots for anthrax and botulin, those were completely experimental too. And the FDA gave emergency-use authorization for poisoning U.S. troops with those Frankenshots in violation of the Nuremberg Code on Medical Experimentation. So they're doing the exact same thing here all over again, and you can't believe anything the FDA is telling you. Likewise, Tony Fauci. That whole project was funded by his NIAID, the National Institute for Allergy and Infectious Diseases. He was put in there by Reagan right at the very beginning to handle this entire program of using DNA genetic engineering for the purpose of the research, development, and testing of biological weapons.

Fauci's NIAID is directly listed as funding COVID-19, and now we know he also was involved in Wuhan BSL-4 funding over there. Likewise, the National Institutes for Health, Francis Collins, you can't believe anything they're telling you either. They are clearly listed as funding the UNC BSL-3 COVID-19 with the Chinese Bat Queen from the Chinese Fort Detrick, along with the U.S. Fort Detrick. Now imagine that. The National Institutes of

Health working with Fort Detrick. It's true. I have the documentation. So you can't believe anything they are telling you either. So it's a supremely dangerous situation.

President Biden expressed his full support for Fauci, so you can't believe what these people are telling you. Indeed, Biden's chief of Staff, Ron Klain, who was behind me at Harvard Law School, he worked for Obama, who was also behind me at Harvard Law School, and Obama made him the Obama Ebola Czar, in charge of covering up these Frankenshots coming out of the USAID BSL-4 in Kenema, Sierra Leone, which murdered well over 12,000 Black Africans. So that's Biden's chief of staff right there, Ron Klain.

So I can't overemphasize how much propaganda everyone is being subjected to here on COVID-19. Now that it's come around, everyone's admitting, yeah, it did come out of that Wuhan BSL-4. Well, fine. But now since they've made this admission, the whole debate has turned around from when I started arguing this point on January 24, 2020, that you have to ask yourself what good are any of these Frankenshots? None. They were all developed on the assumption that it came from the fact that Chinese people were eating bat soup in Wuhan. That, of course, is totally worthless. They are more dangerous than worthless. They are both dangerous *and* worthless. And I'm afraid if you read the incident reports coming out of the U.S. government's own VAERS [Vaccine Adverse Event Reporting System] and also the European Health Agency, it's horrendous already. And I'm afraid like what happened with Gulf War Sickness, we won't be seeing the full implications here maybe for the next two years, but certainly by then it'll be out.

Host: Right. It's highly orchestrated. You spoke to so many other points that I want to inquire of, specifically if you believed in what evidence exists about the substantiation of Fauci's NIH funding of gain-of-function research and the fact that, of course, Peter Daszak admits to being funded. Essentially it's been established on record his activities with respect to the gain of function. You've already kind of covered that pretty comprehensively because you've detailed these government-funded, these taxpayer-funded organizations, entities, and companies that actively, you said, participated in the creation of COVID-19, and then so subsequently you'd think that they'd be able to reverse-engineer, they'd be ready to go quick as anything, because why? Because they participated in the creation, so it would stand to reason that they were already working on the vaccine, the solution. Create the problem and have the solution ready to go and make billions of dollars.

If you could, would you speak to the fact that coming out of Harvard, we all recognize Harvard as one of, if not the most significant, cultivator of world leaders. Every world leader I can think of, at least American world leader, presidents, and what have you, come out of Harvard. Legendary. I heard that you even shared an office, or you had the same office, as Henry Kissinger. True?

FAB: Yes, that's correct. I went to Harvard Law School. Mitt Romney was my 1L section mate. Obama was after me. We had the same jurisprudence teacher. But then during my first year there at Harvard Law School, I applied to the Harvard Graduate School of Arts and Sciences Department of Government to their PhD program, specializing in International Relations, because that program had produced Kissinger before me; and later on, Brzezinski, Huntington, all these U.S. imperial apparatchiks—and I wanted to figure out how these people thought and how they operated, because I was against what they were doing.

So, yes, I did—and that was the number-one ranked program in the world at the time I went there. I'm sure it still is. Kissinger, of course, was a mentor to Klaus Schwab of Davos. But in any event, I then spent two years at Harvard's Center for International Affairs, just like Kissinger, and one year on their Executive Committee, and my first year there they gave me Kissinger's old office. That's correct. So my response to that is there but for the grace of God go I!

So I spent seven years at Harvard, and I have three degrees. I spent two years teaching at Harvard. It doesn't surprise me that Harvard's up to its eyeballs in this, and if you have any doubt about that, about how rotten, corrupt, and despicable Harvard is, you could look at the Jeffrey Epstein scandal, where Jeff Epstein, as we know, is this massive child molester who gave large sums of money to Harvard and to all its star faculty, and they all took pedophile money from Jeff Epstein. What more can I say than that?

What surprised me was for a fellow like Epstein, I guess he figured this was chump change for Harvard chumps, because it surprised me how little they were able to be bought for. Larry Summers's wife—Epstein bought her off for a million dollars. He was the president of Harvard. So you have to understand that Harvard trains people to rule the world, not just the United States, but the world, like Kissinger. Kissinger is the foremost example.

That's why I entered that particular program. Harvard has another program at the Kennedy School, which is an insult, I think, to the name of John Kennedy, but there they just train sort of U.S. imperial bootlickers and apparatchiks. So I went through the real deal. The Harvard Graduate School of Arts and Sciences Department of Government. That goes all the way back, in my political lifetime, to McGeorge Bundy, who taught there ahead of me, and we all know the role he played in the Vietnam War that killed 58,000 young men of my generation and three million Vietnamese. So Harvard's been that way, certainly in my political lifetime. I haven't really studied all of what Harvard was up to before then, but since then, that was my Government Department, for sure.

Host: It begs the question—I'll ask you the same question I asked Robert Kennedy Jr., as you talk about the Kennedy Foundation. You studied alongside, before, a little bit after, so many of the individuals who are part and party to this calamity that we are experiencing at present. Talk about Larry Summers and his role in the 2008–2009 financial crisis. We'll talk about that after, but you mentioned Larry Summers, and wow, I have a paper on him. But the question I asked Robert Kennedy Jr. is, you were educated, associated. Obviously they must have solicited you for your services, your brilliance, your intelligence, your aptitude. How was it that you didn't succumb to global influences?

FAB: Well, you know, I have three sons, and I told them that with those three degrees from Harvard, I could have had all the power, all the money, and all the fame I wanted. Instead, I just decided to use my talents to make the world a better place in the hope that I don't want my three sons to follow in my footsteps, and fortunately they're not. It hasn't been an easy life, but I have encouraged them to use their talents to make the world a better place. That's the way my parents raised me, to use my talents to make the world a better place, and that's why I'm appearing on this program—to give you my assessment of the situation where we stand today, and I guess your viewers will have to draw their own conclusions of what to do now.

Host: The legacy that is of the Western civilization, and I believe it's those principles founded and fostered in the contributions that freedom is not free, but in many instances it's other people who paid for it, so we are so grateful for the service that you continue to provide, the insight, the information, of course the commitment, that you make in the pursuance of truth, freedom, and accountability. And we are calling and lobbying for corporate manslaughter charges, just to mention some of the initiatives that we are looking at undertaking with respect to this mass abomination that has been imposed against the unsuspecting public. It is truly, truly horrific.

FAB: I would add to that, personal criminal charges against Fauci and Collins and everyone involved in the UNC BSL-3 and the Wuhan BSL-4. They should all be prosecuted, yes. And I'll continue working toward that end the best I can. Although I haven't dealt with Robert Kennedy Jr., I do follow his computer list. I think they're doing very good work on COVID-19 and against these Frankenshots, and I would encourage your listeners to sign up for that list, the Children's Health Defense Fund. I think they're doing very good work. Please understand that I'm not here one way or the other as any spokesman or participant in any anti-vax campaign or anything like that. My specialty is biological weapons and so-called vaccines with respect to biological weapons. But on this issue, I think Kennedy and his Children's Health Defense Fund are doing a good job.

Host: Dr. Zalenko suggested that it's not a vaccine. He said that it's more of a gene therapy. That was his professional opinion. You have any sentiment? Any thoughts on that?

FAB: That's why I call it a Frankenshot. I've done a little work against GMO foods, which we called Frankenfoods, and so I call them Frankenshots. If you look at the technology involved, they're actually giving you cells from COVID-19, which as I said before, is an offensive biological warfare weapon. It has been DNA genetically engineered with gain-of-function properties. It has synthetic biology in there that's paid for by the Pentagon, Fort Detrick. It has HIV, the precursor to AIDS, genetically engineered into there and nanotechnology. So why would you want to inject yourself with cells of that nature?

Host: Absolutely.

FAB: We're already seeing the catastrophic consequences that these Frankenshots are having on human beings, and it's just the beginning, I'm afraid.

Host: And on kids, especially. I wish we had more time to talk. I have so many questions, and of course have listed them out, but I recognize that your time is very precious.

FAB: Let me say—you mention the kids. This is Dr. Mengele at Auschwitz work, injecting kids with these Frankenshots. You can read the Nuremberg *Medical/Doctors* case. It's all in there. But what the Nazi doctors were doing—and this is where the Nuremberg Code on Medical Experimentation came from, to prevent something like this from happening again. Injecting Frankenshots into these kids is similar to the hideous experiments that Dr. Mengele did on children at Auschwitz.

Host: And I would suggest that the premise behind the literature, the contents, of your BWATA of 1989, you authored it for the USA. It was passed unanimously by both Houses and is still in place today. We are all looking around bewildered, wondering at what point the side of righteousness and integrity would stand up and hold these parties accountable for their tyrannical and outright unconscionable actions.

We thank you for your contributions and your insights and for spending time with us. Your contributions—I've got two pages of notes. I was trying to interview and take notes at the same time, but phenomenal, Dr. Boyle. I certainly appreciate, again, you taking this time out. It is the Awakening Truth Summit. Any parting notes before we let you go?

FAB: Well, we're in a tough situation here between the COVID-19 and the Frankenshots. I don't think you should let anyone tell you this stuff isn't dangerous. A lot of that going around. I personally think it's an extremely dangerous biological warfare weapon, and then the Frankenshots, it's like a one-two punch against humanity. This is what we are facing now, so I think everyone is going to have to decide in accordance with his or her conscience what they're going to do and how they are going to proceed. That's all I can say.

Host: And it couldn't be said much better than that. Thank you so much, Dr. Francis Boyle, author of *Biowarfare and Terrorism*, the Act of the United States in 1989, and a plethora of books on the subject as well. If we want to purchase, to learn, to investigate more about your work, sir, how do I get ahold of your books?

FAB: *Biowarfare and Terrorism*, you can get on Amazon. It's cheaply priced. It's a paperback, there's no problem.

Host: We're going to make sure we get that information to our viewers, and again, thank you so much, and I hope we get the chance to talk to you again, especially as this calamity continues to evolve. We don't know what's coming next, and certainly it's been dastardly and shocking to this point. So just to have access to your insight, your experience, again intangible, and very much appreciated.

FAB: Well, thank you. I'm very happy to appear here and again. All my best to my friends down there in the Caribbean.

Host: Thanks a lot.

Kissy and Timmy and Me

"You're moving into Kissinger's old office"
Said Bud, the wizened old janitor
And a decent guy at that
"His file cabinets are in there"
Sure enough they were
So it must be true

"And down the hallway there
Is Timothy Leary's old office"
So that must be true too!

Kissy and Timmy
Kissing Cousins in the Vanserg Building
Amazing!

Did they pass in the hall?
Glance at each other?
Say a few words of greeting?
The last probably not

Did they piss in the men's room
Silently standing next to each other?
Staring at the wall
Probably so
There was only one

The counterfactuals of history
What if Timmy had given Kissy acid?
Timmy turn Kissy on?
Maybe the world would have been
A more peaceful place
With Kissinger on acid
It certainly
Could not have been worse

The Kissinger War Prize for Vietnam
Obama got one too
Those Norwegians
Surely have
A wicked sense of humor

Timothy Leary's dead
No! No!
He's on the outside
Looking in
Say the Moody Blues
Bards of My Woodstock Generation

PROFESSOR FRANCIS A. BOYLE

Photo caption: Francis A. Boyle, Associate and Executive Committee Member, Harvard Center for International Affairs, 1978 [third row down, second from left].

CHAPTER 12

INDICTING THOSE RESPONSIBLE FOR THE COVID-19 PANDEMIC AND THE NAZI FRANKENSHOTS (AUGUST 20, 2021)

Alex Jones: Thank you for joining us on this very important emergency Saturday bulletin. I have gotten hundreds of calls on air in the last few months and massive emails. People on the street have said, That Dr. Francis Boyle, can you please get him back on about the Nuremberg Code, about trying to make the military take experimental shots? What are the military rights? How does the military challenge unlawful orders? How do you exercise the law? What do we do?

And so he's the author of the U.S. Biological Weapons Treaty implementing legislation. He has been a big UN head prosecutor that prosecuted Milosevic and others. So he's a lawyer's lawyer on this, with multiple degrees from Harvard, you name it, to be able to lay all this out. And so I'm going to try to shut up here on the Saturday show and give him the floor to just walk through that Nuremberg Code, what's going on with these shots.

But, also, I know that Dr. Boyle doesn't like to digress, but for folks who didn't see the dozen or so interviews he did in the last 18 months here, he predicted everything that would happen. They'd come out with a vaccine that wouldn't work. They'd have quote, booster shots, that didn't work. He predicted it would cause everything that we've seen so far, so, wow. Wherever he wants to begin, it's great to have him here; and we really, really appreciate his time. Dr. Boyle, thank you.

FAB: Well, thank you very much for having me on, Alex, and my best to your viewing audience.

Alex Jones: You just heard my preface, but you're the expert here. Where should we start with this fiasco that you predicted?

FAB: Right now I want to sketch out a strategy for resistance that all of your viewers can undertake if they want to, a resistance to this medical tyranny. And I hope people could pull out a pencil and paper at this time. And I don't mean to sound too much like a law professor here. I try to speak in plain English.

And I will try to present this in plain English. If it departs from that, please interrupt me and ask me to explain. But what we're seeing now is that the Biden administration is working in cahoots with Fauci and all the rest of them, imposing these Frankenshots on the American people.

And you can just see the deaths and disabilities rising up. So I want to point out, then, that there *is* a way we can fight back. And the way we can fight back is the beauty of the Tenth Amendment to the United States Constitution, which says the powers not delegated to the United States by the Constitution nor prohibited by it to the states are reserved to the states respectively or to the people.

So I don't think we're going to get anywhere, or get much help from the federal government because the federal government is all in on the Frankenshots. What I'm suggesting here, then, is that we exercise our rights under the Tenth Amendment to the United States Constitution. And try to get Fauci, Collins, Baric, the Bat Queen, Menachery, Daszak, and everyone else involved in this indicted for murder, and conspiracy to commit murder, at the state and local levels of the United States government. Likewise, I will go through a strategy here that the exact same thing be done over the Frankenshots.

So let me explain the first strategy to try to get Fauci, Collins, Menachery, the Bat Queen, Baric, and Daszak indicted for murder, and conspiracy to commit murder, over the COVID-19 pandemic. Now, I was originally hired here to teach Criminal Law, and I taught it for seven or eight years before I moved over to teach International Human Rights Law, but I still do criminal cases, both for the prosecution and for the defense on matters of principle. Murder is defined at common law. And here, I can't speak for all 50 states of the Union, but we are a national law school here, and we train lawyers to practice law all over the country. So what I am doing here is explaining to you general principles of criminal law that apply in all 50 states of the Union. And here again, we have to focus on the state and local level, because the federal government, the Department of Justice, is now all working in cahoots with Biden and Fauci and Collins and the rest of these people.

So at common law, the common law of most states of the Union, murder is defined as the unlawful killing of a human being with malice aforethought. OK, so let's go through those elements on the pandemic first. On the unlawful killing of a human being. We have a violation of my Biological Weapons Anti-Terrorism Act of 1989. That is a federal crime punishable by life in prison. So we have that element established. Killing of a human being. Yes. Large numbers of people here in America have been killed by the coronavirus pandemic. The probable estimate is that well over a million people now, a million Americans in excess deaths.

All right, then, we come to malice aforethought. Malice aforethought is a legal term of art, and I'm not going to expend a lot of time here, you know, lecturing you and your audience on all the elements of malice aforethought. That would take me four or five days—

Alex Jones: But I plan to come dump gasoline on your house at 2:00 a.m. and hope to burn you and your family out. Does it mean a premeditated plan to hurt somebody?

FAB: I'm going to get into that, and let me explain it here. There are different types, but in this case, with respect to the pandemic, one element of malice aforethought is manifesting grave indifference to human life, grave indifference to human life. Now, if you look at that "Smoking Gun" contract article that we went through before: SARS-like cluster of circulating bat coronavirus poses threat for human emergence. We went through that. It is clear that Fauci, Menachery, the Bat Queen, Baric, Daszak, and Collins knew they were manifesting grave indifference to human life.

Indeed, they have been told, and they knew that this was extremely dangerous and hazardous. There is no question at all about it; that is why the Obama administration put a pause letter on this very existentially dangerous type of gain-of-function work, whereupon Fauci and Collins then tried to whitewash it through Daszak by running it through the Wuhan BSL-4.

So they knew that they were manifesting a grave indifference to human life. So, yes, we have the elements for murder there. The unlawful killing of human beings manifesting malice aforethought with grave indifference to human life. And that is clear again—that would be the case for Menachery and Baric and everyone signed on to that article we discussed before, the SARS-like cluster—

Alex Jones: Well, I'm glad you raised that, but to just interject, you're going back to the last few exchanges with Senator Paul, where you said he nailed Fauci. Fauci even put on conferences called gain of function and defended at a function that he argued that he didn't do that. And so you're just going with, out of the different types of malice aforethought, the bare minimum. If I secretly, you know, start building nuclear weapons next to your house, and one of them leaks or poisons your neighbors, I had malice aforethought because I didn't care that I was doing something basically illegal right next to it—is that what you're saying?

FAB: That's exactly correct, Alex. That is correct. So all of them, on the basis of just this article, and the history of it and what is in there, in my opinion, could be indicted for murder, and conspiracy to commit murder.

Now, this is not going to happen by the federal government because the feds are all in on this with Biden, and he controls the Department of Justice. So what do you have to do? Well, if you have lost a loved one as a result of the coronavirus pandemic, you have to go to your local state's attorney, district attorney, county prosecutor, or attorney general and demand that they convene a grand jury and present this evidence before a grand jury and seek an indictment for murder, and conspiracy to commit murder. Now, these local officials are accountable to you. They are elected by the people of the community, and they are paid for by the people of the community, and they can be reelected or dis-elected by the people of the community. And so they are going to listen to you.

So my advice here is that everyone in this country, in the United States of America, who has lost a loved one—a million of them as a result of this pandemic—go in personally to their state's attorney, district attorney, county prosecutor, attorney general. Bring in that article and all the other evidence that has accumulated in the public record and demand that those multiple prosecutors convene a grand jury and present the case to a grand jury for indictments for murder, and conspiracy to commit murder, against Menachery,

Baric, the Bat Queen, Fauci, Daszak, and Collins, and everyone else who was involved in that project at the UNC BSL-3.

This can be done. You have the power to do it. You will have to get organized to do it. Emails are not enough. My experience is, you know, politicians, I hate to say, don't pay all that much attention to emails, but they do pay attention to personal appearances by the people of the community who elect them and pay for them and reelect them with solid evidence. Get them to convene those grand juries, and indict them for murder, and conspiracy to commit murder.

Now you asked this other question about premeditation and deliberation. I want to make it clear: I do not support the death penalty. I'm a lifelong abolitionist myself, and worked against the death penalty. But that being said, since we are a national law school here, we train lawyers for all over the country. I also have to lecture my law students; I have had to lecture them on capital offenses. A capital offense, a death penalty—in addition to what I have discussed with you so far, also requires on top of unlawful killing of human beings, malice aforethought, premeditation, and deliberation.

That is the additional element for a capital offense. And clearly that is what we have here with Menachery, Baric, the Bat Queen, everyone else on that UNC team, this person from Harvard Medical School, this person from the Food and Drug Administration—which is why you can't believe anything the FDA tells you, and Fauci and Collins. I believe we have more than enough evidence here of premeditation and deliberation. So if your state's attorney, district attorney, county prosecutor, attorney general, believes there is enough evidence there, sure, they could go for a capital offense as well. Fortunately, I live here in the state of Illinois. We do not have the death penalty, and I oppose the death penalty, but as you know, other states in the Union *do* have the death penalty. That would be how you would proceed to make a capital offense against these individuals.

Alex Jones: I'm not a top lawyer like you, but it seems like if you release a bioweapon, even by negligence, because you knew it could happen, that seems like something you'd either go to prison for, for life, or get executed for. And that's why I'm glad you're here. 'Cause you deserved a few weeks off during your summer vacation, you're back, our listeners have been begging for you. They wanted you on about the move with these Frankenshots against the military. And from your experiences, you can help get some of the anthrax shot. The anthrax shot, how they would proceed, but I think you're right starting at the root of the leak and what happened. And now that you've been vindicated—you were here 18 months ago; you were the first to report it.

And then now it's happened. And you sat on this show 18 months ago, 17 months ago, you said that the shot won't work, and that it's going to cause all these problems, and now that's happened. So there's a whole waterfront to cover here, Dr. Boyle. And I've got your letter; we're going to post it on Infowars.com. You're noticed by authority of the Nuremberg Code, that actual Nuremberg Code, which I see at city council meetings, your letters are being brought up. And so people are rediscovering that there's a whole spectrum out there, and people really want to hear what you have to say. So where do you want to start next?

FAB: Right. Well, now I want to deal with the Frankenshots, Alex, how we can fight back on the Frankenshots. And the legal analysis is pretty much the same with the Frankenshots: unlawful killing of a human being with malice aforethought. Unlawful. Let's start with that on the Frankenshots.

Clearly, we have a violation of the Nuremberg Code on Medical Experimentation, and that is a Nuremberg Crime, and it is also a Nuremberg Crime against Humanity. And this is the exact same statute we used to prosecute Nazis at Nuremberg. And let me read for you the appropriate passage here from the Nuremberg Charter: crimes against humanity, namely murder, extermination ... and other inhumane acts committed against any civilian population. Clearly, that's what's going on here with the Frankenshots. We have a Nuremberg Crime and a Nuremberg Crime against Humanity.

Second, then, the killing of a human being from the Frankenshots. Well, we don't have the exact number here. Right now there've been estimates in the tens of thousands now of Americans who have been killed by means of these Frankenshots.

Killing of human beings with malice aforethought. All right, here we get into two other variants of malice of aforethought—namely, an intention to kill or an intention to cause grievous bodily harm. Now maybe the manufacturers of the Frankenshots say, well, you know, we didn't really intend to kill anyone, but they clearly intended to cause grievous bodily harm. That is very clear from the adverse incidents, those reactions now, that are piling up and have been documented in the VAERS reports and also the European Health Agency. And yet, despite that, they are continuing to inflict Frankenshots on the American people, despite this grave harm, grievous harm, to human bodies. So yeah. I think you can make out malice aforethought there, either intention to kill or intention to cause grievous bodily harm.

So again, my advice—this would be a separate and second type of legal action—different from the legal action with respect to the COVID pandemic itself. I think this legal action would be after Slaoui, the Operation Warp Speed director, and then the chief executive officers for Pfizer, BioNTech, and also Moderna and Johnson & Johnson. Those are the three Frankenshots administered here in the United States. And again, you would go into your state's attorney, district attorney, county prosecutor, attorney general, and say, Look, here we have had in your jurisdiction my loved ones who were killed as a result of these Frankenshots—and you would have to produce this evidence, a coroner's report or an autopsy or something like that. And therefore, I want you to convene a grand jury and request the indictment of Slaoui, as well as the chief executive officers for Pfizer—

Alex Jones: Because they can give themselves into the 1986 Reagan Act. That was terrible. Liability protection, but that's for civil. They don't have criminal protection.

FAB: That is correct. Dealing here with criminal accountability, Alex, that the civil protection is not going to help these people; and Moderna and Johnson & Johnson, for murder, and conspiracy to commit murder. And the state's attorney, county prosecutor, district attorney, attorney general, would assemble the case, convene a grand jury, you know, under the Fifth Amendment to the United States Constitution. They have a right, this is a serious offense, to an indictment by a grand jury. So I'm not saying we should short-circuit any legal due process here.

Alex Jones: Doc, Doc, it's great to have you here on a Saturday. Everybody's tuning in. We're going to give you the floor, and it's amazing, but people need to hear this. So just digress. 'Cause I don't want to go as a lawyer and want to hit just the facts, but how did you 18, 19 months ago, predict they bring out shots that didn't work? Predict they'd have boosters? Predict it would cause all these health problems and predict this breakdown? I mean, you were the first, so we're always wanting to know what's coming next.

So if you told us what was going to happen 18 months ago and it came true, I want to focus on how we stop them, and I get that. But if we don't stop them or we don't take action or have legislatures and prosecutors, then what comes next? I know, as a prosecutor, you don't get into the mindset of the killer. We know they did it. But for the public, they have to understand why somebody would do something like this. That's why so much of the public just can't believe this is happening. Just like half the Germans lived right next to death camps. They didn't believe that Hitler was killing people until they took them in and Eisenhower made them look at the dead bodies. I mean, people just can't believe this is happening.

I mean, I'm ranting here. So what is the big picture? 'Cause I know you want to focus on, as a respected top lawyer and a guy who wrote the U.S. weapons law and former top human-rights prosecutor, you want to focus on what you can prove in a court of law. People are listening, but just as a father, I've got four children. As a person, I still can't wrap my mind around how you predicted all this. And I had other scientists talking on it as well. It's all coming true like a nightmare. And then you're getting censored. Now *I'm* getting censored. And what does Google think it's doing? What is the Democratic party or Trump, who hasn't come out against this? What do they think they're involved in? Because this is serious. This isn't like old-fashioned vaccines and some side effects. This is devastating. This is premeditated.

FAB: Right. Biden is going to recommend, and they will soon require, a third round of Frankenshots for everyone. So if the first two didn't kill you, the third will get you for sure. But Alex, what I've just outlined here is what I believe common, ordinary, everyday American citizens can do to fight back now. Go to your state's attorney, district attorney, county prosecutor, attorney general, and demand they convene grand juries for both the Frankenshots and the pandemic itself. I think this can be done. It should be done. And if we start doing it now, we will be fighting back. We will be resisting, and we will be going after the perpetrators for sure.

Alex Jones: You're right. So go right at the fact that it violates the Nuremberg Code; they skipped all the trials up front. This is insanity. Just attack it right at its base is how to stop them.

FAB: Right. And that's why I'm appearing here for you today, to outline this dual legal strategy to go after the people behind the pandemic, to hold them legally accountable on a state and local basis. And also the Frankenshots to hold those people legally accountable on a state and local basis. And despite whatever civil immunity they might have, this is not going to protect them from criminal indictments for murder and conspiracy.

Alex Jones: Given the fact you're only here as a legal scholar going on what legally is happening, I get it. I'm asking you as an American. Why do something so bold and so reckless when even the majority of top scientists say this is terrible, it's going to cause all these problems, and now it's happening and they just keep bullying forward. Why would they do something so insanely aggressive and reckless?

FAB: Well, because we haven't fought back yet. I'm here to explain how I think common, ordinary, everyday Americans can start to fight back. Indeed, there are some states in the Union—I know Massachusetts is one—where people can go into court and file their own criminal complaints as well.

So if you have loved ones who have been killed, murdered, by either the pandemic or the Frankenshots, you have a standing to go into the state's attorney, district attorney, county attorney, and say, my loved one died in your jurisdiction, your jurisdiction here; it was murder. I want you to convene a grand jury and present the evidence to the grand jury. Now, of course, maybe the grand jury will not agree, but I think both you and I conclude the evidence is out there.

Alex Jones: I agree. Spend as much time as you want on it, Dr. Boyle, on that two-pronged approach to stop this with the criminal investigations, criminal indictments, but then separately, the military has been begging for you to come on. I pointed them at previous interviews, and I pointed them toward your letter in the Nuremberg Code. And it's being brought up at city council meetings in Texas and in California and other areas—your letter, but specifically to the military, you helped expose the Gulf War Illness, what was really going on. So the military is calling me, and I'm not a lawyer. And I just point them at your interview, and I know nothing's perfect, but the Pentagon is saying, Oh, well, if you have an exemption, but they make it very hard to get the exemption. What is the real legal position for those in the military when they're trying to make them take this experimental injection?

FAB: My advice is that under military law, you do not have any obligation to obey an illegal order. I've been involved myself over the years, Alex, in defending *pro bono publico*, five GI resistors against war or torture or war crimes. And you have no obligation to obey an illegal order, which in this case would be in violation of the Nuremberg Code on Medical Experimentation, to take these Frankenshots.

So, of course, you need to get yourself a lawyer, and we've discussed this before. I've dealt with JAG [Judge Advocate General] lawyers. I mean no disrespect to JAG lawyers, but at the end of the day, they are in the chain of command. There's only so much they can do for you. So you'll need to get a lawyer; you could get a retired JAG lawyer or JAG judge or civilian counsel willing to push the envelope for you and just invoke your rights in my *Nuremberg Notice*, and say, I am not going to follow this order because it's an illegal order.

Now, then, what would happen is if they want to introduce court-martial proceedings, you have enormous protections under the Uniform Code of Military Justice [UCMJ]. Now, you know, I'm just speaking from my own personal experience. Obviously, it's not what we would expect as civilians, but I think our UCMJ is pretty good if you're a member of the U.S. armed forces. But you're going to need a lawyer to assert all of your rights under the UCMJ.

Now, the last I've read, there are at least 30% or more members of the U.S. armed forces who have so far not taken these Frankenshots. Well, imagine if 30% of the U.S. armed forces assert their right to disobey an illegal order in violation of the Nuremberg Code of Medical Experimentation and say, I'm very sorry, but under military law, I have no obligation to obey an illegal order.

Then what is the military going to do? Are they going to court-martial 30% of the U.S. armed forces? I don't know, but that would be the dilemma that the military would be in today. Are they going to court-martial 30% of the U.S. armed forces or not?

Alex Jones: I think you've hit the heart of the matter. They wanted to get 80, 90% of the public to do this, but because they got about half the U.S. public, 70% of the military to do it, they've got a real problem bullying a giant minority that also has a law on their side.

FAB: That's correct. And so, again, if you want, I wrote a book, *Protesting Power: War, Resistance, and Law* [Rowman and Littlefield, Inc.]. That has a case in there on a failure to obey an illegal order. And we won it, so this case is a precedent.

Alex Jones: Let me stop, because you never, ever tell a story to toot your horn, and go back for me, 'cause you were on over 15 years ago. I remember reading the news articles; it's how we first got you on. You helped stop the experimental anthrax shot that killed tens of thousands of people. They admit that's something. So this is not your first rodeo here.

FAB: Now, if you read my book *Protesting Power: War, Resistance, and Law*, I wrote that for lawyers to explain to them how to use international law, the laws of war, U.S. Constitutional law, and human-rights law, to defend GI resistors as a matter of principle. GI resistors who have opposed illegal, criminal wars or war crimes or torture or things of this nature or illegal orders, it's all there in my book.

And so all your lawyers have to do is get a copy of that book and read through it, and they'll know how to make out this this type of defense. I helped defend U.S. Marine Corps Corporal Jeff Patterson, who was the first military resistor to Bush Sr.'s war against Iraq, and Corporal Patterson refused to go to Saudi Arabia in August, right after Bush Sr. was ordering U.S. armed forces to Saudi Arabia on the grounds that he believed this was just another U.S. war for oil, which was, of course, correct.

But in any event, we defended him on the grounds that the Bush Sr. order to ship off to Saudi Arabia was not authorized by law because it violated the War Powers Clause of the Constitution and Congress's 1973 War Powers Resolution. I was out there at Kaneohe Bay in Hawaii for the preliminary court-martial proceedings. It took about three hours. And the judge took the matter under advisement, and Corporal Patterson was dismissed from the Marine Corps. They did not want to go to the formal court-martial with the posture of that case—

Alex Jones: So your experiences where people have decent counsel on there, on the right, that usually they're able to exercise their freedom.

FAB: Right. So I'm just saying these are very complicated issues.

Alex Jones: Sure, we can't sit up here in generalities and give people a one-size-fits-all, back-of-the-envelope thing to do. You're just saying, here's the history of it. Here's what I've done in the past. And here's what you might want to look at.

FAB: Right. But I think the grounds are for military personnel to say, you know, I'm exercising my right under military law not to obey an illegal order that would clearly violate the Nuremberg Code on Medical Experimentation here.

Alex Jones: And isn't the Nuremberg Code—that's storied, and one of the most respected laws in the world. That's so well known that even the general public knows that. That's a pretty strong international agreement, and that's bad. I know U.S. law, then, follows that. Explain how that works, but that's a very strong thing to hang your hat on, isn't it?

FAB: Yes, of course. And you know, if it were to come to a court-martial, I think we'd do quite well arguing that point, yes. But the point is, we're talking about mass civil resistance here by 30% of the U.S. armed forces who don't want to take these Frankenshots, exercising their rights under U.S. military law, and saying, I'm not going to do it. And then if they are court-martialed, they get civilian counsel and make these types of arguments that, you know, have successfully been made in a military court-martial.

Alex Jones: Let me just digress, Doctor, because this is important, Professor. It's just so interesting, as you've been on my show, probably 50, 60 times in the last 15 years, and you never like to repeat yourself, but you did predict that the vaccine wouldn't work because you couldn't make one for a coronavirus, which they now admit. You did predict these attempts at the passports, the controls. I mean, so it's rare to get you to make predictions, but you were here over a year and a half ago and predicted the world we live in now. You can go wherever you want right now, but the listeners want to hear what you think is coming next if we don't oppose this, because 99% of the time, you want to do legalese and the actual facts of the cases; you can talk about them. But what do you see as an American, as a citizen, about the world we live in right now?

FAB: Well, we're going to be living under a medical dictatorship and totalitarian dictatorship for sure. So we have to fight back, and that's why I'm appearing here on your show today: to give a strategy. I've given three different strategies here, two for civilians on the pandemic and the Frankenshots, and one for the military on the Frankenshots, that they can use to fight back and resist the Frankenshots.

Alex Jones: Wow. OK. Well, amazing. So we've been talking here about 35 minutes. We've got about 30 minutes left with you and your time on this special Saturday show. Please continue, Dr. Boyle, wherever you want to go next, dealing with this medical tyranny you just talked about and how we oppose it and what we can do. I think you're saying it's time for the public to get informed and to start saying, No, it's really up to us.

FAB: Well, I'm not just saying no, but to fight back legally, as I'm saying. I'm not saying you take up arms here or anything like that, but based on my experience, legally, this can be done. It should be done. I think we can succeed, and we can fight back, yes.

Alex Jones: Well, please continue, then.

FAB: Well, that's the strategy I had here, those three points I had: one for the military, two for civilians, and we can control this resistance at the state and local government. We do not have to rely on the federal government that is under the control of Biden, and he's working in cahoots with Fauci. He's made that very clear, and I've been up against Biden twice in my professional career, in his capacity as chairman of the Senate Foreign Relations Committee. The first time, I beat him out. The second time I stopped what he was doing and protected the interests of my people.

You can't believe anything Biden's telling you. My experience is that he is very ruthless, cunning, despite the Uncle Joe–type image. He is very ruthless, cunning, unprincipled, and a typical machine politician. And we now see that in the tyranny of Biden, imposing the Frankenshots to whatever extent he can.

And so basically, hijacking those in the private sector to impose these Frankenshots. So again for our future, the future of our children, we have to resist the Frankenshots, and we have to fight back against the instigators of the pandemic.

Alex Jones: Dr. Boyle, I know because you don't have all the facts, you don't want to go there before we start this interview, and I respect that, but we've learned it's in the news: Owen Shroyer is being indicted. They say for being on the steps of the Capitol. He was with me on January 6; we went up to try to stop it. Bullhorned it.

It's on record we did that. But that's so chilling. I wanted to raise the national strategy for countering the domestic terrorism of Joe Biden from June, two and a half months ago. And it says in here we can put up NBC graphics that are out of this, protesting COVID measures, any claims of election fraud. It says the Pentagon and CIA see you as the main terror threat. You wrote books on this, you warned of this. You were put on a no-fly list yourself. Now we see other people who are totally peaceful Republicans and others and liberal antiwar activists being put on a no-fly list.

Again, this is all going on. What do you, just as a citizen looking at this, because I don't even know what to say about this. I wake up and there's a top Reuters story: FBI find scant evidence U.S. Capitol attack was coordinated. It says Alex Jones and Roger Stone did not coordinate them, investigating me for six months, they subpoenaed us. They know that, and then they indict Owen hours after this. I know you can't speak to that specifically, but what do you make in general of this move to declare protesting and the American people terrorism. To me, this sounds like the pages of *1984* have come true in the real world.

FAB: It's the next step. As I said, it's establishing a totalitarian dictatorship here in the United States. We do not need any type of domestic terrorism statute. We have already enough statutes on the books to deal with whatever acts might be the case. You're correct to point out that this concept of domestic terrorism here in the United States would simply be used by the United States federal government to repress and persecute any type of dissent against United States government federal policy.

I listened to Attorney General Garland's speech on this, and he was completely disingenuous. He tried to cover up the fact that the Levi Guidelines still apply to the FBI. They do not. I think we've discussed this before in one of the many interviews we gave years ago. The Levi Guidelines were established by Attorney General Edward Hirsch Levi to try to stop FBI COINTELPRO operations, which is, you know, basically infiltration of what otherwise might be peaceful, law-abiding groups exercising their First Amendment rights and encouraging them to commit illegal activities—agent provocateurs.

And that's what COINTELPRO was all about. That came out in the Watergate hearings, the Church hearings, and all the scandals related to that. So, President Ford appointed Levi. Levi had been a dean of the University of Chicago Law School when I was an undergraduate there. So I followed this quite closely, and Levi adopted the Levi Guidelines that were supposed to eliminate COINTELPRO. I don't know if they did or they didn't, because I suspect the FBI was still out there in any event. Thought they did rein them in seriously. Now everyone knows after 9/11/2001, Attorney General Ashcroft, who went to the University of Chicago Law School probably when Levi was dean, revoked the Levi Guidelines. Everyone knows that. And the FBI was back into COINTELPRO operations officially. OK. And they've been involved in COINTELPRO operations ever since.

Alex Jones: And for those who don't know, COINTELPRO means harassing and setting up citizens. You're the legal scholar, but how would you define COINTELPRO in one line?

FAB: Spying, agent provocateurs, entrapment.

Alex Jones: It's a war on domestic political opposition.

FAB: That's correct. All right. So Garland in his speech covered up for the FBI and said, Well, as we all know, the FBI has been adhering to the Levi Guidelines since they were promulgated. That's a total lie! Everyone knows that Ashcroft repudiated the Levi Guidelines, and the FBI has been involved in COINTELPRO operations ever since Ashcroft after 9/11 repudiated them.

They've inflicted massive COINTELPRO operations on Muslims all over the United States. And this is not to excuse any type of violent activity here—

Alex Jones: One hundred percent, I'm all against it. I'm experiencing them setting me up and my friends and family in my lifetime, but I had nothing to do with it, so I'm not placing myself as a victim, but I'm really starting to enjoy a little bit of what Martin Luther King and Bobby Kennedy and others—I guess we're enjoying, because to have this agency literally up my rear end, constantly hovering over me, trying to set me up, it's just outrageous.

FAB: Right. As I told you before, they put me on all the U.S. government's terrorist watch lists because I've refused to become an informant for the FBI and the CIA and on my Arab and Muslim clients in violation of their constitutional rights.

Alex Jones: For those who don't know, they came and visited you, didn't they, Dr. Boyle? I know you never like to repeat something you said once. But they came and visited you, and you wouldn't do it, so they came after you.

FAB: Well, they came right to my office in the law school. I mean, can you believe that? Agents in the FBI and CIA come to the office of a law professor at a law school—

Alex Jones: They've come to this office off record before. They did the same thing here.

FAB: Right. So, but the point is that domestic terrorism is being used to oppose any resistance to what the United States federal government might want to do. We don't need any domestic terrorism statute. This is just, as you said, Orwellian. Even after the Anti-Terrorism Effective Death Penalty Act as a result of the bombing of the Murrah Federal Building, that was more than enough on the books there to deal with domestic terrorism.

And then after 9/11/2001, they adopted the USA Patriot Act, which basically set up an American police state, which is what we live under today. There's no question about it. Indeed, I've lectured to lawyers on the USA Patriot Act. And so this will be the next step: domestic terrorism to use to go after peaceful, nonviolent American citizens—left, right, middle—exercising their First Amendment rights to oppose whatever policies the United States federal government is engaged in. Like today, the Frankenshots, arguing this is domestic terrorism and we will have to prosecute them.

Alex Jones: All right, we've got you here on this emergency broadcast. Millions are going to watch it. And I just want to shut up, then, for ten minutes, Dr. Boyle, just what do you want to say about America, the world, Afghanistan, China, geopolitics—anything you want to impart to viewers and listeners? People really respect you. They want to hear from you on that....

You've been very accurate. You said this was a very deadly virus, and I thought it was real as well. I looked at the statistics; the numbers weren't that high. Now I can tell you that I personally have people that I know who have died. Everybody I know knows people who have died. My mother and father right now are literally fighting for their lives. Almost everybody else I know is sick. The hospitals are all completely full, and it's all variants. And the scientists I talked to, the experts I talked to, have been very, very clear that it's sloughing mutants out of this GMO live virus. Just like with the polio vaccine, it causes shedding. And so those are the best numbers we've got that this is. You're right, it was a real virus, very bad out of Wuhan. You said that 18 months ago... I talked to the hospitals, I talked about it... this is a real bio-attack. I've talked to my Pentagon sources. They've all confirmed it.

And this year it looks like five times worse than where we were last summer at this time, as we're about to go into the fall. I mean, I'm a guy who's a tough guy, but I'm scared. I mean, I'm really shook up right now. I know how serious this is. Almost everyone I know in the last two months has been sick.

Some people, like I said, are not getting better in two, three weeks. So that's—I know you're a lawyer and a scholar—but just in general, looking at this and what they've done, and Fauci, and we know it was made in the lab. Let's start there. What is it like to be vindicated, and everything you said since 17, 18, 19 months ago has come true—Peter Daszak on video saying, Yeah, we were developing a vaccine.

We can bind five viruses. You already have other documents. They didn't hide it. And then the lies to Congress, and then they get away with it. 'Cause I'm not a homicidal person. I'm a loving guy, and I'm not going to kill anybody. I'm just saying I'd like the courts to arrest these people. I'd like to see them on death row. They are assaulting us. And I feel like a coward and a pathetic worm sitting here, taking it so I feel better getting you on to talk about the legal parameters here. So that's a lot I just threw out there. Where do you want to take that?

FAB: Right. Well, Alex, I remember at the very beginning of our conversations, I did mention how lethal I thought the Wuhan coronavirus was. I said it was about in the area of 15%. I noticed that in his last interchange with Dr. Fauci, Senator Ron Paul also said 15%.

Alex Jones: He's definitely listening to you because you've got the best info. So continue.

FAB: Well, I don't know if Senator Paul was listening to me or not. As you know, Senator Paul is a medical doctor. He's an ophthalmologist—that's a highly specialized area of medicine, board certified.

Alex Jones: He explains in that last confrontation that he was first going to be basically a pathologist and then went to eye surgery for money. So his original training is in all that.

FAB: Right. So Senator Paul said 15%, and that's what I said originally. And I know one of your colleagues there said, well, he thought that was an exaggeration, but this is extremely dangerous. Yes. And we have to treat it that way. And again, that's why I appear here on your show today, to come up with three different strategies for fighting back. One, the indictment, state and local basis against Fauci and Collins and Baric and the rest of them for murder, and conspiracy to commit murder.

Second, a separate indictment against Slaoui and the chief executive officers there at Pfizer, BioNTech, Moderna, Johnson & Johnson, for murder, and conspiracy to commit murder. And then the third one, a legal strategy for the members of our U.S. armed forces, now the 30% or so who don't want to take the Frankenshots.

So we're all in this together. We have to fight back together. Yes, we also have to resist this whole concept of domestic terrorism that is going to be turned against all of us. I mean, as far as the U.S. government is concerned, sir, I'm a domestic terrorist. When I applied to get out of my Social Security benefits, I filled out the form online. No problem. And what happened? I got a call from the Social Security agency up there in Chicago, saying, Well, you're on the computer alert system here, and you are going to have to go into a personal interview to Social Security down there in Champaign. So I had to go in there to a personal interview for about an hour and convince the Social Security agent that I was not a terrorist.

I kid you not. This is what is going on in this country. If they've done this to me, you can imagine what they're going to do to you. We have to fight back. We have to stop the pandemic. We have to stop the Frankenshots. We must stop the further development of a totalitarian police state that is clearly coming under the guise of this medical tyranny. I mean, you can just listen to Fauci. He speaks out of both sides of his mouth. I mean, Senator Paul—

Alex Jones: And I want to get back to that, but you sat here a year ago, over a year ago, and you said we're in a two-front war. Now I think we're in a three-front war. What were the two fronts you said 15 months ago?

FAB: The two-front war was the pandemic and the Frankenshots. And now I'd say it's this whole notion of domestic terrorism, right? As I said, we don't need any concept of domestic terrorism here in the United States. We do not need a law. There are more than enough laws on the books. My guess is that under the currently operative COINTELPRO, the FBI has everyone infiltrated all up the kazoo anywhere.

Alex Jones: I wake up this morning at 5:30 and I go to Google alerts, and there's my name, and it says Jones cleared. And then I get a call from one of my crew members who went, Hey, they went and visited a lady I know. Who, I don't even know. They were asking her about me three days ago. So I know you as a lawyer don't wanna get into it because you don't know the facts. I don't either. It's just bizarre to be like top news story: Jones cleared. And then Owen, no criminal record, former sports broadcaster, Mr. America, is he indicted for being there with me? I mean, he was there with me. We didn't do anything.

We tried to stop it on video. So I'm not even scared, 'cause I'm innocent. It's a very weird feeling like when I'm going 70 in a 68. Oh God, there's a cop, I'm gonna get a ticket. I go, I'm sorry. I take the ticket. It's a weird feeling.

Dr. Boyle, in law, as a human to have not done anything wrong and to actually not have fear, it's more of sadness for the country. Like really? They've indicted Owen for being a journalist outside the Capitol? I'm just freaked out. I can't believe Americans have turned into this.

FAB: Well, to give you an example, when the FBI and the CIA came to interrogate me in my own law office, the first question was: Why are you giving all these interviews all over the world?

So much for the First Amendment, right? They couldn't care less.

Alex Jones: They were letting you know the problem was your ... positions.

FAB: Right! You know, it's preposterous. They didn't care about the First Amendment. They didn't care about the Fourth Amendment, the Fifth Amendment, the Sixth Amendment, the Seventh Amendment. Just in my case alone, this is what we're dealing with. The FBI is completely out of anyone's control, whatever Garland says.

Alex Jones: Let me just tell you the story, 'cause with you they were at least up front. This is happening like seven or eight times where a national TV host or an international newspaper editor, they want an interview, so you go, Let's go to dinner. And I don't do this anymore.

After the last time this happened, like eight years ago, when I quit doing it and you're at dinner, they make sure your phone's not on. They go, Listen, I'm really here with the CIA, and we just want you to stop this right now. And we can really work with you. Another time it was a Mossad agent. Another time it was the FBI. And later, they had people contact me about, Hey, you gonna do what we said? And then when I didn't do what they said, bad things happen. But I mean, it's like the Mafia. And so I guess most people, Dr. Boyle, we'll put ourselves in a club that doesn't—we get those visits and don't roll over. Can you imagine how many Americans, and I don't blame them, don't know how to deal with stuff like that?

FAB: Well, that's correct. You should never meet with any of these people without having a lawyer with you, that's correct.

Alex Jones: They tell you they're the editor of *The Atlantic*. Or they're with *Vanity Fair* or whatever. And then they're really an operative.

FAB: Sure. After 9/11/2001, there had been, before then, a presidential order that covert agents should not be members of the press or working with the press or things of that nature. And after 9/11/2001, Bush Jr. lifted that order. So yeah, you have to understand, when you're dealing with the media, you could be dealing with some type of covert agent.

Alex Jones: And the weird thing is, they're playing spy, harassing a prominent, respected lawyer or a talk-show host. We're just normal people. I mean, you've got a PhD that hardly anybody else has. You're a special guy, but it's like, they think just because they're the CIA or the FBI, we're supposed to be a doormat to them, like we don't have any rights. And I've even seen Psaki say, Oh, U.S. citizens don't get priority out of Kabul. They've got to pay money, but others don't. Where is this pissing on Americans leading to? Why do they do that?

FAB: Well, I guess they just don't care, Alex. They have all the power, and they figure they can get away with it, and that's what's happening. But the real dangers here are the Frankenshots. Biden's now going to recommend, and soon they're going to require, a third round of Frankenshots for everyone that are going to kill a lot of people off, that they haven't killed off already.

And remember, based on my experience, having defended *pro bono publico* Captain Dr. Yolanda Hewitt-Vaughn, who refused to give the Frankenshots in Gulf War I. Out of 500,000 inoculated—and these are ballpark figures because the Pentagon still lies about them because they know they committed a Nuremberg Crime on our own troops—but out of 500,000 troops inoculated, about 11,000 were killed, and about 100,000 were disabled. And those were healthy young men and women in the U.S. armed forces. So you can extrapolate from there what a third round of these Frankenshots is going to do. The Gulf War Sickness was produced by the first set of Frankenshots. We're already seeing massive adverse reactions to the current COVID Frankenshots. And it's just begun, indeed.

As I said before, it took me two years to figure out that the Gulf War Frankenshots had produced this humanitarian catastrophe known as Gulf

War Sickness. That Gulf War Sickness and Frankenshots, also, they infected health-care workers. And next of kin and members of the family, and that indicated there was a biological warfare agent at work, probably going back to those first Gulf War Frankenshots. So I'm afraid that certainly in the next two years, if we don't stop these Frankenshots now, who knows how many will die and how many will be disabled?

Alex Jones: In closing here on Saturday, I appreciate your time, Dr. Boyle. Thank God you and others were able to stop the experimental anthrax shots before. So we should be able to do it. And the numbers vary from the swine flu vaccine that killed 20 or 30 people they debated, but they suspended that over a few deaths when already the deaths in the VAERS reporting system were in the tens of thousands. And so I just, again, wonder why they're doing this exercise of power.

FAB: They're going for broke, Alex! I think that's all we can say that's going on here. This is a massive push by the financial elite, the power elite. And they're going for all the power. This is it. Absolutely.

Alex Jones: You never plugged one of your books, and I've read three or four of them, but how do people find your books that you've written? So many people really should read them, especially lawyers out there.

FAB: Well, you can just hit my name on Google or Amazon, and all the books will come out. But for the members of U.S. armed forces and their lawyers, the important book is *Protesting Power: War, Resistance, and Law*. It explains how to make these arguments in U.S. military court-martial proceedings. It's basically written for lawyers, but you can read it on your own. And certainly if 30% of the U.S. armed forces just say, I'm not taking the Frankenshots, I have a right under U.S. military law to resist an illegal order. And you know, if you're going to court-martial me, so be it. And then you proceed to exercise all the rights you have under the Uniform Code of Military Justice. Well, if 30% of the U.S. armed forces do that, the whole system will break down.

Alex Jones: Even if 10% did. All right. And again, we're going to post this interview. It is going out Saturday, and we're going to post an archive of this on Infowars.com and Freeworldnews.tv. We'll put the Nuremberg Code up there, and the short, very simple and sweet letter also that Dr. Boyle has put out for folks, because that is very, very important, letting people know the basics of their rights.

As usual, thank you for joining us. I hope you had a great vacation. It's good to have you back, Dr. Boyle, and have a rest this weekend. Thank you so much.

FAB: Well, thanks for having me on, Alex, and to get the message out to all of my fellow American citizens who are in dire danger now from these Frankenshots. We must resist, and also the members of our military who are also in great danger here. They have to resist too.

Alex Jones: Thank you, Dr. Boyle, and we salute you. God bless. Thank you.

FAB: You too, Alex. Bye.

...

CHAPTER 13

PROSECUTING FAUCI, SLAOUI ET AL., FOR THE COVID-19 PANDEMIC AND FRANKENSHOTS

Professor Francis A. Boyle
Before the 9/11 Lawyers Committee 20th Anniversary Conference
From 9/11-Anthrax to the Pandemic: Life & Liberty in the Balance
September 11, 2021

David Meiswinkle: The next great speaker we have is Francis Boyle. Let me tell you a little bit about Francis. Francis Boyle is a University of Illinois College of Law professor and the author of the United States implementing legislation for the 1972 Biological Weapons Convention, also known as the Biological Weapons Anti-Terrorism Act of 1989 that was passed unanimously by both Houses of the United States Congress and signed into law by President George Bush Sr. with the approval of the United States Department of Justice. The story is told in his book *Biowarfare and Terrorism* [Clarity Press: 2005]. So I want to introduce Francis Boyle here.

And you know I first heard Francis right at the beginning of this pandemic. We didn't know each other at the time, but I'm watching this guy, he's talking about Wuhan, he's talking about bioweapons. I'm saying, "Let me listen to him." I was really impressed, and then I went back to try to watch it again, and it was taken down by YouTube, I believe. So he was censored right from the beginning, but he seemed to be right on point, as we say. So, Francis, thank you very much for being here, and please teach us.

FAB: Well, thank you very much for having me on. My best to your viewing audience. I did want to express my sincere condolences to the families, next of kin, and friends of those who suffered and died 20 years ago today. And that's why I am here today: to try to point a direction to where we can go from here.

You all heard President Biden's horrendous diktat to the American people that we must take these Frankenshots. I did some work against genetically modified organisms—GMO foods—they were called Frankenfoods. I will call these things Frankenshots because they are not to be dignified with the word *vaccines*. And I'm here today to explain how we can fight back against a medical dictatorship that is currently being imposed upon us by Biden and his people. And here, I'm just talking about the Americans, but I've consulted in Israel and other countries.

Here, I'm just talking about us Americans and the Tenth Amendment of the United States Constitution, which clearly says: "The powers not delegated to the United States by the Constitution, nor prohibited by it to the States, are reserved to the States respectively, or to the people." That's us! And what I want to outline here today is the mechanism and means whereby we can get everyone involved in the COVID-19 pandemic prosecuted for murder, and conspiracy to commit murder; and then second, everyone involved in these Frankenshots can be prosecuted for murder, and conspiracy to commit murder, on a state and local basis all over this country.

We know that the whole federal government is in the tank there for Biden. You can't believe anything they are telling you. It's just been a pile of lies from the get-go, even under Trump. But we do have here in the United States, states attorneys, district attorneys, attorneys general, county prosecutors, et cetera. Last time I looked into this, there were over 400 of these local prosecutors; and I am recommending here today a strategy for common, ordinary, everyday citizens who live in their territorial jurisdictions to go into these local prosecutors and demand the prosecution of the people involved.

I'm going to explain how this happens in a minute. But these are local prosecutors, not federal prosecutors. Biden's made it clear he's working with Fauci against us, and he controls the Department of Justice under Garland. They're not going to help us. But these local prosecutors, they are elected by us, their salaries are paid by us, and they can be dis-elected by us. It's that simple. And so we need to get people organized and go in and demand these indictments and prosecutions by these local prosecutors. For what?

Well, let me start with the pandemic itself. And here we have the very famous article that I have lectured on before. You can Google it; it might still be up there: "SARS-like cluster of circulating bat coronavirus pose threat for human emergence." And it's clear if you read this article that COVID-19 is an offensive biological warfare weapon with gain-of-function properties. Also, according to Montagnier and the Indian scientists, it has HIV DNA genetically engineered into it. It has also been aerosolized by means of nanotechnology. The Wuhan BSL-4 bragged that they had been able to apply nanotechnology to viruses.

So my argument here, then, is that everyone involved in this contract can be prosecuted for murder, and conspiracy to commit murder. Why? I was originally hired here to teach Criminal Law to law students and future lawyers, and I taught it for seven or eight years before I moved over into teaching International Human Rights Law. But I still do criminal cases both for the defense and the prosecution on matters of principle.

Murder has a definition in Anglo-American common law that would apply to all states of the Union except, as you know, Louisiana, which has a civil law system. I haven't studied their civil law system. But every other state in the Union has a common-law definition of murder. What is murder? It's the unlawful killing of human beings with malice aforethought. All right, let's go through the elements with respect to the pandemic.

Unlawful. OK, everyone involved in this project at the UNC BSL-3 manufacturing COVID was acting in violation of my BWATA of 1989 that was passed unanimously by both Houses of the United States Congress and signed into law by President George Bush Sr. with the approval of the United States Department of Justice. So who was involved?

Menachery, the University of North Carolina. There were several others involved here from the University of North Carolina, including Ralph Baric.

The National Center for Toxicological Research, the Food and Drug Administration, they mention this fellow's name. Think about that for a second. The FDA was involved in the development of an offensive biological warfare weapon with gain-of-function properties using synthetic biology and, we will see, working with Fort Detrick and the Chinese Bat Queen from the Wuhan BSL-4, which was also China's first Fort Detrick. That's why you can't believe anything the FDA is telling you about the safety of any of these Frankenshots. Indeed, the FDA is up to their eyeballs in offensive biological warfare Nazi death science. It's that simple, and we'll continue from there.

Two foreign institutes, fine. I'm not going to get into those here.

The Department of Cancer Immunology and AIDS, Dana Farber Cancer Institute, Department of Medicine Harvard Medical School. I'm a triple alumnus of Harvard. Notice that Harvard Medical School is involved in developing an offensive biological warfare weapon with gain-of-function properties that has HIV DNA genetically engineered right into it and working with Fort Detrick and the Chinese Bat Queen from the Wuhan BSL-4, China's Fort Detrick. That's also clear from this article.

Imagine that. Harvard working with Fort Detrick. As a matter of fact, Harvard is also a sponsoring institution for the Wuhan BSL-4, which is China's Fort Detrick. And the chair of the Harvard chemistry department, Lieber, worked on applying nanotechnology with Fort Detrick. And Lieber was also over at Wuhan working with Chinese scientists on applying nanotechnology to biology and also chemistry. I told you the Wuhan BSL-4 bragged that they had applied nanotechnology to viruses. Why do you apply nanotechnology? To aerosolize it. That's why. For aerial delivery to human beings so we breathe it in. Reports from scientists at MIT are that COVID-19 can travel up to 28 feet, and at Cornell, 21 feet. And that's thanks to nanotechnology.

The next person on this contract, the Chinese Bat Queen, Zhengli-Li Shi. The infamous Chinese Bat Queen and a director there at the Wuhan BSL-4. One of the founders of the Chinese Fort Detrick is over there working at the University of North Carolina to develop COVID-19.

And then, of course, Fort Detrick is mentioned in that article. They were involved in that UNC BSL-3 too, working with the Chinese Bat Queen and everyone else there.

In addition, then, if you read to the end of this article, it is funded by the National Institutes of Health under Francis Collins. He knew all about it. You can't believe anything Collins is telling you. He's lying.

And also the National Institute for Allergy and Infectious Diseases, that's Tony Fauci. So of course you can't believe anything he's telling you either.

And by the way, Harvard Medical School—Biden hired this Dr. Walensky, head of the CDC, from Harvard Medical School. So of course you can't believe anything she's telling you. And the CDC has been up to its eyeballs in offensive biological warfare Nazi death science dirty work since the beginning of the Reagan Administration when Reagan and his neocons put Tony Fauci in charge of research, development, testing, and using DNA genetic engineering, and now synthetic biology, to manufacture every type of hideous biological warfare weapon you can possibly imagine, as well as COVID-19. So all these people should be indicted for murder, and conspiracy to commit murder.

Now what's the next stage? Killing human beings. The estimate is excess deaths here in the United States are about a million people. As for the dangers of SARS-CoV-2, I have a book here by Professor Zubay and his graduate students at the Columbia University Biology Department that was written in 2005, long before the current controversy arose. On page 188 of Professor Zubay's book it says: "The overall death rate of SARS patients is 14–15%." That was SARS 1. COVID is SARS 2. COVID SARS 2 is SARS1 on Steroids. So this is extremely dangerous.

Now we come to the final element of murder: malice aforethought. Malice aforethought is a term of art. I have to lecture my law students for four days or so going through all the different elements of malice of forethought. But here, the critical element of malice aforethought is acting with grave indifference to human life. That is an element of malice aforethought. So you can have malice aforethought with people acting with grave indifference to human life. And if you read the article here "SARS-like clusters . . . ," they admit that they were acting with grave indifference to human life. They knew how dangerous this was, and they went about it anyway. All that has now been documented from the public record. I've been saying this right from the get-go of the pandemic on January 24, 2020.

So we have all the elements there for murder by everyone I mentioned here. So I advise all of you listening to go out and buttonhole your local prosecutor. And don't send emails; politicians don't respond to emails. They respond to face-to-face contact. Say, I want you to convene a grand jury; I want you to present this evidence to the grand jury; I want you to try to get the return of an indictment for murder against Menachery, Baric, the Bat Queen, Francis Collins, the Harvard Medical School person, Tony Fauci, the FDA person, the rest of them, as well as conspiracy to commit murder. I believe the evidence is there.

The last time I looked, there were over 400 or so of these local prosecutors around the country. I think we can get at least one of them to get indictments for murder, and conspiracy to commit murder, for everyone involved here on this contract for the development and research and manufacture of this offensive biological warfare weapon known as COVID-19.

Now let me move to the Frankenshots, and there's no other word for them. I'm not going to dignify them by calling them vaccines or alleged vaccines. Just like Frankenfoods are to foods, Frankenshots are to shots. And I want to make it clear: I'm not part of any anti-vax movement. I go vax by vax in evaluating them.

But here on the Frankenshots, let me go through the elements there as well. Unlawful killing of a human being with malice aforethought. Unlawful killing. A clear-cut, blatant violation of the Nuremberg Code on Medical Experimentation. That is a Nuremberg Crime under international law for which we, the United States, prosecuted, convicted, and executed some Nazi doctors. That's exactly right.

In addition, the Frankenshots violate the Nuremberg Crime against Humanity. It was President Franklin Roosevelt's idea to set up the Nuremberg Tribunal. It was our idea. And in the charter setting up the Nuremberg Tribunal, there were three crimes: war crimes, crimes against humanity, and crimes against peace.

Let me quote for you crimes against humanity. This is from the Nuremberg Charter that we signed, which was President Roosevelt's idea: "CRIMES AGAINST HUMANITY: namely, murder, extermination . . . and other inhumane acts committed against any civilian population . . ." This was put in there for the express purpose of prosecuting the Nazi persecution of the German Jews, their own citizens. And that is exactly what Biden and his henchpeople are doing to us Americans today. And this Nuremberg Crime against Humanity is in the Nuremberg Charter of 1945. It is in the Nuremberg Judgment of 1946. It is in the Nuremberg Principles of 1950. They are all generally recognized as basic, customary international criminal law all over the world.

So we have unlawful killing. So now we come to the element of malice aforethought for the Frankenshots. And here, two other elements of malice aforethought: intention to kill, or intention to cause grievous bodily harm. So the people responsible for the Frankenshots will say, "Well, we never intended to kill anyone." OK. Maybe they didn't. But they certainly intended to cause grievous bodily harm on human beings. That has been documented right from the very get-go of the administration of the Frankenshots. People are dying soon after. I don't know the exact figures. You can look at the VAERS statistics and multiply by 100. You can look at the European Health Agency.

And those who do not die are subjected to serious, life-threatening, lifelong disabilities. So in my opinion, yes, we have the malice aforethought of intention to cause grievous bodily harm for the Frankenshots.

So what I would also recommend, then, is a second cause of action here for people all over the country to go into their local prosecutors, states attorneys, district attorneys, county prosecutors, attorneys general, and say: I've lost loved ones living in your jurisdiction to the Frankenshots. Or I've lost friends. I have autopsy reports, I have coroners' reports saying this. And I want you to convene a grand jury and return an indictment for murder, and conspiracy to commit murder, against the people primarily behind these Frankenshots. And that would be Slaoui, the director of Operation Warp Speed. You know: Beam me up, Scotty! And the chief executive officers and scientists at, I would say, Pfizer, BioNTech, Moderna, and Johnson & Johnson. Those are the Frankenshots being used here in the United States. And Health and Human Services Secretaries for Trump and Biden. And we want you to return an indictment against these people from this grand jury. It could be the same grand jury going after the people responsible for the pandemic, for a second set of indictments here for murder, and conspiracy to commit murder, for the Frankenshots. I think the legal theories are sound, but we basically need the American people to get organized and go out and do this.

Finally, as you know, President Biden has ordered all U.S. military personnel to take these Frankenshots, so in my concluding words here—I know I'm sort of running out of time—I am a lawyer, I try to deal with my allotted time. The military, as you know, had been ordered to take these Frankenshots. I helped defend Captain Dr. Yolanda Hewitt-Vaughn, who refused to give the Frankenshots for Gulf War I that resulted in the Gulf War Sickness.

Out of 500,000 troops inoculated—the Pentagon lies about the figures because they know they committed a Nuremberg Crime on our own troops—but out of 500,000 inoculated, 11,000 died, and about 100,000 were disabled. And those, I suspect, are underestimates. That's the Gulf War Sickness, and that was inflicted upon our fairly healthy young men and women in our armed forces. You can extrapolate from there what is going to happen to the general population with these Frankenshots that are far more dangerous than the Gulf War I Frankenshots. Likewise, the Gulf War I Frankenshots infected health-care workers who were treating them, indicating that a biological warfare agent was at work. And also infected family members, indicating that a biological warfare agent was at work. I suspect we are going to see this breaking out all over in the next two years.

So my advice to members of the armed forces is that if you are given an order, whether orally or in writing, to take the Frankenshots, be respectful, because they'll get you for contempt of a superior officer. Don't lose your cool. And say, "Sir, I respectfully decline to take these Frankenshots. This is an illegal order in violation of the Nuremberg Code on Medical Experimentation that is a Nuremberg Crime under international law; and it is illegal also under the Nuremberg Charter, Judgment, and Principles that the United States government was responsible for at Nuremberg and we prosecuted, convicted, and executed Nazis for violating this body of law; and so, sir, I respectfully decline to take these Frankenshots."

Now my advice to the military at this point is with all due respect to JAG officers—I've worked with them, they're fine. But JAG officers can only do so much for you. JAG lawyers, they are in the chain of command. You are going to have to go out and get civilian attorneys who can exercise and assert your rights under the Uniform Code of Military Justice [UCMJ]. You have very substantial rights under the Uniform Code of Military Justice, and it is a well-known principle of military law that you have no obligation to obey an illegal order.

I established that in the court-martial of the very first GI resister to Gulf War I, U.S. Marine Corporal Jeff Patterson, who refused to ship out to Saudi Arabia when ordered to by President Bush Sr., saying that this was just another U.S. imperialist war for oil, which it was. He was charged with failure to obey a lawful order. I went out to Kaneohe Bay for the preliminary court-martial proceedings. I was out there arguing for three and a half hours that this order was illegal, not authorized by law. And the judge took it under advisement, and about ten days later, Patterson was out of the Marine Corps. They did not want to go to trial with this posture of the case. How I did that is explained in my book *Protesting Power: War, Resistance, and Law* [Rowman & Littlefield Press: 2008]. So my advice would be get copies of that book, line up your civilian defense lawyers—all military bases have former retired JAG lawyers and JAG judges or civilian lawyers around them who specialize in the UCMJ.

This is very complicated to do. You can't really do it on your own, so get yourself civilian defense counsel. But what you *can* do on your own in the military personnel I'm speaking to is say, "Sir I respectfully decline to carry out your illegal order that I take this Frankenshot in violation of the Nuremberg Code on Medical Experimentation and in violation of the Nuremberg Charter, Judgment, and Principles."

Thank you very much. I think I did it just on time. Thank you.

...

CHAPTER 14

MY ADVICE TO THE BRITISH PEOPLE (SEPTEMBER 16, 2021)

(Jason Liosatos is the host of *Outside the Box* in the U.K.)

Jason Liosatos: Good evening, everybody. A very important show tonight. Very important. Probably one of the most important shows ever. We've got Dr. Professor Francis Boyle on the show again. Thank you, Professor Boyle, for your very, very precious time.

FAB: Well, Jason, thanks so much for having me, and my best to all my friends over there in Britain.

Jason Liosatos: Well, it's great you've come on again. I'm very honored. I'll just introduce you. People mostly know that you're a human-rights lawyer and professor of International Law. You know, at the University of Illinois there, you've done so many things. You served as counsel for Bosnia, and you supported the rights of Palestinians, indigenous people. You supported the Gulf War Syndrome problems they were having there—I was talking about that back in the day as well. And here, just in case people forgot about that, out of 500,000 soldiers vaxed, 11,000 were killed, 100,000 disabled. Most people don't even know about this stuff.

And I think it was the FDA that gave the emergency authorization for that, if I remember rightly. And the Gulf War Syndrome, they trashed them, no longer depleted uranium. That's another story I covered. But you know, it's an amazing situation we're in, and you were on with Alex Jones. Thanks, Alex, for your work if you're watching ... Fauci has been absolutely exposed. Now he's still lying as he's exposed. Thankfully, people like Dell

Victoria have taken the NIH to task; we can't trust the corrupt Biden, Fauci, Johnson. You know, we've got Dr. Charles Hoffler, exposing what's going on now, with all the blood clots from these dreadful Frankenshots, as you call them. So we're coming to a real head and, you know, the Mengele experiments on kids; and you were saying with Alex, Professor Boyle, you know, this is what's going on. Now. People have to send their kids to school, or they can't work—no vax, no job, no food.

And it is a breach of the Nuremberg Code, people. If you don't send your kids to school, you can't work. If you can't work, you can't pay a mortgage. You can't pay your mortgage, you can't eat. So they're holding people for ransom. They know. And it's a dreadful situation. So thank you for coming on. You fought Biden back when, and here we go again, with that dreadful man and club. You know, Professor, where do you want to start with this? We need help here in England, and I spoke to a lawyer today who's pressing charges against the government elsewhere in the world, I can't quite say where at the moment. But we're going to be hopefully getting some work with him. And I know you've said before your work with other solicitors and lawyers in other countries, if you could help—you've done so much good work. Thank you for everything you've done.

FAB: Well, thank you, Jason. Just commenting on Boris Johnson, you remember our first interview—I was willing to give him the benefit of the doubt. But no more. As you know, he's not just pursuing a policy of so-called herd immunity, which is a joke. But now the philosophy is "Let it rip." That's even been reported over there. So basically, he's eliminating any protections the British people might have. He's sending your children back to school, right into the jaws of death. I was just reading in the *Financial Times*, it's so bad out there in Scotland that they have to draft the military to come in and run their ambulances for them. So we have to seriously consider the responsibility of Boris Johnson, under the Nuremberg Charter, Judgment, and Principles that that we used to prosecute Nazis, for the policies he's pursuing here.

And let me quote for you, Jason, the Nuremberg Charter, which Britain signed and helped prosecute Nazis at Nuremberg, and rightfully so. This is the definition: There were three crimes: crimes against peace, war crimes, and crimes against humanity. Crimes against humanity apply in war or peace. So you don't need war to have a crime against humanity. And here, I believe is what Prime Minister Johnson is pursuing. Article 6(c), quote: "Crimes against humanity: namely murder, extermination . . . and other inhumane acts committed against any civilian population." I believe those would be the appropriate elements of crimes against humanity: murder, extermination, and other inhumane acts committed against any civilian population. And notice, crimes against humanity was put in there to deal expressly with the Nazi persecution of their own Jewish citizens. So these were citizens of Germany who were Jewish, and under other provisions of international law, like war crimes or whatever, that wouldn't qualify. But they made this crimes against humanity. Well, I'm submitting, I'm arguing here today, that's exactly what Boris Johnson is doing to his own British citizens, a Nuremberg Crime against Humanity: murder, extermination, and other inhumane acts committed against any civilian population.

In addition, I would hope your British lawyers could look into my suggestion of initiating criminal proceedings against Johnson, and also the relevant members of his cabinet. Well, he's now shuffled—I don't know who the Minister of Health is these days, and his scientific advisers on this, the SAGE people, for murder, and conspiracy to commit murder. And let me go through the elements here of murder. Because I was originally hired here to teach Criminal Law, substantive Criminal Law. And I taught it for six or seven years before I moved over to teach International Human Rights Law. But I still do criminal work, defense or prosecution, on matters of principle. And we in the United States and Britain, not technically Scotland, but the rest of Britain, share in common the Anglo-American common-law definition of murder. So let me run through that here with you.

Jason Liosatos: I was just going to say I'll put your book up on screen now—

FAB: Sure.

Jason Liosatos: Hang on then, Professor, because this is important, because the reason this is important is because you've been there. It's just one of the books, *World Politics, Human Rights, and International Law*. But also—

FAB: It's me arguing at the International Court of Justice, on genocide for the Republic of Bosnia and Herzegovina. And that's my book *Biowarfare and*

Terrorism, not that you will not find this particular argument here. *United Ireland*, trying to promote peace with justice for Protestants, Catholics, and Jews in Northern Ireland. *Protesting Power*, yes, that's very important. That book was written for lawyers on how to use international law, international human-rights law, the laws of war, U.S. constitutional law, criminal law, in cases, and it might be of use to your British lawyers.

But let me run through the elements of murder, Jason. As I said, we have in common the Anglo-American common law of murder. Now Scotland has a different legal system. I've been up there to Scotland, I've argued in Scottish court, so I'm not including Scotland here. But I am including the rest of the U.K. and the Anglo-American common-law murder, which I used to teach here, train lawyers for the last 43 years. And the Anglo-American common-law definition of murder is unlawful killing of a human being with malice aforethought. Unlawful killing of a human being with malice aforethought.

Now let's break that down, Jason. Unlawful. OK. I have already established that I believe Johnson is committing a Nuremberg Crime against humanity. And, indeed, I've been up in Scotland to argue these points: the Nuremberg Charter, Judgment, and Principles in the case of the Trident Two Thousand Ploughshares that you can find online, though it's spelled British p-l-o-u-g-h-s-h-a-r-e-s, and was qualified as an expert on these matters in Scottish court and argued these points for close to three hours up there, got directed verdicts and acquittals for all the defendants. Well, so unlawful. The Nuremberg Crime against humanity, for sure. Killing of human beings. Jason, could you tell me, I'm sorry, I don't know, what is the number of excess deaths now, in Britain, since the pandemic started? Do you have a ballpark figure on it? You may know that the *Financial Times* had a story on this, country by country in Europe. And I just forget, deaths versus excess deaths.

Jason Liosatos: I've completely forgotten, and that's the truth. I've gone blank as you've asked me, so I've written it down so many times. They've still got amnesia, I'm afraid to see.

FAB: But it's, you know, tens of thousands.

Jason Liosatos: A tremendous amount. Yeah.

FAB: Right. The *Financial Times* has a story on this. Not that long ago, where they went through not just deaths but excess deaths. The excess deaths are almost twice the reported deaths, because governments are covering it up. So you can get that information in the *Financial Times*.

Jason Liosatos: I'll pull that story up and put it underneath this short gap, right?

FAB: So with malice aforethought. Malice aforethought is a term of art. And there are different types of malice aforethought. But here, I think with the statements made by Prime Minister Johnson right from the beginning, and you remember the first interview I gave you, I was commenting on his speech that I just read in the *Financial Times* on herd immunity. And I said, Well, you know, that's the Nazi philosophy of "useless eaters" is what he's pursuing. Well, now it's "Let it rip," which is, you know, even worse than that. One of the elements, I think here, then, is the manifestation of grave indifference to human life. So Johnson said, Well, I'm not intending to kill anyone. But clearly, in his policies, from that first speech he gave that we interviewed on—you might want to put a link up to that one too at some point. Until now, today, where he's eliminating all restrictions on anything, sending children back into the jaws of death, and the teachers as well. He is clearly manifesting a grave indifference to human life, and the grave indifference to the life of his own people. Getting back to the Nazi crime against humanity.

So I believe that under the Anglo-American common-law definition of murder, we see that Johnson and his health advisers and his scientific advisers could be indicted for murder, and conspiracy to commit murder. Now, you know, I'm familiar with Anglo-American common law. I studied all that at Harvard Law School, many different areas—we share in common, torts, property, contracts. But I'm not an expert on how the British court system actually works. I've worked with your solicitors and barristers over there over the years—you have very fine legal talent—but they're the ones, then, who will have to figure out how best to apply this analysis in the British court system.

For example, here in the United States, we have states attorneys, district attorneys, county prosecutors, borough prosecutors, attorneys general, who have authority, each one of them, to convene a grand jury and seek an indictment. So I don't know to what extent that could be done over in Britain—that is, to go to your local prosecutor and ask your local prosecutor to convene a grand jury and secure indictments for murder, and conspiracy to commit murder, against Johnson and his henchpeople. But I would recommend that to stop what is, you know, this crime against humanity on the British people, I would say almost tantamount to genocide, except the problem there is genocide has, you know, he's murdering his own people. This is his own people. So technically, it's hard to argue genocide, but clearly a crime against humanity and murder, and conspiracy to commit murder. So that would be my advice. But you really need to talk to your solicitors and barristers over there to figure out what's the best approach to take to implement this.

Now Britain also is a party to the Genocide Convention. And you do have domestic implementing legislation for the Genocide Convention. You need to look into that. Likewise, Britain is a party to the Rome Statute for the International Criminal Court. And the Rome Statute for the International Criminal Court, likewise, incorporates this Nuremberg definition of a crime against humanity. So that needs to be investigated by your—I do not recall if Britain has domestic implementing legislation for the Rome Statute for the International Criminal Court. I haven't researched that. But if it does, I think your solicitors and barristers can consider moving against Johnson and his cabal, for those reasons as well, Jason. I provide these arguments, I certainly defer to the judgment of your solicitors and barristers, on how to implement my recommendations, and I'm happy to work with them, if they want to work with me on this campaign.

And I've done this here. I've started this here in the United States, a similar campaign against Fauci, Collins, all their people here, both for the pandemic and then also for the Frankenshots. So what can I say, I think we're in a desperate situation here. And I think we have to fight back. Plus, the local prosecutors are accountable to the people in the districts and the boroughs where they live. I take it over there they are elected by the people, your communities, and they're accountable to them. Here in the United States, we pay their salaries. I don't know how it works out there in Britain. And I think they'd be amenable to these arguments as long as they can be properly presented to them.

Jason Liosatos: Thanks, Professor Boyle. That's fantastic. All of that. And what I'm doing, we've got a very important meeting this evening. When I finish this, and we will, it's a gentleman over from America who knows quite a bit about this kind of thing. I'm waiting for a call back from a barrister and a lawyer now, and I'll be phoning in another one tomorrow. And it's taken a long time, but we're definitely building a bit of a picture, Professor Boyle, so thank you.

FAB: Let me also say, Jason, that I think the people of the communities here need to pressure their local prosecutors to do this, and go into their local prosecutors and say, Look here, the following people in our community, your community, have died because of the Johnson policies. And we pay your bills, we elected you, we can dis-elect you—we want you to convene a grand jury and present the case for indictments for murder, and conspiracy to commit murder. Now, of course, the grand jury might not return an indictment. OK, that's the way the system works. But I think the case is there.

It would need to be, you know, compiled by barristers and solicitors to present to the prosecutors. But I think we need pressure from the British people at the grassroots level. Because, unfortunately, as you know, Johnson controls the Parliament, and he has a very wide majority there. So I don't think you're going to get anything out of the Johnson Parliament, between you and me. I mean, there could be some people there who raise parliamentary questions to embarrass him and accuse him of murder, and conspiracy to commit murder, and a Nuremberg Crime against humanity against his own people. Yes, that should be done, and put Johnson on the spot. But because of his huge majority there in Parliament, I think you're going to have to work at a village, borough, district basis—the British people getting together and demanding that their local prosecutors do this. We're trying to do that here in the United States.

Jason Liosatos: It's amazing, Professor Boyle, and what amazes me is that, of course, we all know that—I will take too long on this—but what we all know is those people around Johnson and in the inner circles, the outer circles, they've all got mortgages to pay, they've got kids in college, then they've been threatened. Shut up, or well, if people don't even have to threaten them, they know if they speak up, they're out.

Now, the greatest thing I find now, Professor Boyle, is that people are self-censoring themselves. Who knows the truth is amazing. Even people in the circles around you where I am, they won't put their name to anything like our talk here, right? Not even a little tick or a little like, because they know our current employment or a future employer will punish them. And again, it's that threat—no job, no food, no house, no this, and look at all the people who—

FAB: Jason, let me say this, please. Circulate this interview all over Britain so that the British people can hear my advice and hopefully act on it. Because, as you pointed out in your beginning statement, our survival is at stake here.

Jason Liosatos: The future of humanity is at stake here. And the problem is, they know what's going on. They know how many people are becoming ill. Countless people are coming up to me. A lovely man I know came up to me and said that his wife mustn't get this vaccination... she's in a wheelchair. These people are dying. Endless, endless stories...

FAB: Well, let me let me also go through, then, the Frankenshots argument.

Jason Liosatos: Please. Yeah.

FAB: All right. And here, again, I would argue that this is murder, and conspiracy to commit murder, by those in the Johnson administration who are foisting these Frankenshots on you. So we go through the elements again of murder, unlawful killing of human beings with malice aforethought. Clearly, as we discussed before, Jason, Frankenshots violate the Nuremberg Code on Medical Experimentation. This is an international crime. It's blatant. It's obvious. Killing of human beings again. I apologize, I don't have the figures of excess deaths there in Britain. I just don't have it off the top of my head. And then malice aforethought. And here we're dealing with a different element of malice aforethought. Johnson will say, Well, we're intending to heal people, save people, not kill them. Well, OK, maybe. But another element of malice aforethought is intention to cause grievous bodily harm. Grievous bodily harm under the Anglo-American common law of crimes.

And clearly, what we have seen with the Frankenshots is grievous bodily harm, and they know it. All you have to look at is the European Health Agency figures on adverse reactions to the Frankenshots. And it's very clear, you know, whatever they might have said at the beginning, it's very clear, even right from the beginning, right there reported there in Britain, some of the first nurses who took it had severe allergic reactions; and now you have large numbers of death and disability, people hospitalized. So I would argue here on the Frankenshots that you have malice aforethought causing grievous bodily harm. And conspiracy to commit murder as well. So this would be a second type of legal action—to go after all those involved in Frankenshots up from Johnson and his cabal, separate because the elements involved the legal elements, as I described them.

And again, go to your local prosecutors, tell them, Look, the following people in your community have died as a result of the Frankenshots. And we want you to convene a grand jury and get an indictment against Johnson and the relevant officials. I'm not saying all of them for murder, and conspiracy to commit murder. It could be the same grand jury; it would just be a separate set of indictments. So I would recommend that too. And again, it's really going to be up to the British people to demand this from their local prosecutors with the assistance of British barristers and solicitors. I'm happy to work with them, and we're pursuing that same strategy here in the United States with those responsible for the Frankenshots.

Jason Liosatos: Well, that's the great thing about you, Professor Boyle. You could create a template that can work—I know they're slightly different legal things on either side of the water.

FAB: Yes, the procedures are different. And the court system is different. But the law on murder is the same. That's the critical point. It's the Anglo-American common law of murder, and conspiracy to commit murder, which I taught here in the United States for six or seven years.

Jason Liosatos: And the disease that you're trying to try to cure or punish if you'd like. I don't mean the disease of the so-called. But I mean this is amazing. And there are people like Dr. Chuck, there's so much proof, Professor Boyle, it's unbelievable, and they're all being blackballed, like you. Everyone's being banned. Anyone who speaks the truth. Ban them, ban them, ban them, right. But Dr. Charles Hoffa was interested in—he used that diameter or whatever it was called test on his own patients who had the jab within seven days, and 60-something percent of them all had tiny blood clots around the cells in their lungs, which he said never go away. And that's a fact, and look what happened—boom, he's sort of been blackballed off everywhere. And this guy's proven it. This is terrible.

I'm speaking to people every day. It is a crime against humanity. There's absolutely no doubt about it. And that lovely lady Dolly—she spoke on Alex Jones ... her husband had this terrible thing that was out there, you said initially it was a bioweapon and everything. And he was in terrible trouble. He was there, they wanted to put him on a ventilator. They wanted to do all these things to him, put him on remdesivir, and she said, No, we want 10,000 mils of whatever it was, vitamin C and everything. They refused, they refused. They've got their set pattern when people come in. I know so many people who've had put on their death certificates from their brothers, mothers, sisters, fathers, that they've got COVID, and it's a crime against humanity.

Thank God, the truth is coming up like smelling salts now, again and again and again, Professor Boyle. It cannot be. The sad thing for me is in a place where I live, Totten, as in Devon, the so-called spiritual, advanced sort of society of thinking beings, they're often the very last people to actually look at the truth. I'm shocked. I'm really, really shocked that they will not look at it. They're sending their kids to the slaughterhouse basically, to get the vaccinations. It's a terrible, terrible thing. But the tide's turning, isn't it? You see a turning of the tide.

FAB: That's why I've appeared now, to give you three interviews to help turn the tide there with the British people. I think your government is hopeless under Boris Johnson, I've made that clear in the beginning, but we do have to understand that this is not a regular disease or anything like that. It's an offensive biological warfare weapon with gain-of-function properties. It has HIV DNA genetically engineered into it. It's been nanotechnologized to facilitate its dissemination. It's extremely dangerous. The lethality rate is about 15%. So that is what is facing us.

Jason Liosatos: Funded by Fauci and the NIH.

FAB: That's correct. It was the contract on this, which I've read, and I've discussed with you before, this was all done jointly by the University of North

Carolina, their BSL-3, and the Wuhan BSL-4, which was China's first Fort Detrick; and at the UNC BSL-3, America's Fort Detrick was there working on this. As well as the FDA—they were helping develop it, so you can't believe anything the FDA says. They're up to their eyeballs in COVID. Likewise, the Harvard Medical School there was involved. I'm a triple Harvard alum. Why would Harvard Medical School be working with Fort Detrick? Think about that. And then Dr. Rachel Walensky, who Biden appointed as head of the CDC. She's from the Harvard Medical School, so you can't believe anything they're telling you. You can't believe anything the CDC is telling you. You can't believe anything the WHO is telling you.

I do get the *Financial Times.* I do follow some of the British media. Seems to me you can't believe anything Johnson is telling you. Even these SAGE people, I think, certainly dropped the ball. Between you and me, I don't know them personally. But it doesn't seem to me that the SAGE members have come out and told the truth to the British people about what's going on here. I have nothing against them personally; I don't know who they are.

Jason Liosatos: One final question in the last two minutes. Not putting you on the spot here, you know, but I want to ask you this. Clearly, whatever has happened, whether it was an accident or purposely unleashed, is another thing, you know, that's another story, but whether it was or wasn't, this is being used as a Trojan horse to bring in the digital reset. We know that for a fact. Schwab talked about it in *COVID-19: The Great Reset.* I've got the book there. The Rockefeller Foundation has talked about it in Operation Lockstep, but I want to ask you this. What is this? Are they purposely trying to depopulate people? You've said yourself they've got the God complex, the Nazi people. The Nazi regime thought they were superior. What do you think they're trying to achieve?

FAB: I think it's first de-population, and second, setting up a medical police state. I think that's what's going on right now. It's a twofold process.

Jason Liosatos: Thank you. Thank you for that.

FAB: As for Schwab, he studied at the Kennedy School at Harvard. And his mentor was Henry Kissinger. And I went through the exact same PhD program at Harvard that had Kissinger before me, the Harvard Graduate School of Arts and Sciences Department of Government, where they train future professors of political science. They even gave me Kissinger's old office there at the Harvard Center for International Affairs. He's a total Machiavelli. That's the type of people we are dealing with here.

Jason Liosatos: Thank you, and they've got to be stopped.

FAB: Schwab has protégés all over the world. I think Merkel was a Schwab scholar; Trudeau and many others were Schwab people. So that's what we are dealing with here, Jason. I know it's hard to accept, but I believe we're dealing here with people with the Nazi philosophy, Übermensch versus Untermensch. They're the übermensch. And we are the untermensch. And like the Jews, we can be exterminated and reduced. Hitler, you know, had a population of 12 million Jews, and he took care of close to 6 million of them. Population reduction. So I'm afraid that is the agenda, population reduction. And then second, a police state like George Orwell's *1984.* It's a grim future.

You know, I have to give it to you straight, Jason, and to the British people. I think this is what we are fighting against. And that's why I came here with these two different strategies, to recommend to the British people to fight back against Johnson and his cabal over his "Let it rip" attitude toward the pandemic that's sending British children into the jaws of death. And then Johnson and the rest of them for the Frankenshots.

Jason Liosatos: Thanks, Professor Boyle. Anything else before you sign off? You've been great to come on again. Thank you so much. Anything else you want to mention before you go?

FAB: Well, the British people had a revolution before, as you recall, and it was against King Charles. So it seems to me we need a revolution against King Boris in Britain, right? That's what we're going to need here to try to stop this.

Jason Liosatos: Thanks, Professor Boyle. We've really appreciated you being on the show.

FAB: I think the British people need to take this by the horns themselves. They cannot rely on anyone else to save them. They are going to have to save themselves here. I think lawyers will help, but they're going to have to save themselves.

Jason Liosatos: The amazing thing is, Professor Boyle, they're being literally blackmailed into a corner—you don't get this, you don't get that, you don't get that, you don't get that. Ultimately, you don't eat, you don't function. That's it. It's the greatest crime against humanity I've ever heard of. It's unbelievable, and it's done in a very scheming way.

FAB: You really have to go back to the Nazis there in World War II to find, in my opinion, historically, anything equivalent to this, Jason. I think you're correct about that.

Jason Liosatos: Thanks, Dr. Boyle. Where's the best place to find you? For instance, if someone needs to find you?

FAB: Just send me an email.

Jason Liosatos: Send you an email, OK. Thanks for your tremendous courage over the years. And thank you for your courage now, to come forward again, in this critical crossroads for humanity, and to speak on our shows. And we do really appreciate you very much. Thank you so much, Professor Boyle.

FAB: Well, thanks a lot. Again, my best to the British people. Good luck here.

...

CHAPTER 15

MY ADVICE TO THE ISRAELI PEOPLE (OCTOBER 15, 2021)

(The host is a journalist broadcasting in Israel. The interview was set up by the Israeli human-rights law firm I mentioned in chapter 4, which is suing China over the COVID-19 pandemic. I am working with them on the lawsuit.)

Host: Tonight we have on the show Professor Francis Boyle. He drafted the U.S. domestic implementing legislation for the Convention against the use of bioweapons. And today he is here from the department of International Law at Illinois University. We are happy to have you on the show, Professor. Tonight on the board are journalists Shay Shelley and Philippe Jean Jandrok, writer and investigator.

Dr. Boyle, my friend Philippe and I are honored to interview you about the dramatic situation we've had to live with since the end of 2019 with the coronavirus crisis. The situation in Israel is one of the worst in the world. We have been a laboratory of experimentation for the Pfizer laboratory, with the complete collaboration of the Israeli government. Let's not waste time and go straight to the question. First off, do you think vaccines are used as a bioweapon of mass destruction?

FAB: Well, thank you for having me, and my best to your viewing audience. I agree with what you are saying about the Israeli population being used as lab rats by Pfizer/BioNTech. These, I call them Frankenshots, because that's what they are, clearly violate the Nuremberg Code on Medical Experimentation that was applied at Nuremberg against the Nazi doctors. One of the requirements of the Nuremberg Code—and that makes it an international crime—is that experimental vaccines must be first tried out on animals, it clearly says that. And we know that for the Pfizer/BioNTech Frankenshots, they didn't do that. It was not done. So I regret to report that it seems to me that Pfizer/BioNTech is using you Israelis as their lab rats. And that's what this is all about. And this violates the Nuremberg Code on Medical Experimentation. It is a Nuremberg Crime. And it also violates the Nuremberg Charter, Judgment, and Principles of 1945–1946–1950 for a prohibition on crimes against humanity, which clearly states are, namely: "murder, extermination ... and other inhumane acts committed against any civilian population." And I should point out to my Israeli friends that Nuremberg "crimes against humanity" was specifically put in there to criminalize what Hitler and the Nazis did to the German Jews. I won't give you a lengthy lecture here, because we don't have that time. But that's why it was put in there. And I'm afraid that when it comes to all Israelis, Arabs, and Jews, everyone else, we're seeing history repeat itself here.

Host: Well, first of all, I'm asking again, you said in an interview with Alex Jones in December 2020 that you think the vaccines are a weapon of mass destruction. Can you support that claim?

FAB: Well, I think COVID-19 is a biological warfare weapon.

Host: We're speaking about the vaccines right now that are killing a huge amount of people all around the world.

FAB: Oh, yes. Well, the Pfizer/BioNTech vaccine and Moderna were both funded by the Pentagon's Department of Advanced Research Projects Agency. That is correct. And so that is where the seed money came for this, and I did quote in the Alex Jones interview the technical details of this—let me see if I have them right here at hand. But that is very clear if this comes from the Pentagon, and DARPA that has all of their—

OK, here we go. Now this is for the Moderna technology, biotechnology Frankenshot, but the same applies to Pfizer/BioNTech that is being used there in Israel. This is for the messenger RNA technology. "DARPA awards Moderna Therapeutics a grant up to $25 million to develop Messenger RNA Therapeutics," but that's a joke. And the same agency, DARPA, was behind the technology for Pfizer/BioNTech. And what this says is a messenger RNA can be designed to tap directly into the body's natural processes to produce antibodies, et cetera, et cetera. So they're going right into your body itself. You know, the rest of it is here, if you want to read it, but I read the exact same thing I discussed with Alex Jones.

Host: So now you are claiming that the shots are bioweapons?

FAB: They're part of it, yes. The COVID is a bioweapon. And it does appear that the Frankenshots, the messenger RNA Frankenshots, are part of it too. Yes.

Host: So you can approve the sentence that you think the vaccines are bioweapons?

FAB: I think it's part of the system that they put together. Yes, it does appear there.

Host: OK, so we have a confirmation. Thank you very much, Doctor. Mr. Philippe, you can ask your question. Thank you.

Philippe: Yeah. So we have prepared all kinds of questions. But the debate now, it's taking us a little bit away. I have a question for you, Doctor, because you're specialized in bioweapons and all those complicated things about war and what we can use and what we cannot use, and you have been an expert in America for years. You're some kind of a huge reference in the world. And today, in America, the media, the mainstream media, they don't let you talk at all. Why? Because, first, you were the first reference; and today, they don't want to hear you, and you have to talk on the Alex Jones show or on our show. How come? Because you're still one of the greatest specialists in the law for warfare and for the viruses and war viruses, and war against the enemies. And today, the situation is quite terrible, because we the people, we became the enemy. So what can you say about this?

FAB: Right. Well, this goes back to the fact that I was the first person to publicly state that the anthrax attacks here in the United States in October of 2001 came out of the United States government biological warfare program and laboratory. And that was November 1, 2001, at a conference held by the Council for Responsible Genetics at Harvard Divinity School, where I was chairing a panel or a workshop against biological weapons. And I said this live to Fox TV that was covering that. Then I came back to my office and said it on Pacifica Radio Network, which went out nationwide. Then I was interviewed by the BBC on this. So the whole world heard me, and then an order was given that I was never to be interviewed again, by any mainstream news media in the Western world on biological warfare weapons. And that order has held up until today, so that's exactly why they still bar me from speaking.

Indeed, it's even worse than that. I guess it was May of 2020. The Associated Press, which provides most of the news feeds here in the United States and around the world, assigned three reporters to do a hit-and-smear job on me for 90 minutes. Well, I'm a lawyer, I argue my case to everyone, I answered all their questions for 90 minutes. And then in February 2021, they disseminated this hit-and-smear job against me all over the world. According to my research assistant, there were close to 58,000 hits on news media sources all over the world. So it's clear that someone has given an order to make sure that my viewpoints are not heard. So in fairness, Alex Jones has been the only one permitting me to speak freely on these matters.

Philippe: So they don't want the truth to be told.

FAB: That's exactly correct. And that's also because of the previous work I did that you have here in the United States alone. As of 2015, 13,000 so-called life scientists, I call them death scientists, are involved in the research, development, testing, and stockpiling of offensive biological warfare weapons. We have an offensive biological warfare weapons industry here in the United States. Starting after 2001 until 2015, they had spent $100 billion on it. Which to give you an idea, the Manhattan Project, to develop the atom bomb, in constant dollars, was only $40 billion. So it's clearly a weapon.

Philippe: It was not the same time, the Manhattan Project.

FAB: Well, this is in constant dollars. As of 2015, it would have been $40 billion. And since—that's why I said constant dollars—since about 2015, they have spent about $6 billion more per year to research, develop, and test offensive biological warfare weapons; and so you have literally thousands of scientists, laboratories, and corporations making money off of this. And I've also stated that all Biosafety Level 3 and 4 labs should be shut down immediately to prevent another pandemic. Well, they'd all be out of business, every one of them. And so you have all these jobs at stake. And the drug companies are making money off of these Frankenshots, and they all advertise on the mainstream news media. So, of course, my viewpoints have been completely suppressed here in the United States, and not just in the United States, but in the mainstream Western news media. They haven't heard of me in France or Germany or Britain or anywhere else.

Philippe: I have another question. Because what you said is very important that the multibillion-dollar industry was working on those so-called vaccines, which are not vaccines because they're modifying the genetics of human beings. So today we are accusing China to be the scapegoat, to be the criminal, but it seems that America helped China build these so-called vaccines.

FAB: That is exactly correct. In the interviews I've given, I have pointed out what I call the smoking-gun article: "SARS like cluster of circulating bat coronavirus pose threat for human emergence," and you will see that working with the Bat Queen there from the Wuhan BSL-4. We have to understand that the Wuhan BSL-4 is China's Fort Detrick. So you have these people from the University of North Carolina, they were all working before that at the University of North Carolina, BSL-3. And on this contract, this article you have, several of them are professors there from the University of North Carolina, working with the Bat Queen from the Wuhan BSL-4, it's all on there.

And, in addition, you have the Food and Drug Administration. Let me repeat that. You have the American Food and Drug Administration that is approving all of these Frankenshots. And now the boosters you can read about today, working on this development of COVID-19, it says they're right under contract. So, of course, they are rotten, corrupt, and despicable, up to their eyeballs in COVID-19. And you can't trust or believe anything they are saying.

Likewise, you have someone from the Harvard Medical School. I have three degrees from Harvard. And the Harvard Medical School. Now this woman Walensky is head of the CDC, the Centers for Disease Control. They likewise give the second level of approval to these Frankenshots. And so, of course, you can't believe anything she's saying. Indeed, Harvard was one of the sponsoring institutions of the Wuhan BSL-4. This contract also says that Fort Detrick itself was involved in the development of COVID-19. Working with the Bat Queen from the Wuhan BSL-4, which is China's Fort Detrick. Likewise, the WHO was a sponsoring institution of the Wuhan BSL-4. So, of course, you can't believe anything the WHO is saying.

Finally, this research was paid for by the National Institutes of Health here in the United States. Francis Collins is the director; and the National Institute for Allergies and Infectious Diseases: Tony Fauci. So, of course, they, too, are all up to their eyeballs in this Nazi biowarfare death science dirty work.

And let me go back to one point that Shay made about vaccines and biological weapons. You see the way this works is this: You first develop an offensive biological warfare weapon using DNA genetic engineering, and now synthetic biology, which is involved in COVID-19. Then when you have done that, you then develop a vaccine. In the event that there is blowback on your own people, you have to have a vaccine. So these vaccines, what I call Frankenshots, are part of this biological warfare weapon system. They go together. That is why DARPA funded the messenger RNA technology. The Pentagon's DARPA funded this messenger RNA technology behind the Pfizer/BioNTech Frankenshot that has now been inflicted on all the Israeli people. And Moderna. And then the Pentagon's Fort Detrick was involved in developing COVID-19. So, of course, the right hand of the Pentagon knew exactly what the left hand of the Pentagon was doing.

Host: I'm sorry, Doctor, we are very short on time.

FAB: That's fine, I'll take whatever time you want.

Host: Thank you. What do you think is the ultimate goal of the vaccines?

FAB: The ultimate goal? Depopulation. There's no question about it.

Host: How many people do you think they want to depopulate now?

FAB: Well, Shay, let me say this. I oppose the—

Host: I'm talking about your personal opinion. Now I'm not talking about your research or something. What's your opinion? What's your view about that?

FAB: It's depopulation, and it's exterminating human beings, right? We saw this before with the Nazis. Not only did they exterminate millions of Jews, they exterminated 26 million Soviets, millions of Slavs. This is a Nazi mentality involved here. That's what's going on, in my opinion.

Host: But now it's going to be in the billions, not millions, this time.

FAB: Well, all I can do is give you my experience in opposing the Gulf War Frankenshots in the Bush Sr. Gulf War against Iraq. I came to the defense of the doctor who refused to give those Frankenshots, two of them, for botulin and anthrax. Out of 500,000 U.S. troops inoculated, those Frankenshots killed approximately 11,000 U.S. troops and disabled 100,000 U.S. troops. And those were healthy young men and women in the U.S. Armed Forces. So you can extrapolate from there, Shay. That, I think, is a floor of what we're talking about here. A floor, not a ceiling.

Host: OK. Do you think that there is a global holocaust, and who do you think is responsible for the holocaust?

FAB: I'm sorry, could you repeat that more slowly?

Host: Yeah. I said, do you think there is a global holocaust? And who is in charge of this holocaust?

FAB: Well, I think that certainly what we're dealing with here is a cabal of Nazi biowarfare death scientists that is transnational. And it is funded, certainly, by Bill Gates and others. Gates is an investor in BioNTech. And you have there in Israel, the Pfizer/BioNTech vaccine Frankenshot.

Host: What about the Rothschild family? Are they involved? Do you think that they are involved in this scam?

FAB: I don't know about the Rothschild family. The Rockefeller Foundation has supported eugenics for quite some time, that is well known. And the Nazis were influenced by the Rockefeller Foundation. I have no opinion about the Rothschild family.

Host: Thank you very much. Philippe?

Philippe: Yes.

FAB: I don't mean to interrupt you, Philippe, but I want to explain the relationship between the vaccines and the weapon. They go together; they are a system.

Philippe: I know, because I'm doing lots of research. Again, and you have given us the answer that I wanted to hear from you. Because it's a point of view that I have, that it's a kind of conglomerate that we don't know those people, but they are all working internationally against the people, against the human race, which is quite incredible. Because the French, the Germans, the Italians, some of the Spanish, I don't know, the politics, they are all working together to realize this, this holocaust in a global situation. Because the Nazis there were contained in Germany and the east of Europe. They were not in America, they were not in Spain, for example. But it was contained. But today, the holocaust is all over the world.

We are all concerned by these catastrophic events, by these murders, the mass murders, and it's quite incredible to see how easy it is to realize today. I mean, they decided two years ago to eliminate the people, and they do it like nothing. It's incredible. And the people there are like the Jews, but at home, they don't need to be in camps. They are killing them at home, just by the so-called vaccine. This is incredible. I cannot believe this, but we are living it today, which is quite difficult for everyone.

FAB: Right, you have to read the *Doctors/Medical* case from Nuremberg. And, you know, this is sort of like Dr. Mengele at Auschwitz, but on a global scale, as you're pointing out, Philippe. As I see it, I'm not trying to scare anyone or sound sensationalist here, but historically this is the only precedent we have for, I think, what's going on here, and so we have to learn from that precedent.

Philippe: But they don't learn from that.

FAB: Well, some of us have learned, right?

Philippe: Yeah, some of us. Shay, you can finish if you want.

Host: Thank you, Doctor. You made a claim before that the Zionist regime committed genocide and include war crimes. Do you?

FAB: Could you please repeat that again so I can get it?

Host: Okay, I'll do it again. Thank you. You made a claim before that the Zionist regime committed genocide and includes the war criminals. Do you think that the State of Israel was established to concentrate all the Jews from all over the world and murder them as part of the Final Solution?

FAB: Well, Shay, right now, how else can you see what's going on here that Europe after the end of the Second World War moved all the Jews to Palestine, most of them, and they're all there today, sitting there in Israel, and now they are being subjected to these Nazi COVID Frankenshots. That does seem to be they're going to kill you all. I thought, you know, that we have learned that should not be the case. But I don't know what else to say here, I'm afraid. If you look at the projections, I've given you the extrapolations. I'm afraid we're going to see large numbers of deaths there among the Jewish population in Israel. Yes, maybe the rest of the world too. But I want to state quite clearly to my Israeli friends, you are being used as lab rats by Pfizer/BioNTech, and Bill Gates, in violation of the Nuremberg Code on Medical Experimentation. This is a Nazi crime that has been inflicted upon you.

Host: Do you think that this time the Nazis are going to pay for this holocaust, not like Nuremberg, where I think only 20 people were in charge of crimes against humanity? Do you think that they are going to pay on Judgment Day?

FAB: You know, Shay, that was the problem after World War II. The United States only engaged in a partial de-Nazification of Germany. It was stopped dead in its tracks once the Cold War broke out between the United States and the Soviet Union. A good friend of mine, Mary Kaufman, was in charge of prosecuting I. G. Farben, all the German industrialists. And when the Americans decided that they wanted the German industrialists, even though they were Nazis, to work for them, that prosecution was sabotaged. So what will happen with what's going on here today?

I sent you, Shay, a speech I just gave about how we in the United States of America can go after and prosecute all of the individuals I just mentioned to you here today who were involved in the development of the COVID-19 biological warfare weapon, and also are involved in the Frankenshots. How this turns out, I don't know. All I can do is start the process myself and see what happens.

Host: Professor, thank you very much. Unfortunately, our time is very, very short. Philippe, do you want to say anything else to the professor?

Philippe: Just a last word. We know that Dr. Fauci has lied all the way. And I hope he will be judged for the terrible things he did against the American people and all the people all over the world, because he is one of the masters and the masterminds who obeys Bill Gates and the Rockefeller Foundation. And this is absolutely terrible. And I'm ashamed that those people are today pretending that they're scientists, because they don't do science. They only do crime and mass depopulation. That's the conclusion that I have.

FAB: Well, that's exactly why I'm giving you this interview here today. I've given interviews all over the world to people who will speak to me, because all of humanity, we are in this together. I think this is World War III here that we're dealing with. And, unfortunately, the Jews are being used as the guinea pigs here, the lab rats, by Pfizer/BioNTech and Bill Gates. And I hate to say that. I had thought we had learned the lessons of World War II. And we have not.

Host: Thank you very much, Professor Francis Boyle, for this interview. My friend Philippe, thank you very much. We wish you a very nice weekend, from Israel. And to our audience. Thank you for being with us. And good night.

FAB: Well, thank you again. My best to my friends in Israel and Palestine too. Thank you.

Host: Thank you all. Bye-bye.

...

CHAPTER 16

PROFESSOR BOYLE SAYS THE U.S. GOVERNMENT IS UP TO THEIR EYEBALLS IN COVID-19 CRIMES (OCTOBER 21, 2021)

Kristina Borjesson: Welcome to the *Whistleblower Newsroom*. I'm Kristina Borjesson. As the get-vaxed noose tightens now for children, my guest today is coming forward with a plan for triggering prosecutions all over the United States against the criminals he alleges were involved in funding and creating the lab-engineered COVID virus; and the criminals responsible for creating and disseminating experimental vaccines that have, he says, and continue to, kill and maim people by the tens of thousands.

Professor Francis Boyle is a human-rights lawyer who has taught Criminal Law and is now teaching International Law at the University of Illinois. In 1989, President Bush Sr. signed into law the Biological Weapons Anti-Terrorism Act that had been called for and drafted by Professor Boyle after he learned that U.S. government labs directed by Dr. Anthony Fauci were abusing genetic engineering to develop offensive biological agents. Today, Dr. Fauci is in charge of the U.S. government's response to, and policies for, the COVID pandemic. Boyle's 2005 book, titled *Biowarfare and Terrorism*, details the dangerous and illegal actions taken by several U.S. government administrations that made COVID-19 inevitable. Welcome, Francis.

FAB: Thank you very much, Kristina, for having me. I'm very happy to be here once again, and my best to your viewing audience. Well, I don't mean to toot my own horn here, but I did draft the U.S. domestic implementing legislation for the Biological Weapons Convention, known as the Biological Weapons Anti-Terrorism Act of 1989, which was passed unanimously by both

Houses of the United States Congress, signed into law by President George Bush Sr. and with the approval of the United States Department of Justice.

Kristina Borjesson: And you did that during the Reagan era, because of Fauci. Could you talk about that? Fauci goes all the way back to then?

FAB: Well, that's correct, Kristina. What spurred me into action, the Council for Responsible Genetics at that time, no longer there, headquartered in Cambridge, Massachusetts, had some of the top life scientists in the world—Harvard, MIT—and they asked me to get involved in order to handle their biological warfare weapons work against it. So it turned out that the Reagan administration and its neocons were engaged in the illegal, unlawful use of DNA genetic engineering, to research, develop, test, and stockpile biological warfare weapons.

So the Council asked me to hold a briefing on Capitol Hill for members of Congress on this. I believe that was September 13, 1985. And in this briefing, at the end, I said that we really needed domestic implementing legislation for the Biological Weapons Convention to make this activity a crime, which it had not been before that.

Kristina Borjesson: And who was in charge of this activity at that time?

FAB: Well, it started with Reagan and the neocons. And, yes, pursuant to this strategy, Reagan appointed Tony Fauci head of NIAID, the National Institute of Allergy and Infectious Diseases, to carry it out. That was around about 1984 to 1985. So Fauci has been up to his eyeballs in this Nazi biowarfare death science dirty work since then.

Kristina Borjesson: He was carrying out the genetic tests? The genetic modification?

FAB: He was in charge of it. Even the *New York Times* reported that 95% of this work, this Nazi biowarfare death science work, was under the auspices of Fauci, yes.

Kristina Borjesson: OK.

FAB: So I went to work. The Council asked me to draft the domestic implementing legislation, which I did do. And we then proceeded to lobby it through Congress. And that was finally done in 1989, passed unanimously by both Houses of Congress, signed into law by President Bush Sr., and with the approval of the U.S. Department of Justice. You can read that early work I did in my book *The Future of International Law and American Foreign Policy*. And then the latest book on that is my *Biowarfare and Terrorism*, which does not contain the early work I did against Reagan and the rest of them. My publisher felt that was ancient history, so we picked up pretty much with the second book with the anthrax attacks of October 2001.

Kristina Borjesson: Wait a second, let's be clear, because I just want to be very clear. Article I of the Convention says that it obligates the state contracting parties, never, in any circumstances, to develop, produce, stockpile, or otherwise acquire or retain microbial or other biological agents or toxins, whatever their origin or method of production of types and in quantities that have no justification for prophylactic, protective, or other peaceful purposes.

FAB: That's correct. And the problem was that, clearly, that language applied to the use of DNA genetic engineering. But the Reaganites, including Fauci, claimed that, well, they were doing this for peaceful purposes, which was a total lie. So I wanted to make sure that there were no loopholes here that could even be exploited, arguably, for the research, development, and testing of biological weapons, including DNA genetic engineering. At the time of the drafting of the Biological Weapons Convention, finally approved in 1972, DNA genetic engineering was just in its infancy. So I wanted to make it clear that all of this activity was a crime under United States law, which it was not; it was illegal under the Biological Weapons Convention. But I wanted to make sure it was a crime. And it is a felony punishable by life imprisonment. The Department of Justice wanted me, instead, to include the death penalty. I'm a lifelong abolitionist against the death penalty, so after several rounds of negotiations, they let me keep life imprisonment in there.

Kristina Borjesson: Well, so if Fauci was in charge of this, and he continued doing this, why wasn't he prosecuted?

FAB: Because all this was being done under the auspices of the United States government itself, including the Pentagon; they were involved in Fort Dietrick. So, you know, they're not going to prosecute Fauci.

Kristina Borjesson: Then why have a convention at all?

FAB: I did the best I could. I'm just a lawyer. And I decided to shore up this convention and make it clear it was a crime, which it was not before my implementing legislation.

Kristina Borjesson: But it was signed off by the government. You know, everybody signed off on it.

FAB: It was signed off, yes, by President Bush Sr. Reagan fought us tooth and nail, because the Reaganites knew full well I was going directly after all of their programs, to use DNA genetic engineering to create advanced biological weapon systems. So they fought tooth and nail, but when Bush Sr. came in there, they dropped the opposition. And I had to do some more work, et cetera. But we got it approved.

Kristina Borjesson: OK, because I want to look at all the problems, the loopholes and things that have also been taken—

FAB: There are no loopholes in my legislation.

Kristina Borjesson: The actual loophole is the Defense Department continued to do it because they could.

FAB: That's correct. And the CIA kept doing it too. There was no doubt about that. The CIA continued—they have biological warfare programs, even including smallpox—they have it.

Kristina Borjesson: So are those two agencies above the law?

FAB: Of course they are. Who has ever held the CIA or the Pentagon accountable for anything? I regret to say that. I entered Harvard Law School on

September 7, 1971, and have tried to hold the CIA and the Pentagon accountable for all the atrocities they have committed all over the world. It's very difficult to do.

I do want to point out one thing about my Biological Weapons Anti-Terrorism Act that also criminalized the use of synthetic biology, which is the current rage today, synthetic biology. It turns out that synthetic biology was envisioned and paid for and sponsored by the Pentagon's DARPA, the Defense Advanced Research Program Agency. All right, so synthetic biology is a wholly owned industry by the Pentagon going on today. So whenever you hear these great marvels of synthetic biology, just understand this is Pentagon DARPA work. And I criminalized that too. I anticipated it. And I criminalized that as well.

Kristina Borjesson: And who can be held accountable under your legislation if the main people who are doing the development of these bioweapons are not accountable? . . . I feel like they're using that almost as a fig leaf, you know. Well, we have this convention, you know, you're not allowed to do it. And yet they do it.

FAB: That's correct. And that's why when you earlier this summer asked me to appear again, I said, "Why don't you wait until I have all this worked out?" So now I have it all worked out. And this goes back to then. I mean, it takes time to figure these things out.

Kristina Borjesson: Yes, it does.

FAB: So this, then, is my current proposal thinking this out, which is that under the Tenth Amendment of the United States Constitution, the states of the Union have authority to deal with these people. So what I have done starting on September 11 of this year, the 20th anniversary of the attacks there in New York, is to launch a campaign to get everyone involved in the COVID-19 research, development, testing—from the U.S. citizens including, you know, Fauci, Daszak, the officials from the FDA, officials from other U.S. agencies involved in this—indicted for murder, and conspiracy to commit murder, by state and local prosecutors, not the feds.

This is the problem. With my statute, it was not enforced, because the federal government, and in particular, the Pentagon, the CIA, and the

National Institutes of Health under Fauci and Collins—who just resigned because the proverbial *merde* is going to hit the fan, pardon my French—to get them indicted for murder, and conspiracy to commit murder, by local prosecutors. That would be states attorneys, district attorneys, county attorneys, and attorneys general all over the country. That would avoid the problem of having to get the federal government indicting, because that's not going to happen. Biden appointed Fauci as his top scientific adviser, so he's in the tank with Fauci. And Garland is fully Biden's man over there at the Department of Injustice.

So the feds aren't going to do it. So there are well over 400—last time I've looked into this—state and local prosecutors all over the country. And what I am doing is encouraging them to convene a grand jury on the basis of evidence already in the public record; and start to get these officials, especially Fauci and Collins, indicted for murder, and conspiracy to commit murder.

Kristina Borjesson: You have to tell the audience who Collins is.

FAB: Collins is the director of the National Institutes of Health, who paid for all this research to develop COVID-19. And he just quit. Because he knows all the documents are now coming out that he authorized and paid for, both at the University of North Carolina BSL-3. And at the Wuhan BSL-4, which is China's Fort Detrick.

Kristina Borjesson: BSL means Biosafety labs 3 and 4, which are the ones that were the highest, the most dangerous viruses worked with.

FAB: Yes, that's correct. So that is a campaign. I started on September 11, on the 20th anniversary, and that's why I wanted to talk with you after I had given that lecture, and try to explain it. This was a conference of my fellow lawyers, so I was trying to explain it to them, get their feedback if they had any problem with it, and they didn't,

Kristina Borjesson: You know, this reminds me a lot of Vince Bugliosi prosecuting George Bush for murder, where he was saying we should go to the attorneys general and prosecutors around the country and charge him for murder of, you know, individuals charging him with murder for the murder of their children, et cetera, for the war in Iraq. So this sounds very similar to me. I would like to ask you—

FAB: Let me agree with you on that. You see, I was doing the exact same thing myself with lawyers in different states of the Union, and tried to get Bush Jr. and the rest of them like Colin Powell indicted for murder, and conspiracy to commit murder, for U.S. troops in Iraq who died in Iraq subject to from where these prosecutors were located. Vince heard of me. And he contacted me; he published a whole book on it.

I just published an interview I gave on it outlining the theory—you can see it in my book *Tackling America's Toughest Questions.* So then Vince heard about me and contacted me, and we agreed to—I read his book—and we agreed to work together. Now, Vince, you know, he's older than I, but he was actually prosecuting. So he went after this from a somewhat different perspective than I did. I'm a law professor. I spent seven years or so teaching Criminal Law here. I was originally hired to teach Criminal Law before I moved over to teach International Human Rights Law. But we reached the same conclusion. And so he did agree to go in with me, but then unfortunately, Vince died. If you're interested, you could read Vince's book.

Kristina Borjesson: I have. And I knew Vince. So let's say, you know, I'm a mother who lost my child to COVID. Or I'm a woman who lost my husband to COVID. I go to the state prosecutor. And what do I present as proof of murder?

FAB: Well, you would go to whatever your local prosecutor is. We've organized all sorts of different ways all over the country. We have—

Kristina Borjesson: Your county prosecutors.

FAB: You might have a county prosecutor, you might have a district attorney, I can't say exactly. And you also have an attorney general. I'd go to all of them. And what you do is you could take a lot of the interviews, materials, I've given since the beginning of the pandemic—they're all out there on Google—and I did send you my paper that I gave at this conference of lawyers. So you take this into your local prosecutor and say, I want you to convene a grand jury, and I elected you, and I'm paying your bills, I'm paying your salary, and I can dis-elect you if I have to. And not just you, but you go in there with your friends. You lost your babies or your spouses or whatever, and say that's what we want you to do. And you then put together the evidence to present to the grand jury, and Professor Boyle is more than happy to help you, free of charge, to catalog this evidence for you.

As you know, I've been giving interviews on this since January 24, 2020, when I first blew the whistle that COVID-19 was an offensive biological warfare weapon with gain-of-function properties, that makes it more lethal and more infectious. And, in addition, has HIV DNA genetically engineered right into it. I blew the whistle on it. So I've given innumerable interviews since then that are out there on the internet, but it would really be for you to pressure the states attorney, to agree to move forward. I'm happy to work with the states attorney to give that states attorney, district attorney, county prosecutor, references to all the interviews I've given and the evidence I have used, and then it would be for the prosecutor to present this evidence to the grand jury.

Kristina Borjesson: OK, I'm going to say something that I think would be an interesting thing to do. And I think it would motivate people more to do it because it sounds like a big task for somebody who's already heartbroken and whatnot and feels, you know, that the noose is constantly tightening on vaccines and so on . . . . What if you were to draft not really an affidavit, but I don't know what you would call, it a brief or something? Instead of asking people to go research all the things that you've said and done, put it all in one in document that they can present as their case.

FAB: I do have all that in one document.

Kristina Borjesson: I wish you'd send that to me.

FAB: In late April 2020, some Israeli human-rights lawyers asked me to get involved in their lawsuit against China, in Israeli courts, over the COVID-19 pandemic. So I agreed to get involved because I thought this was very important litigation. And I did prepare a declaration for them that they then filed against China, and the Israeli attorney general then served my declaration on China. So that has been published. I have a new book titled *World Politics,*

Human Rights, and International Law, and I put the declaration right in there and explained the basic outline.

Kristina Borjesson: I would like to have that link, if there's a link to it. I'd like to have it.

FAB: If you remind me, I can send it to you.

Kristina Borjesson: You talked about malice aforethought . . .

FAB: I was originally hired, as I said, to teach Criminal Law. So murder at common law, which would be the case in every state of the Union except Louisiana. They have a civil law system. I haven't studied down there in Louisiana. Murder is defined as the unlawful killing of a human being with malice aforethought. Unlawful is a violation of my Biological Weapons Anti-Terrorism Act of 1989. Killing. My guess now is that we have maybe 1.3 million excess deaths as a result of the COVID-19 pandemic, just here in America.

And malice aforethought. There are different variants of malice aforethought, but in this case, I believe the best approach is to take the element, grave indifference of human life, that is an element of malice aforethought. So what Fauci, and indeed—if you read the contracts and everything, they admit with this gain-of-function work—the studies show they knew that it could create a pandemic again, among human beings, and they didn't care. They knew the risks, and they went forward. So I think there is enough documentary evidence out there already for a local prosecutor to convince a grand jury that these individuals had malice aforethought, defined as manifesting grave indifference to human life.

Kristina Borjesson: Now let's talk about the individuals. We talked about Fauci, right? We talked about Francis Collins, who was the geneticist who actually worked with Wuhan, right?

FAB: That's correct. And he was given an award by the Chinese military for all the great work he did with them. Fauci, Peter Daszak—he was up to his eyeballs in this.

Kristina Borjesson: Tell our audience who Peter Daszak is, please.

FAB: Well, he's head of EcoHealth Alliance, and he was working to fund and direct all this Nazi biowarfare death science work over at the Wuhan BSL-4.

Kristina Borjesson: EcoHealth Alliance. Is that an NGO?

FAB: Yeah, it's a private corporation that he heads up. In addition, if you look at the contract for this, you have Menachery at the University of North Carolina. You have Baric at the University of North Carolina.

Kristina Borjesson: Those are the two who were working on the gain of function at the University of North Carolina until they were told to stop because it was illegal, right?

FAB: They were told to stop because it was existentially dangerous. And then what they did was working with Daszak—they then moved this work to the Wuhan BSL-4 and continued to do that.

Kristina Borjesson: Now is that in itself a crime, to do that?

FAB: I guess it'd be defrauding the United States government and conspiracy to defraud the United States government, and that's pretty small potatoes. And again, that would have to be prosecuted by the feds. And, of course, they're not going to do any prosecutions.

Kristina Borjesson: If they were sending it over to Wuhan, to continue the development of this, obviously they had an interest in having that done, and Wuhan was going to share something back for doing that. They didn't just give it to Wuhan. It's got to be more than defrauding the United States. It's basically outsourcing the work because you're told not to do it here, even though you want the product of the work.

FAB: Yes, it's a violation of my Biological Weapons Anti-Terrorism Act. And when it leaked the way it did, I would argue it's murder, and conspiracy to commit murder. The other people involved here, there's a fellow from the

Food and Drug Administration. Now think about that for a minute, Kristina. The Food and Drug Administration was up to its eyeballs working with Fort Detrick, the Chinese Bat Queen, and Wuhan BSL-4, China's Fort Detrick, to develop COVID-19. It is the FDA now that is approving all the so-called vaccines that are also existentially dangerous. I call them Frankenshots, because that's really what they are. So the FDA is completely compromised here—you cannot listen to anything they are saying about the safety of these vaccines, these Frankenshots, their approval, or anything else. They've been up to their eyeballs in the development of COVID-19.

In addition, involved in the development of COVID-19 at the UNC BSL-3 was the Harvard Medical School. It says right there, Department of Cancer Immunology at the Dana Farber Cancer Institute, Department of Medicine, Harvard Medical School. Now, you know, Biden's current director of the CDC, Walensky, is from the Harvard Medical School. You can't believe anything she is telling you. Nothing. Harvard Medical School was involved in this right from the very get-go, this COVID-19 pandemic. And, indeed, Harvard was a sponsoring institution of the Wuhan BSL-4. Think about that, Harvard was a sponsoring institution of the Biosafety lab for China's Fort Detrick. We know for a fact that the chair of the Harvard Chemical Chemistry Department, Lieber, worked with Fort Detrick. He is an expert on nanotechnology, applying nanotechnology to biological weapons and chemical weapons. Harvard knew he was working for Fort Dietrick.

Kristina Borjesson: And that's for aerosolized, right? The virus so that it came into the lungs.

FAB: That is exactly right. Aerosolization, Kristina, is a tip-off of a biological weapons program, because that's how human beings get infected, by breathing through the air. Lieber was over there at Wuhan with his own lab, courtesy of the Chinese 1000 Talents Program, and the Wuhan BSL-4 bragged on their webpage that they had applied nanotechnology to viruses. So in other words, they were able to aerosolize this COVID-19 at their BSL-4, which they really couldn't have done at the UNC BSL-3.

Aerosolization of biological warfare weapons is so dangerous that you have to wear a moon suit with a portable air supply. That's how dangerous it is. That is why COVID-19 travels by air. There was one scientist at MIT who said it traveled 28 feet. I think another at Cornell said 21 feet. So that is how dangerous this is.

Kristina Borjesson: This six-feet distancing is BS.

FAB: That's correct. All of it is intended to lull the American people into a false sense of security here. And now they're sending our kids back to school, and the CDC, under Walensky, reduced that to three feet. She's a very evil person, despite you know, whatever you see on TV. She knows exactly what she is doing.

But let me continue here. I won't go through everyone on this contract. It's all there in writing. But finally comes the Wuhan Bat Queen when she was over there working at the UNC BSL-3 to give it gain-of-function properties making it more lethal, more infectious. Indeed, she took over there a synthetic biology SARS, and then they souped it up. This is SARS on Steroids.

Also on this contract is Fort Detrick itself. They were providing cells to the UNC BSL-3, right. So you can see why the federal government under Biden is not going to prosecute any of these people. That is why we have to go to local prosecutors, states attorneys, district attorneys, county prosecutors—anyone who has the authority to convene a grand jury can present this evidence and get an indictment. Yes, that's my campaign that I started on September 11, and this lecture I gave to this lawyers organization, which I sent you, you are free to distribute if you want to.

Kristina Borjesson: What I find interesting here is that people are not thinking in terms of how basically on this lower level, China, China is our enemy. China has just, you know, come up with this missile that goes around the world in two seconds or whatever, they're our enemy, we got to go after, and then at the higher level, our government, our defense department, other agencies, are actually working *with* the Chinese.

FAB: That is exactly correct. That can be documented from the public record. And indeed, there's more evidence coming out every day. Today, *The Intercept* had an article on this.

Kristina Borjesson: Well, I don't know. That makes me feel like a deer in the headlights, you know, because basically, at the higher level, all these criminal acts are taking place and the laws that address them, it's like they're too big to indict or prosecute. So who are these laws for?

FAB: That's why I'm saying that we have to take our case to the local prosecutors who have been elected by the people of their territorial jurisdiction. Their salaries are paid by the people of their territorial jurisdiction, and they can be reelected or dis-elected. So popular pressure can be brought to bear on the state and local prosecutors.

Kristina Borjesson: I think it's a really good idea for a campaign. But I also think that the prosecutors and attorneys general are all going to look at this and think, *Wow, this is a situation that's way above my pay grade.* And, you know, there's going to be a lot of fear.

FAB: I think the response is, by the local people, we pay your salaries, and we elected you. So you better pay attention to what we want you to do. Obviously, it's not for them to indict these people. I'm recommending they convene a grand jury, and let the grand jury, citizens of our peers, decide to return the indictment. Now out of the over 400, I think Bugliosi had the exact number there in his book. I'm hopeful that we can get at least one prosecutor with the courage, integrity, and principles to do this with public support behind him or her.

Kristina Borjesson: I think if you develop a victim's package of legal materials, and make it available to anybody who wants to do this, I think that would be amazing, because people will do it. The people who have lost loved ones will do it.

FAB: There's a new book that just came out with all the evidence in there by a Ms. Sharri Markson: *What Really Happened in Wuhan* [Harpers Collins]. It just came out. And I just finished reading the book. It's all in there.

Kristina Borjesson: I know. But you understand how people, the average person who is completely overwhelmed by this whole thing, is not going to read that huge book. I'll bring her on as my guest. And she'll share the contents of her book. But what they need to be able to do is walk into the prosecutor with something in their hands, a package that says, OK, here's my case, you know, please look at this.

FAB: What I would recommend is they walk in here with the paper I gave you, and this book, and say, Here it is, study this. And if you want to talk to Professor Boyle, he'll talk to you about it, and then convene a grand jury, because everything I just read in this book just came out. It's got the sources; it's all there in one book. And that's all they'll need—one book and my essay that I sent to you outlining the legal theory, but the facts are now all in this book.

Now, Kristina, let me get into the Frankenshots themselves. And what we have here—they are existentially dangerous. If you read the technical literature on the current Frankenshots available: AstraZeneca, Moderna, Pfizer, BioNTech, Johnson & Johnson, they all give you live cells of COVID-19. Let me repeat that: they all give you live cells of COVID-19. So in other words, they are injecting into their victims' bodies an offensive biological warfare weapon, cells with gain-of-function properties to make it more lethal and more infectious, and with HIV, the precursor of AIDS, DNA genetically engineered right into it. That is what we are facing with these Frankenshots. And we already have large numbers of Americans who have died as a result of these Frankenshots. A minimum figure I have seen is 45,000. Another figure I have seen is 200,000. I don't know, precisely, the numbers.

Kristina Borjesson: And they're hiding the numbers so we don't know.

FAB: Of course they're lying about the numbers. So I recommend the same thing here. Namely, that people who want to stop these Frankenshots—and you know your mayor out there, DeBlasio—he wants to inject everyone with the Frankenshots, even little kids; they're now moving into little kids.

Kristina Borjesson: Yeah, Biden has just said, Oh, warp speed for the kids now.

FAB: His [Jeff] Zients fellow today just said, Well, yeah, we're gonna have mandatory Frankenshots, even for little kids at some point. That's in today's *New York Times*. So the strategy is the same. You go into your local prosecutor and you say, I want the people behind these Frankenshots to be indicted for murder, and conspiracy to commit murder. And in this case, the elements of murder, unlawful killing of human beings with malice aforethought. Unlawful, a clear-cut violation of the Nuremberg Code on Medical Experimentation that the United States government used to prosecute Nazi doctors.

I think I sent you my lecture I gave on that. If not, remind me, and I'll send it again. That's how dangerous this is. It's a slam-dunk violation. The Nuremberg Code on Medical Experimentation requires the—I won't go through all the violations, as almost every provision has been violated—but the keynote here is that it requires animal testing before testing on human beings. There has been no animal testing for any of these Frankenshots. We human beings are being used as the lab rats for Pfizer, BioNTech, Moderna, and Johnson & Johnson. AstraZeneca is not available in this country, so fine. And by the way, Johnson & Johnson are the same people who gave us the opioid epidemic here in the United States, and also gave us asbestos in their baby powder that has given large numbers of women cancer of the ovaries. Why would you trust any of these people?

And so what we want you to do is get a second set of indictments for the chief executive officers and the scientific officers for murder, and conspiracy to commit murder. And here, the malice-aforethought element would be another variant of malice aforethought. And this is Anglo-American common law, either the intention to kill or intention to cause grievous bodily harm. And clearly we know that from the very get-go of the administration of these Frankenshots, they have been killing people and/or causing grievous bodily harm to them. That can be established. So the chief executive officers, the chief scientific officers of these organizations, the companies that are heading the drug companies that have put these together, and then people like Fauci and Walensky for conspiracy.

Kristina Borjesson: Why not the president?

FAB: That. obviously. would complicate and politicize the whole matter. In the Watergate investigations, Leon Jaworski did commission a staff memorandum by his lawyers who concluded that while a president is sitting, he is immune from prosecution except for murder. So, yes, that could be done. But under the circumstances, with Biden that'd be highly politicized. And I think a state or local prosecutor might conclude: That is above my pay grade.

Kristina Borjesson: What about the heads of the agencies? The CDC?

FAB: Well, as I said, Collins and Fauci and Walensky for sure, for conspiracy to commit murder. Yes.

Kristina Borjesson: And could people who are being forced to take the vaccine or lose their jobs—take the vaccine or you can't travel here—do they have a case?

FAB: Again, my advice at this point would be for those who have lost loved ones or friends, to make this argument to their local prosecutor. And I think if we could even get one of them to convince the grand jury to return an indictment, the whole house of cards would collapse. And by the way, one of the other points here in the Pfizer/BioNTech Frankenshot, which is the predominant one here in the United States, one of the investors in BioNTech is Bill Gates. So it might be possible to implicate Gates, I don't know, for conspiracy to commit murder. I noticed that Robert F. Kennedy Jr. is coming out with a book soon. I've listened to him discuss it on a podcast that deals with Fauci, but he also has more evidence in there about Gates going around and orchestrating it all. So I'm not expressing an opinion yet about Gates. But he was a financier of this, and he's been heavily involved.

Kristina Borjesson: Globally, the Gates Foundation has been involved. As a matter of fact, I've been talking to Indian lawyers and researchers, and they have just submitted a huge complaint to the prime minister, et cetera, where they detail how the Gates Foundation basically hijacked India's health system to force these vaccines on the Indians by these public/private partnerships. In other words, you know, they would get in partnership with these Indian health agencies and then the other agencies, where they couldn't have partnerships, they had people that they paid. And all the decisions, obviously, were made in favor of pushing the vaccine and suppressing early treatment—you know, successful early treatment options. So they're going after everybody, including Gates. They're going after all the agencies.

FAB: For now, I want to see some more evidence before I recommend pursuing an indictment against Gates. I'm talking about here in the United States.

Kristina Borjesson: But if you want to look at a road map of how the Gates Foundation operated in a huge country . . .

FAB: I'm totally aware of how they've operated. That would be the agenda here. And you're the first—I gave this lecture September 11, but I had a strict 25-minute time limit on that lecture monitored by Chat. So there was only so much I could say, and you're the first journalist here in the United States I'm giving this story to at length, and this strategy to. I did not answer any questions there in the September 11 lecture.

Kristina Borjesson: I'll make sure this gets out as far and wide as possible. I still think that there's that upper layer that somehow has to be addressed. And I don't know how, if they're above the law.

FAB: Well, we'll get to it. But we have to start somewhere, and in any prosecutions, you start at the bottom and work your way up. So that is what we're going to have to do here. We're going to have to start at the bottom at the grassroots level—the American people pressuring states attorneys, county attorneys, attorneys general, district attorneys—to get indictments from grand juries, and then we'll take it the next step. Right.

Kristina Borjesson: Well, it's interesting, you know. I was inspired to reach out to you, I think I told you in my email, because I had gone to see *No Time to Die*, the new James Bond movie, which is surprise, surprise, about viruses that target specific populations, and there's one scene, for example, where Bond goes into a big party, and they release the aerosolized virus through, you know, a sprinkler system or whatever, and everybody dies except for him because everybody has been biologically targeted.

FAB: The Pentagon has been working on ethnic-specific biological warfare weapons. We know that, and you can read about that in *Biowarfare and Terrorism.* The CIA was working with the criminal, racist Afrikaner apartheid regime to develop ethnic-specific biological weapons to use against the Black people in South Africa. So they have been working on them. I don't know if they have succeeded. But they have been working on these for quite some time, and the neoconservatives going back to Reagan recommend that they do this type of genocidal biological warfare. So this is a reality on the planning books. Whether they've actually done this, I don't know. Because so far, I haven't been able to track down that evidence.

Kristina Borjesson: You know, it's interesting, because, again, in this film, it's even more specific than that, because they have a huge database of individuals that they have targeted for a virus genetically engineered for that individual alone.

FAB: Well, we know that the United States government has been over in Russia, harvesting their DNA. And that I've been interviewed by the Russian news media on this. And certainly, that is for the purpose of developing an ethnic-specific biological warfare weapon against the Russians, which is, you know, it won't cover everyone over there. But it's the Great Russian ethnic minority group. There have also been reports that they have been doing it in China, and you basically have the Han ethnic group. It would be harder to do that here in the United States, because we're multiethnic. To target the people of the United States, we've got everyone over here. But some of these countries with high degrees of genetic homogeneity, like the Blacks in South Africa, the Great Russians, the Han, it is conceivable, and we've been working on certainly the Pentagon and the CIA. Whether they have succeeded on this, I don't know, because I haven't seen that evidence.

Kristina Borjesson: You know, in the end, to turn this ship of death around, it just seems to me that there has to be some kind of almost a spiritual transformation at the highest levels, like people in the Defense Department and in the CIA. I mean, they're trained to become pathological. A lot of them. But I mean, somebody has to turn the ship around at that level.

FAB: That is, well, we have to do it again, from the ground up. I've worked with grassroots movements all over the country for peace, justice, human rights, ever since I started teaching here in 1978. I am appearing here because, I think, you know, the American people, if you take your case out to them at a state and local basis, at a grassroots basis, they have common sense, decency, and morality. I think it's hopeless at the top.

You know, Kristina, I went through the exact same PhD program at Harvard that produced Kissinger and Brzezinski before me, the Harvard Graduate School of Arts and Sciences, Department of Government. These people are trained to be Nazis. That's what happens at these elite schools like Harvard, the University of Chicago, where I went as an undergrad, the home of the neocons. So those people are hopeless. I'm counting on the common, ordinary, good-faith, common-sense morality of the American people. And that's why I've launched this campaign. And that's why I am appearing here today with you. I hope you will do your best to get it out as widely as possible among the American people, and I appreciate your taking this time to do this interview with me.

Kristina Borjesson: My pleasure.

FAB: Thanks.

Morton Mecklosky, State University of New York at Stony Brook Radio, WUSB 90.1, interviews Francis A. Boyle on June 9, 2008

Morton Mecklosky: You're listening to WUSB here at Stony Brook, and I have Francis A. Boyle, professor of law. I just had Vincent Bugliosi on talking about his book *The Prosecution of George W. Bush for Murder.* He's a significant prosecutor. I think he got the case against Manson. What's your sense of the legality and presenting the case against the president for murder?

FAB: Right, Mort. I've been working on this myself for the last several weeks with people in Maine, Vermont, Connecticut, New York, New Jersey, North Carolina, and Illinois. Then Vince Bugliosi's book came out. He had heard of me and gave me a call. We had a long talk about it last week and agreed to join forces and work together. I think there is a compelling case for indicting President Bush for murdering U.S. troops in Iraq. Right now, the official figure—if you believe it—is 4,089 dead U.S. soldiers, marines, sailors.

I used to teach Criminal Law here; in fact, I was originally hired to teach Criminal Law. Murder is defined by common law as the unlawful killing of a human being with malice aforethought. Generally speaking, you will find a definition along those lines in almost every state of the Union because they are all based on the common-law definition.

Now let's parse that definition: "Unlawful." In this case, the war against Iraq was a war of aggression by President Bush in violation of the United Nations Charter. In fact, he had twice tried to get authorization by the United Nations Security Council to launch that war and failed. So currently we have the "unlawful" part being fulfilled.

"Killing": Under the law, it does not require that you actually pull the trigger on someone. For example, you could push someone in front of an L train, and that would be enough. In this case, Bush ordered these now almost 4,100 dead U.S. soldiers into a meat grinder in Iraq, where they were killed, and it was very clear there were going to be casualties when he gave these orders.

So unlawful killing of a "human being": These 4,100 dead soldiers are our mothers, our fathers, our brothers, our sisters, our sons, and our daughters.

They have been murdered by Bush, Cheney, Rice, Rumsfeld, and the rest of them with "malice aforethought." Malice, malicious. I think we all know what that means—mainly, that Bush lied about Iraq from the get-go. That became very clear certainly starting in the summer of 2002 now, as verified by Scott McClellan in the publicity related to his new book [*What Happened*]. Here, you have the White House spokesperson verifying a very detailed propaganda campaign put into effect in the summer of 2002 to try to sell a war of aggression against Iraq.

Finally the last element: "aforethought." Namely, that they thought about it beforehand before they did this. It is very clear that the war against Iraq had been planned right after they entered the White House, and even before.

In addition, for a first-degree murder charge on top of these elements, you also have to establish what is called "premeditation and deliberation." Truly, here we have had this death and destruction in Iraq premeditated and deliberated by these Bush people since at least when they came to power in January 2001. So I think there is a compelling case that can be made for murder and also first-degree murder, which can be a capital offense—not that I support the death penalty.

What Vince Bugliosi and I are both recommending is that this matter be considered by every district attorney and state attorney general in the United States of America. What we are recommending is that people living in a community where there are dead U.S. soldiers get together a group and set up a meeting with the local district attorney—a democratically elected official for that county—where there is at least one dead U.S. soldier, and go in and meet with the district attorney; bring in Mr. Bugliosi's book; and demand that Bush, Cheney, Rice, and Rumsfeld at least be indicted for murdering that dead U.S. soldier in the district attorney's county—and also for conspiracy to commit murder.

Conspiracy is defined at common will as an agreement between at least two people to do an illegal act or to do a lawful act by illegal means. Clearly, what has happened here is an agreement among Bush, Cheney, and Rice, who are still in power, and Rumsfeld, to commit an illegal act of murder of that dead U.S. soldier.

Unfortunately, if you take a look at the math and Mr. Bugliosi's book, you will see that there are dead soldiers now all over the country, and there are going to be more. They are dying every day, if you follow the count in the *New York Times*; they have the names and ranks and locations where these soldiers come from. So Vince Bugliosi and I want to stop this. If we don't do something now, these deaths will mount and continue since Bush has made that clear that the war will go on. Indeed it could escalate between now and the time they leave office in late January of 2009.

As for the question of whether or not a sitting president can be indicted, Mr. Bugliosi did express sort of an offhand opinion in his book that he didn't think so. But in our conversation, I hope I did convince him that in fact there is authority for indicting a sitting president for murder, and I sent him those materials. That would be the following sources: First, during the Nixon impeachment proceedings, Professor Raoul Berger of the Harvard Law School, who at that time was this country's leading constitutional law historian, did a very important law-review article expressing his opinion that a sitting president could be indicted. Second, at the time Leon Jaworski, the second special prosecutor of Nixon after Nixon had fired Archie Cox, obtained an opinion from his legal staff to the effect that a sitting president could be indicted for crimes. Although in his memoirs Jaworski took the position that he personally did not think the crimes for which Nixon was guilty warranted prosecuting a sitting president, he did state his opinion in his memoirs that he felt certainly that a sitting president should and could be indicted for murder. There are some more recent law-review articles generated out of the Clinton impeachment proceedings to the effect that a sitting president can be indicted. Indeed, it was reported that the lawyers on the Ken Starr staff also did a memo, which I haven't seen, to the effect that a sitting president could be indicted. So I don't believe that this is an obstacle.

Again, what we are recommending is that people from the community where there is a dead soldier get together, probably try to line up veterans to go in with you from the Iraqi Veterans Against the War—perhaps there might be next of kin who are outraged, and I know many are by the deaths of their loved ones—to get into this group and demand that the district attorney convene a grand jury and indict Bush, Cheney, Rice, and Rumsfeld for murder, and conspiracy to commit murder, of that dead soldier. So that is where we stand. Mr. Bugliosi and I agreed late last week to join forces on this matter, and I do recommend his book [*The Prosecution of George W. Bush for Murder*]. The first 175 pages lay out the case for indictment.

Morton Mecklosky: Now, the charge of murder is just on the U.S. troops, not on the Iraqis?

FAB: Right. The district attorneys here in the United States would not have jurisdiction to prosecute for dead Iraqis—unfortunately, I don't see it. It might be possible in a new administration for federal prosecutors to indict for dead Iraqis as war crimes. There is jurisdiction in the United States federal law for indicting for war crimes. But right now, all the U.S. federal prosecutors have been appointed by Bush, so of course they're not going to be convening a grand jury to indict the president who appointed them. The difference here is that the district attorneys and states' attorneys are not part of the federal government.

They have been elected by the people of the states where they live, or the district attorneys for the counties where they live, and have broad discretion, if not an obligation, to inquire into this matter and certainly at least convene a grand jury and to present the case to the grand jury, who, after all, are the citizens of their community. Let the members of the grand jury decide whether or not to return an indictment against the president. This is a democratic process. It would be the people, the grand jury of that county, to make that decision after reviewing the evidence presented by the district attorney.

The second reason, and I think this is very important—not only to stop further death and destruction in Iraq, including as you correctly point out the dead people in Iraq who had been killed and murdered by Bush now somewhere in the area of 1.2 million—is that Bush and Cheney might escalate into a war against Iran. Today on Antiwar.com is this article by Gareth Porter pointing out that last summer Cheney tried very hard to bomb the Iranian Republican Guards, knowing full well it would escalate into a full-scale war between Iran and the United States; he was headed off by the Pentagon and their military officers.

Porter also points out that Cheney has now done an end run around all of them by getting rid of Admiral Fallon, the head of U.S. Central Command, who was dismissed because of his opposition to war against Iran; and bringing in General Petraeus, now heading U.S. Central Command, who is serving Cheney. So there is a very real risk that if we do not stop these people now, they will attack Iran in a war they know will escalate to a major confrontation between Iran and United States. They could do this anytime between now and January 20, 2009, when they leave office.

Let us remember that after President Bush Sr. lost to Clinton in 1992, after the election but before Clinton came to power, Bush Sr. invaded Somalia—there was no restraint on him. But my guess is an attack on Iran between now and November will be decided in accordance with domestic political considerations: namely, will it help McCain win or not. But after the elections in November, anything can happen. There is no restraint on this president or vice president, and in my opinion they have to be removed from office as soon as possible, and stopped.

Morton Mecklosky: All right, while I agree with both you and Bugliosi, would the American public support such a move?

FAB: I don't know, Mort. That's why I am on your program today, to discuss this campaign.

Morton Mecklosky: I am sure that there are going to be several people who would be willing to go to the DA's office and ask them to bring in a grand jury. But the district attorneys and the politicians are afraid of going against the will of the people.

FAB: Well, that's the point, though, Mort. What is the will of the people here? You see, we found this out in our impeachment campaign in Congress. We went to the United States Congress and the appropriate authorities there, and they have ignored the will of the people in Washington, D.C. So now we are bringing it one step down to the real grassroots level, which is the district attorney, who is accountable to the people of a county that is very small: We have here in Champaign County about 180,000 people. So here we are trying to bring a campaign down to the real grassroots level and not target Washington, D.C., but to target whoever your district attorney is and to get the people living in that county to say that we want the president indicted. There are hundreds of district attorneys all over the country. That's why I believe, and I know Mr. Bugliosi, that we can at least find one, and then we can take it from there.

Morton Mecklosky: Now, let's assume that within some community the district attorney is moved to respond and he convenes a grand jury. Suppose that does take place. What's the scenario that follows that? What is the grand jury then to do?

FAB: It's like any other criminal grand jury. The district attorney would go in before the grand jury, present the evidence against President Bush on murder, and basically lay out the case that I just mentioned to you and also in Mr. Bugliosi's book. Now, he's got 175 pages there in the first part of the book laying out the case that he would present to the grand jury. The DA could subpoena witnesses like Mr. McClellan. Then it would be for the grand jury to decide whether or not to return an indictment against them. This is democracy at work at the very lowest level here in America, Mort, as our Founding Fathers saw it. Remember that there is a constitutional protection that you have to have a grand jury indict you for any type of serious offense in this country. So the grand jury is a branch of our democracy. Then if the indictment is returned, it will be up to the district attorney to pursue the prosecution, as he would any other case: issue an arrest warrant that would be valid nationwide under the Full Faith and Credit Clause of the United States Constitution.

Morton Mecklosky: OK, now if they call witnesses and subpoena people in the administration, could these people go to the government, to the president, and the attorney general could tell them that they don't have to appear? Is that possible?

FAB: Yes, this has happened already, right. Congress has subpoenaed Karl Rove, Harriet Miers, and Josh Bolton. The three of them have told Congress to take a hike. Right? What has Congress done but cave in? They have gone to court to try to enforce their subpoenas, which is a cop-out. Everyone knows this is a cop-out. Congress can enforce its own subpoenas. They have their own sergeant-at-arms; they have their own jail. He can go out and arrest them, and he can bring them back and incarcerate these people if he wants to. But Congress is not going to do it. So they copped out by going to federal court to try to enforce their own subpoenas.

The federal courts are not going to pull Congress's chestnuts out of the fire for Congress. It is up to Congress to enforce its own powers. And they have not done that. Indeed, as we know since the Reagan administration, the federal courts have now been stacked with these right-wing, totalitarian members of the Federalist Society, which you and I have discussed before. Two-thirds of all federal judges now have been appointed pretty much by Reagan, Bush Sr., and Bush Jr., and most of them are members of the Federalist Society. People know this—I mean, sensible people, and lawyers certainly know that the courts are not going to enforce these subpoenas. It's really for Congress to enforce its own subpoenas, and right now they have made it clear they are not going to do it.

That's the problem we found repeatedly in dealing with Congress, at least in my experience from 13 March 2003 on, trying to get Congressman John Conyers and the other Democratic members of the House Judiciary Committee to put in Bills of Impeachment against Bush, Cheney, Rumsfeld, and Ashcroft. They are not going to do it. Pelosi and the Democrats were put in power in Congress after the 2006 elections, and what does Pelosi say but impeachment is off the table and that's that. So the question is, what do we do now? Well, of course, we do have to keep pressuring Congressman Conyers on impeachment. Ramsey Clark has a campaign on for as much pressure as possible by July 4. Again, I have worked with Ramsey on this project too. But the Washington Democrats are part of the problem, not the solution, so we have to move on to the next stage, and the next stage, as I see it, and as Bugliosi sees it, is indicting Bush for murder.

Morton Mecklosky: Do you want to speak to the validity of the charges of murder against the president, the vice president? On what grounds?

FAB: Well, I think I did go through those elements, Mort. Again, murder is defined as the unlawful killing of a human being with malice aforethought. I went through each one of those elements for you, and then I also went through the requirements for first-degree murder, which would be in addition to those elements: premeditation and deliberation. Each one of those elements would have to be proved beyond a reasonable doubt by the district attorney to the satisfaction of a regular jury. I believe the evidence is there. I think the case can be made. But again, it would really be for a grand jury to decide if the evidence is there, can that case be made, and then to return an indictment.

Morton Mecklosky: OK, if members of the community were to attempt to engage the district attorney to bring charges against the president, should there be anything they should do prior to that? Should they let the public know through newspaper and media coverage of such an event?

FAB: Yes. What we would like to do is to set off a grassroots movement nationwide. I think they should have a look at Mr. Bugliosi's book, the first 175 pages. The case is crystal clear in there, and have a little study group, read through the book, and if they agree with the conclusion, put together their group to approach the DA. Again, my advice would be to also incorporate some Iraqi Veterans Against the War, the Vietnam Veterans Against the War, and of course, you have to be sensitive here, but if there are next of kin of dead soldiers in that community who feel very strongly that they want the president indicted, include them. I know many of them do. I have been following these comments some of the next of kin have made after the deaths have been reported to them. Bring in the next of kin to the district attorney, and demand an indictment. Set up a press conference before and after the meeting with the district attorney. I think that is very important. Then try to replicate this all over the country where there are dead soldiers.

Unfortunately, as of today, there are 4,089 of them reported. The number is probably higher than that because they have a long history of never properly reporting dead soldiers, especially in any of the Special Forces and their operations. I really don't know what the exact number is, but I am sure that it is substantially more than 4,089.

Morton Mecklosky: Now, there are members of the community who are opposed to the president and his policies but will say this will not take place, and we should be satisfied that the president is not going to be president for the coming administration. What's your response to them?

FAB: My response is that the president is still murdering U.S. troops in Iraq, as we speak today. These troops were sent over there in our name, and I personally believe that as citizens of the United States, we have to do everything humanly possible to stop Bush from murdering more U.S. troops in Iraq. If we just sit back and don't do anything, there could be another 100, 200, who knows how many dead U.S. soldiers in Iraq, between now and January 20. There's no guarantee that Obama is going to win this election. It very well could be that the Bush administration will decide to instigate some type of war against Iran in order to help McCain. And McCain would be just as bad on Iraq and Iran as Bush is, so the death and destruction will continue. I don't think any of us should sit on our haunches in the hope and expectation that somehow Obama is going to win and stop everything come January 2009. I believe we would be derelict in our duties as American citizens to not stop this death and destruction against our own troops, let alone the people of Iraq.

Morton Mecklosky: There are going to be people who are going to have a little difficulty with this, that the president murdered the troops. They are going to say he might be responsible for their deaths because he sent them into combat when he shouldn't have done that, but the ones who are killing them is not the president, it's the al-Qaeda and the Iraqis who don't want us there.

FAB: Yes, it's the doctrine of transferred intent, I mean, again, if you push someone in front of an L train and they are run over and killed, they are dead. You push someone into a meat grinder, and they are killed by the meat grinder, you still kill them. So the president knew he was pushing U.S. armed forces illegally into a meat grinder, and they were going to be killed, and he knows it today, and they are still being killed today. So Mr. Bugliosi goes through some of these technical, legal doctrines on transferred intent and things of that nature in his book, if you are interested in reading it.

Morton Mecklosky: OK, I'm recommending the listeners get the book and also contact others who have similar points of view on the war, and its being illegal and the culpability of the president and others in the administration for the deaths of the troops who went over there, and then meet at least informally and set up some sort of a schedule that you recommend. Read the book, set up a study group, contact veterans who are opposed to the war, and then go and meet with the district attorney, and also engage the local media on the issue. Tell them this is what the plan is, we are going to indict the president for starting the war, and hold them responsible for the death of our troops.

FAB: That's the problem, Mort, with Vietnam. We never held any of those leaders accountable for Vietnam. Fifty-eight thousand men of my generation were murdered in Vietnam, and eventually McNamara came out in his book *In Retrospect* and basically said, Yes, I lied to the American people about Vietnam out of loyalty to President Johnson.

We never held any of them accountable. McNamara and Kissinger are still running around today on the lecture circuit. We have to make an attempt here and now to hold Bush, Cheney, Rice, and Rumsfeld accountable for what they have done in murdering United States armed forces, and if we do not, the death and destruction is going to continue.

Morton Mecklosky: All right. Wasn't there an attempt to hold Kissinger responsible for crimes against humanity—for example, what happened in Chile, and doesn't he have difficulty when he leaves the country? Aren't there warrants out there for him in foreign countries?

FAB: That is correct. But not here in the United States. I did work with some people up in Canada trying to get Kissinger prosecuted up in Canada. We were not able to do it. They did try to get him in Paris, and he got out of the country. I believe they are trying to get him in Spain for what he did in Chile. But again, the problem is that we Americans cannot be relying on foreign courts and foreign countries to pull our chestnuts out of the fire. These are our leaders, and we have to hold them accountable. Now what happened in Vietnam is a terrible tragedy. I had friends who were murdered over there, others whose lives were ruined, but you know that was a generation ago. Iraq is today, and we have to stop this.

We have to hold these leaders criminally accountable to stop it and to make sure it doesn't happen again, because otherwise it *will* happen again, and it very well could happen in Iran. If Cheney and Bush attack Iran, as we discussed before, they will set off a regional war over there that I shudder to think could degenerate into a Third World War given the current arrangement of great powers and what everyone has said. Even Bush has threatened World War III over Iran.

After President Putin went to Iran and said he didn't think that Iran was really moving toward nuclear weapons, Bush gave a speech basically threatening World War III over Iran. That threat was not directed at Iran, it was directed at Putin. Then Putin responded later on over these planned U.S. missiles in the Czech Republic and Poland by raising the spectre of another Cuban missile crisis, that this could be a Cuban missile crisis in reverse. I lived through the Cuban missile crisis. If you studied what actually happened there, we came a hairbreadth's away from nuclear Armageddon. This is a very dangerous situation here, and again if you read Gareth Porter this morning on Antiwar.com, you know that Cheney is still chomping on the bit to attack Iran, knowing full well it will escalate into a major war.

Morton Mecklosky: All right. I agree that we shouldn't count on other countries to do our work for us in bringing these people to justice. They did try that with Rumsfeld in Germany.

FAB: Mike Ratner tried twice over there, and the Germans gave two different excuses. Right. But the point is, as you correctly pointed out, Mort, is that we have to prosecute our own criminals over here. With all due respect to

Mike Ratner, I have been involved in efforts to hold our government officials accountable in foreign countries, but if we can't do it here, then what's the point? We have to do it here; we are American citizens. These people were elected by us; we have to hold them accountable; they murdered our own troops.

Morton Mecklosky: I think what it takes is how do we convince our neighbors that what you are saying is not only true but something we have to do? I think that's a problem. Most people don't want to get involved in these things.

FAB: Basically, we need a spark plug in each community. I've heard from several over the last few weeks. I've been working on this, and there are people calling me up saying, What should I do, how do I get involved, and where do I go from here? I think that is the importance of this interview with you.

Morton Mecklosky: Right.

FAB: As has happened in any type of grassroots democratic movement, Mort, in my lifetime going back to civil rights for Black people, straight on through, you need just common, ordinary, everyday leaders from the community. Someone to say I can make a difference, and I'm going to do it. Then as for the technical aspect of it, it's all there in Bugliosi's book. Get a copy for the district attorney too, set up the meeting, demand the indictment.

Morton Mecklosky: Sometime ago I tried to contact a former student of mine to get some town meetings together where people can discuss the war and what we can do about it. I would think announcements should be made that there will be town meetings, if we can get them where the public is invited to participate in this problem. You don't want them to wait as we did. I'm remembering studying for an exam during the Cuban Missile Crisis, and I put the book down and said, Why am I studying when the world can come to an end?

FAB: That's right. I remember myself during the Cuban Missile Crisis saying, Hey I'm only 12 years old, and the whole world is about to blow up; I can do a better job than this. That's what sparked my interest in international relations. So I think you are right; we have to have town meetings.

Morton Mecklosky: Right, and there are towns in the country that are doing that. I mentioned that Bugliosi said that up in Vermont, some towns and communities have given their police departments the order to arrest Bush, should he be in the area.

FAB: I've been working with people up in Vermont, Maine, Connecticut, North Carolina. I've been working with them and advising them, and now we're moving on to this next step.

Morton Mecklosky: Great. There must a considerable number of DAs, and at least one of them out there who will have the courage to say this is the right thing to do. We're going to bring charges of murder against the president.

FAB: Right, there are hundreds of counties. The country at the grassroots basic level is organized by counties, and there are hundreds of them out there and hundreds of DAs. So we are hoping to get at least just one to start this ball rolling.

Morton Mecklosky: The president and the politicians, whether or not they know it, violate all the rules for rational discourse, and the public doesn't want to get involved in thinking deeply about anything. They cannot process information that's really painful, so they go for the slogans, and that's why we're in the condition we're in. I had Marjorie Cohn on a couple of weeks ago, and she is saying that all we have to do is educate the people. I had to tell her, Marjorie, they don't want to know what you're telling them. They'll shut it down. They don't want to know the pain that's in the message you're giving them. They'd rather think we're the greatest country in the world, we're the good people in the world, and you're going to tell them things like telling a kid that his father is a hit man in organized crime.

FAB: I think the best way to deal with that is to bring along enough pictures of dead soldiers, and let people contemplate dead soldiers in their community. We have several of them out here in the Champaign-Urbana area. I would say once a month I'm reading stories about dead soldiers in this community. I think if you were to bring blown-up pictures of these young men and women and realize we're talking here about human beings and fellow Americans who lived in our communities, maybe that is going to drive it home. The *New York Times* has done a great service by periodically publishing all those pictures of all the U.S. troops murdered in Iraq by Bush, and maybe these pictures can bring this home.

Morton Mecklosky: All right, I appreciate again what you are doing. This time we have a group meeting on Saturdays protesting the counter-protesters, and enough of them are veterans, and it's very difficult because, you know, veterans are difficult.

FAB: And even then, we do have the Iraqi Veterans Against the War, and that's now headed by my former client Staff Sergeant Camilo Mejia, who was the first Iraq war resistor. So you've got to work with the Iraqi war veterans and tap into them to give you that type of credibility. And then, second, we still have the Vietnam Veterans Against the War going back to the Vietnam War, and they are very active in resisting this war. And get them involved as well, again to provide that type of credibility in dealing with the community and with the district attorney.

Morton Mecklosky: Right, there's still enough of the veterans out there who paid their price. They feel they never challenged the authority that sent them into the war that maybe they should have.

FAB: Bertrand Russell wrote a very famous book called *Power*, in which he said that all governments basically work the same way: they're run by a very small elite in their own interest. And that is true of Western liberal democracies. The difference is that the Western liberal democracies are far more effective at covering and masking elite control than dictatorships. As Russell saw it, the only time the veil falls in Western liberal democracy is either an economic depression or a defeat in war. In those two cases, then, the people finally realize that they have been lied to by their rulers, and that there is a small elite who have been governing all along.

Morton Mecklosky: Are we going to have to really lose this war and be destroyed before we finally go after the ones who've brought us to this point, and by the time it's over, it's too late?

FAB: That's why I'm recommending we go after them now before there is a total disaster over there, to prevent a disaster, because as you correctly point out, if we wait until there is a disaster, then it will be too late. We need a preemptive indictment now, because I don't think that if they set off a major war over there, that there's much we can do at that point.

Morton Mecklosky: I'm thinking of the poor souls in prewar Germany who were opposed to Hitler. They died, also, as a consequence of his policy, even though they opposed him. Those bombs we put upon Germany didn't discriminate—everybody died. The consequences of a war, everything is going to happen, and the United States—I don't know if you have considered this as a positive, the consequences of the Bush administration—it is very nearly the demise of the U.S. as an empire.

FAB: You know, *Counterpunch* has been making that point. The problem I have with that is that it's just murdering too many people. I mean, the human costs for me are just unacceptable, and I personally just can't stand by and see United States troops be used as cannon fodder and 1.2 million people killed in Iraq. As human beings, whatever we think of the American Empire, we have an obligation to stop this by whatever means we can.

Morton Mecklosky: OK, take care. You are listening to WUSB at Stony Brook. Those of you who are involved in the protest against the president's policies against the U.S. Empire, pay attention to the suggestions. And those of us who meet on Saturdays to stop the war and stop U.S. aggression, perhaps we can meet this coming Saturday and talk about tracking down a DA who can bring charges against the president.

...

CHAPTER 17

CRIMINAL SABOTAGE BY THE U.S. SPOOKS ESTABLISHMENT AND THE U.S. SCIENTIFIC/MEDICAL ESTABLISHMENTS OVER THE COVID-19 PANDEMIC

From Michael T. McCaul, House GOP Foreign Affairs Comm., The Origins of COVID-19: An Investigation of the Wuhan Institute of Virology **{WIV}** ***63-66 (August 2021):***

VII. APPENDIX

Timeline of the WIV Lab Leak and the Start of the COVID-19 Pandemic

April 2012: Six miners working in a copper mine located in a cave in Yunnan province of the PRC fall ill. Between the ages of 30 and 63, the workers presented to a hospital in Kunming with persistent coughs, fevers, head and chest pains, and breathing difficulties. Three of the six died.

Late 2012–2015: Researchers from the WIV collect samples from bats in the cave.

2015–2017: Shi Zheng-Ii, Ben Hu, Peter Daszak, and Linfa Wang jointly publish research on the isolation of novel coronaviruses. They conduct gain-of-function research, testing novel and genetically manipulated coronaviruses against mice and other animals expressing human immune systems. At times they collaborate with Ralph Baric.

2018–2019: Shi, Hu, and other researchers at the WIV infect transgenic mice and civets, expressing human immune systems with unpublished novel and genetically modified coronaviruses.

July 4, 2019: The PRC's Ministry of Science and Technology orders a review of several grants, including grant no. 2013FY113500. This is the grant that funded the collection of hundreds of coronaviruses and bat samples from the cave in Yunnan province.

July 16, 2019: The WIV publishes a tender requesting bids to conduct renovation on the hazardous waste treatment system at the Wuhan National Biosafety Lab (WNBL). The closing date was July 31.

Late August/Early September 2019: One or more researchers become accidentally infected with SARS-CoV-2, which was either collected in the Yunnan cave, or the result of gain-offunction research at the WIV. They travel by metro in central Wuhan, spreading the virus.

September 12, 2019: At 12:00 a.m. local time, Wuhan University issues a statement announcing lab inspections. Between 2:00 a.m. and 3:00 a.m., the WIV's viral sequence and sample database is taken offline. At 7:09 p.m., the WIV publishes a tender requesting bids to provide security services at the WNBL.

September–October 2019: Car traffic at hospitals surrounding the WIV headquarters, as well as the shuttle stop for the WNBL, shows a steady increase before hitting its highest levels in 2.5 years. Baidu search terms for COVID-19-related symptoms increase in a corresponding manner.

Late October–Early November 2019: The international athletes return home, carrying SARS-CoV-2 around the world.

November 21, 2019: A four-year-old boy from Milan, Italy, develops a cough. His samples will later test positive for COVID-19.

November 27, 2019: Samples of wastewater are collected in Brazil that will later test positive for the presence of SARS-CoV-2 RNA.

December 1, 2019: The CCP's [Chinese Communist Party's] first "official" case of COVID-19 become infected.

Late 2019: Major General Chen Wei arrives in Wuhan, taking over the WNBL BSL-4 Lab.

December 27, 2019: A Chinese genomic company reportedly sequenced most of the virus in Wuhan, and results showed a similarity to SARS. Zhang Jixian, a doctor from Hubei Provincial Hospital of Integrated Chinese and Western Medicine, tells PRC [People's Republic of China] health authorities that a novel disease affecting some 180 patients was caused by a new coronavirus.

December 29, 2019: Wuhan Municipal CDC organized an expert team to investigate after the Hubei Provincial Hospital of Integrated Chinese and Western Medicine and other hospitals find additional cases.

December 30, 2019: Doctors in Wuhan report positive tests for "SARS Coronavirus" to local health officials. Under the 2005 International Health Regulations, the PRC is required to report these results to the WHO within 24 hours. They do not.

December 31, 2019: WHO officials in Geneva become aware of media reports regarding an outbreak in Wuhan and direct the WHO China Country Office to investigate.

January 2020: Linfa Wang meets with collaborators at the WIV, likely including Shi and Hu.

January 1, 2020: A Hubei Provincial Health Commission official orders gene-sequencing companies and labs who had already determined the novel virus was similar to SARS to stop testing and to destroy existing samples. Dr. Li Wenliang is detained for "rumormongering."

January 2, 2020: The WIV completes gene sequencing of the virus, but the CCP does not share the sequence or inform the WHO. The PRC aggressively highlights the detentions of the Wuhan doctors.

January 3, 2020: China's National Health Commission orders institutions not to publish any information related to the "unknown disease" and orders labs to transfer samples to CCP-controlled national institutions or destroy them.

January 11–12, 2020: After a researcher in Shanghai leaks the gene sequence online, the CCP transmits the WIV's gene-sequencing information that was completed ten days earlier to the WHO. The Shanghai lab where the researcher works is ordered to close.

January 14, 2020: Xi Jinping is warned by a top Chinese health official that a pandemic is occurring.
January 18, 2020: Linfa Wang departs Wuhan.

January 20, 2020: WIV researchers submitted an article claiming that SARS-CoV-2 is natural in origin. The article renames ID4991 as RaTG13 and contains false information about when the genomic sequence for the virus was obtained.

January 23, 2020: The CCP institutes a citywide lockdown of Wuhan. However, before the lockdown goes into effect, an estimated five million people leave the city.

Last Week of January 2020: Daszak and other outside experts edit a letter to be sent by the presidents of the National Academies of Sciences, Engineering, and Medicine to the White House Office of Science and Technology Policy. Daszak pushes for language to address "conspiracy theories."

January 30, 2020: One week after declining to do so, [Dr.] Tedros [at the WHO] declares a Public Health Emergency of International Concern.

Late January—-Early February 2020: PRC researchers, likely those at the WIV, request Peter Daszak's assistance in responding to suggestions of a lab leak or genetic manipulation of SARS-CoV-2. Daszak helps edit the National Academies of Sciences, Engineering, and Medicine's response to the White House Office of Science and Technology Policy on the origins of COVID-19.

February 3, 2020: The WIV researchers' paper submitted on January 20 is published by *Nature* online.

February 6, 2020 at 12:43:40 a.m.: Daszak sends the draft *Lancet* statement, which cites the Feb. 3 WIV paper, to Wang, Baric, and others, asking them to join as cosigners. Within hours, Wang calls him, informs Daszak that he will not sign, and requests that neither Daszak nor Baric sign.

February 6, 2020 (Afternoon): At 3:16 p.m., Daszak sends a High Important email to Baric, forwarding Wang's request, and informing Baric that the statement will be "put out in a way that doesn't link it back to our collaboration." At 4:01 p.m., Baric agrees to not sign the statement.

February 7, 2020: Dr. Li, who first shared the positive SARS test results with his classmates via WeChat, dies from COVID-19.

February 9, 2020: The death toll for COVID-19 surpasses that of SARS.

February 15, 2020: The first death from COVID-19 outside of Asia occurs in France.

February 16, 2020: WHO and PRC officials begin a nine-day "WHO-China Joint Mission on Coronavirus Disease 2019" and travel to the PRC to examine the outbreak and origin of COVID-19. Many team members, including at least one American, were not allowed to visit Wuhan.

February 18, 2020: The Daszak statement is published by the *Lancet* online, which references the letter from the U.S. National Academies of Sciences, Engineering, and Medicine he helped write, and the WIV' s February 3 paper on the origins of COVID-19. Despite drafting the letter, Daszak is not listed as the corresponding author.

February 25, 2020: For the first time, more new cases are reported outside of the PRC than within.

February 26, 2020: The WHO–China Joint Mission issues its findings, praising the PRC for its handling of the outbreak.

February 29, 2020: The first reported COVID-19 death in the United States occurs.

March 11, 2020: The WHO officially declares the COVID-19 outbreak a pandemic after 114 countries had already reported 118,000 cases, including more than 1,000 in the United States.

November 17, 2020: As a result of public pressure, Shi, Hu, and other WIV researchers publish an addendum to their February 3 paper, confirming that RaTG13 was ID4991 collected from the cave in Yunnan, and revealing they collected 293 coronaviruses from the cave between 2012 and 2015.

June 15, 2021: The presidents of the U.S. National Academies of Sciences, Engineering, and Medicine release a statement saying, "Let scientific evidence determine origin of SARS-CoV-2."

June 21, 2021: After public pressure, Daszak updates his public disclosure form for the *Lancet* statement. He does not mention the WIV or that the statement was drafted at the request of PRC researchers.

July 5, 2021: Daszak and 23 of the original 27 authors release an update to their February 2021 statement, walking back their labeling of public debate around the source of the virus as "conspiracy theories."

In a story published in the *New York Times* on May 22, 2020, by Barnes and Goldman, titled *Host of Virus Alarms Ignored by a Single-Minded President*, the authors reported that President Trump was not informed of the dangers of the COVID-19 pandemic until his Presidential Daily Briefing on the morning of January 23, 2020; and also that his Presidential Daily Briefer, Beth Sanner, "underplayed the dangers when she first mentioned the virus to him on Jan. 23." According to this story, this was confirmed by President Trump himself when he "insisted that the intelligence agencies gave him inadequate warnings about the threat of the virus, describing it as 'not a big deal.'"

This account from the *New York Times* was also confirmed by Bob Woodward in his book *Rage* (2020), on pages 229–230:

> At the White House that day [January 23, 2020] halfway through the Top Secret President's Daily Brief in the Oval Office, chief briefer Beth Sanner told President Trump at that point the intelligence community had a pretty benign take on the coronavirus.
>
> "Just like the flu," Sanner said in terms of severity. "We don't think it's as deadly as SARS. We do not believe this is going to be a global pandemic," she said.

Amazing! Astounding! Excuse Me! Are You Serious?

The American people spend about $82 billion per year on so-called intelligence, and that is the best the U.S. Spooks Establishment can do? This is criminal malpractice by the U.S. Spooks Establishment at the very minimum.

And as I will further argue in this chapter, it was criminal sabotage by the U.S. Spooks Establishment and the U.S. Scientific/Medical Establishments (1) not to have briefed President Trump until January 23, 2020 about the COVID-19 pandemic; and also to (2) underplay its significance and existential dangers. These conclusions and the following analysis are not at all intended to excuse President Trump's criminal mismanagement of the COVID pandemic once he was informed about it by the U.S. Spooks Establishment on the morning of January 23, 2020.

As a matter of fact, on the very next morning of January 24, 2020—24 hours later— working on my own in my office and after a very brief period of research on the internet and free of charge and as a public service, I was able to conclude that COVID-19 was an offensive biological warfare weapon that had leaked out of the Wuhan BSL-4 with gain-of-function properties that rendered it existentially dangerous. And I had surmised those conclusions with my biowarfare friends one week before, on January 17, 2020, as indicated by my email to them reprinted earlier in chapter 1 of this book.

Therefore, that very morning on January 24, 2020, about 24 hours after the Presidential Daily Briefing of Trump, I put out my worldwide *Alert* to that effect that you can read in the beginning pages of this book. Obviously, something is seriously wrong here! Things do not add up! Let me analyze them as best I can based upon the evidence as of now in the public record, adduced above in the House Minority Report *Timeline*, that I find to be eminently credible after careful examination of it, and based upon, and corroborated by, other sources in the public record.

If I knew all these facts as of the morning of January 24, 2020, just by sitting there in my office and on my computer doing research on the internet, then of course the U.S. Spooks Establishment and the U.S. Scientific/Medical Establishments must have known these exact same facts long before I did: that COVID-19 is an offensive biological warfare weapon with gain-of function properties that rendered it existentially dangerous, and that it had leaked out of the Wuhan BSL-4. Otherwise, why are we, the American people, spending more than $82 billion per year on so-called intelligence by the U.S. Spooks Establishment—and billions more dollars every year on the U.S. Scientific/Medical Establishment that contains its own "Intelligence" Service? When I could figure out these facts all by myself free of charge and as a public service just working on my office computer over the internet? Give me a break! Give me the $82 billion! I can do a better job than all of them put together! In fact, I did so by going public with my conclusions on January 24, 2020, which *they* never did.

I have been up against the U.S. Spooks Establishment from the very beginning of my career as a lawyer in 1977. U.S. Spooks are not dumb. They know exactly what they're doing! Indeed, Harvard was overrun with Spooks when I was a student there from 1971 to 1978. And Harvard has been overrun with Spooks from at least when the Harvard faculty returned to campus after fighting the Axis powers with the OSS at the end of World War II. Nothing wrong with that! Commendable! But then the Harvard OSS faculty Spooks recruited the next generation of Spooks for the CIA—JFK's *The Best and the Brightest* (1972) that gave us the Vietnam War.

That Harvard Spooks recruitment process still goes on today. The same is true for all the other Ivy League universities. Most leading universities have resident Spook professors on their faculties who recruit their top students for the Spooks Establishment. We are now dealing with the sons and the daughters of JFK's *The Best and The Brightest* in the U.S. Spooks Establishment and elsewhere throughout the American foreign affairs and war/defense and counterterrorism establishments.

For example, the current Chief Spook of Biden's U.S. Spooks Establishment is Avril Haines, who was behind me in college at the University of Chicago, one of the top liberal arts and science colleges in the country, if not the world. Q.E.D. Having dated University of Chicago college women when I was an undergraduate there from 1968 to 1971, I can assure you they are all as smart as a whip! Otherwise, they would not have been admitted. Despite her yoga-adept reputation, Haines must not be underestimated in her capacity for evil. She has played a decisive role in covering up the origins of the COVID-19 pandemic coming out of the Wuhan BSL-4.

Now let me return to the critical elements of the *Timeline* quoted extensively above:

> **Late Aug./Early Sept. 2019:** One or more researchers become accidentally infected with SARS-CoV-2, which was either collected in the Yunnan cave, or the result of gain-offunction research at the WIV. They travel by metro in central Wuhan, spreading the virus.

Sept. 12, 2019: At 12:00 a.m. local time, Wuhan University issues a statement announcing lab inspections. Between 2:00 a.m. and 3:00 a.m., the WIV's viral sequence and sample database is taken offline. At 7:09 p.m., the WIV publishes a tender requesting bids to provide security services at the WNBL.

Sept.–Oct. 2019: Car traffic at hospitals surrounding the WIV headquarters, as well as the shuttle stop for the WNBL, shows a steady increase before hitting its highest levels in 2.5 years. Baidu search terms for COVID-19-related symptoms increase in a corresponding manner.

I submit that the U.S. Spooks Establishment knew no later than mid-September 2019 that there had been a leak of an existentially dangerous offensive biological warfare weapon from the Wuhan BSL-4, which is China's Fort Detrick. The U.S. Spooks Establishment had the benefit of NSA communications intercepts, NRO satellite imagery, et cetera, et cetera, ad nauseam, and their own Spooks in situ at Wuhan reporting back to them about what was going on at that Wuhan BSL-4—China's Fort Detrick. The U.S. Spooks Establishment had China's first Fort Detrick at the Wuhan BSL-4 intercepted and infiltrated all up and down their kazoos. They probably knew who was flushing the Wuhan BSL-4 toilets at the time of the swoosh!

Then I surmise that the U.S. Spooks Establishment contacted Fort Detrick in order to know exactly what they were dealing with at China's Fort Detrick. At the same time, the U.S. Spooks Establishment called up on their computers that NIAID/NIH contract at the UNC BSL-3 with the Chinese Bat Queen from the Wuhan BSL-4 and Fort Detrick for definitive confirmation. The U.S. Spooks Establishment easily figured this all out around mid-September 2019, exactly as I did on the morning of January 24, 2020, just sitting in my office with nothing more than a computer and the internet.

Likewise, in mid-September 2019, I am sure that the U.S. Spooks Establishment called up Tony Fauci at NIAID and his boss, Francis Collins at NIH, and told them that something was seriously awry at the Wuhan BSL-4: "Houston, we have a problem!" I am sure Tony Fauci called up Wuhan on his NIAID computer to find the contract that he had with Ralph Baric at the UNC BSL-3 with the Chinese Bat Queen working there from the Wuhan

BSL-4 along with Fort Detrick. Likewise, Francis Collins called up the same contract on his NIH computer. Both Fauci/NIAID and Collins/NIH were funding that project at the UNC BSL-3 with the Chinese Bat Queen from the Wuhan BSL-4 and Fort Detrick to do their gain-of-function work on a synthetic SARS coronavirus, as I have already established in the earlier pages of this book.

Even CDC director Redfield admitted as much in his CNN interview on March 26, 2021:

> Robert Redfield, former director of the Centers for Disease Control and Prevention, told CNN Friday he believes the virus that causes COVID-19 was accidentally released from a lab in Wuhan, China.
>
> He offered no explanation for this idea other than to say as a virologist, he does not believe the virus could have been so contagious when it jumped directly from an animal to a person. Instead, he contends it was manipulated in a Wuhan research laboratory to become more contagious and then accidentally released by a worker in September or October 2019, a few months before coming to public attention.
>
> —*USA Today,* March 26, 2021

Of course they all knew way back then! Both the U.S. Spooks Establishment and the U.S. Scientific/Medical Establishments knew full well no later than mid-September 2019 that COVID-19 was an existentially dangerous offensive biowarfare weapon with gain-of-function properties that had leaked out of the Wuhan BSL-4, China's Fort Detrick. Do the U.S. Spooks Establishment and the U.S. Scientific/Medical Establishments really expect the American people to believe that they were not keeping close tabs with a fine-tooth comb on what was happening at China's first Fort Detrick?

Why, then, did they not alert President Trump in mid-September 2019? Why did they not alert the U.S. Congress in mid-September 2019? Why did they not alert the American people in mid-September 2019? Why did they not alert the entire world in mid-September 2019 so that we all could have taken adequate precautions to protect ourselves from COVID-19 while it was still in Wuhan, and could have been contained there around the middle of September 2019?

This entire worldwide pandemic could have been prevented by the U.S. Spooks Establishment and the U.S. Scientific/Medical Establishments taking prompt and effective action as of no later than mid-September 2019 to have the awesome and formidable powers of the United States government make sure that the Chinese Communist Dictator-on-Steroids Chairman President Xi drastically contained the spread of the pandemic to Wuhan and to China—or else! Steps could have been taken to read the proverbial riot act to the Chinese Communist Dictator-on-Steroids Chairman President Xi that he had better immediately and effectively stop and contain the spread of the pandemic in mid-September 2019 to Wuhan and to China! Instead, the U.S. Spooks Establishment and the U.S. Scientific/Medical Establishments said and did nothing! They all let the global COVID-19 pandemic proceed forthwith from Wuhan, China. Why?

This criminal nonfeasance by the U.S. Spooks Establishment and the U.S. Scientific/Medical Establishments by not doing anything to prevent or stop the worldwide COVID-19 pandemic when they had evidence of it by mid-September 2019 can be explained by the fact that the U.S. Scientific/Medical Establishments and the U.S. Spooks Establishment were, and still are, up to their eyeballs in developing every type of hideous offensive Nazi biowarfare death science dirty work weapon possibly imaginable at their own BSL-3s and their own BSL-4s, like the Wuhan BSL-4 and China's Fort Detrick, including at Fort Detrick itself.

They also knew that this Nazi death science dirty work included the very UNC BSL-3 where COVID-19 was manufactured with the Bat Queen from the Wuhan BSL-4—China's Fort Detrick—and Fort Detrick itself. I have already established that in the introduction to this book: 13,000 American Nazi Death Scientists Hard at Work as of 2015! I am not going to repeat any of that analysis here.

So the U.S. Spooks Establishment and the U.S. Scientific/Medical Establishments said and did nothing and let the global COVID-19 pandemic proceed forthwith from Wuhan, China. CYA! They were all trying to cover up their own joint violations of the Biological Weapons Convention of 1972 and of my Biological Weapons Anti-Terrorism Act of 1989 that would subject them all to life imprisonment. And for those exact same reasons, the U.S. Scientific/Medical Establishments and the U.S. Spooks Establishment have been lying and covering up and spinning and disinforming the American people and Congress and the world about the COVID-19 pandemic and then about their Nazi COVID-19 Frankenshots right from the very get-go. They all fear life imprisonment under my BWATA if the truth ever gets out to the American people and to the peoples of the world, who will undoubtedly demand all of their heads on platters.

This, then, can account for the fabled tabletop exercise *cum* war-game at Johns Hopkins University on October 18, 2019, titled *Event 2001*, which uncannily simulated a global coronavirus pandemic. They knew full well that the COVID-19 pandemic was coming, and they were dry-running how to "manage" it while doing nothing to prevent it. They just let the worldwide COVID-19 pandemic happen to the American people and the peoples of the world. If the U.S. Spooks Establishment and the U.S. Scientific/Medical Establishments had acted promptly and effectively to alert President Trump and the U.S. Congress and the American people and the people of the world about the existential dangers of COVID 19 in mid-September 2019 at the United Nations Security Council, like the United States government had done during the Cuban Missile Crisis of 1962, we very well might not have had the global COVID-19 pandemic here in the United States or elsewhere around the world.

Meanwhile, the Chinese Communist Dictator-on-Steroids Chairman President Xi allowed millions of Chinese to leave the epicenter of the pandemic at Wuhan China in mid-January 2020 for the celebration of the Chinese New Year. Large numbers of them traveled all over the world, bringing COVID-19 with them—including here to the University of Illinois at Urbana-Champaign. The dunderheads in the campus administration and the Champaign-Urbana Health Authority did not place returning Wuhan Chinese students into the two-week quarantine, as required by the CDC health protocol at the time, but instead let them wander around campus and town and into classes with flimsy face masks (on their honor to wear them), thus spreading COVID-19 all over this community. Community spread, indeed! Courtesy of the University of Illinois.

Chairman President Xi knew full well that the Wuhan BSL-4 was an offensive biological warfare weapons factory. It was China's first Fort Detrick. Chairman President Xi himself was out there at the Wuhan BSL-4. He knew exactly what they were doing there: research, development, testing, manufacturing, and stockpiling of every hideous type of offensive Nazi biological warfare death science dirty work weapon that is possibly imaginable—just like Fort Detrick. Chairman President Xi wanted his own Fort Detrick in order to keep up with the Big Boys in Weapons of Mass Destruction: the Americans, the British, and the Russians. Hence, China's Wuhan BSL-4.

And when Chairman President Xi let millions of Chinese leave the city of Wuhan and China at the height of the pandemic in mid-January 2020, he knew full well that they would spread COVID-19 all over the world. Clearly, this was a Nuremberg Crime Against Humanity that was inflicted by Chairman President Xi and the Chinese Communist government, verging on outright genocide against all humanity: "murder, extermination . . . and other inhumane acts committed against any civilian population." I guess Chairman President Xi's calculation was that "misery loves company." Since COVID-19 was already going to cause a COVID-19 pandemic in China, Chairman President Xi decided to release and unleash COVID-19 upon the rest of the world and create a global pandemic. I suspect that as Chairman President Xi saw it, instead of China sinking into the sea of COVID-19 all by itself, the entire world would be in the same boat, sinking into the sea of COVID-19 with the PRC. That way, China wouldn't lose its competitive edge with the rest of the world, and especially with the United States, Russia, and Europe.

As of this writing, well over one million American citizens have died because of this criminal sabotage by the U.S. Spooks Establishment and the U.S. Scientific/Medical Establishment. In previous chapters of this book, I described how the American people can begin to hold them all criminally accountable in United States courts for their criminal, homicidal, and genocidal behavior. We the People of the United States of America must act now to bring them all to justice and stop the COVID-19 pandemic and their Nazi COVID-19 Frankenshots in this country and then the rest of the world. We must not go quietly into that dark night! I, for one, will not!

. . .

CHAPTER 18

THE FRANKENSHOT: USING THE LAW TO CHASE THOSE RESPONSIBLE FOR HARMING THE AMERICAN PEOPLE: A SPECIAL INTERVIEW WITH FRANCIS A. BOYLE (NOVEMBER 28, 2021)

Story-at-a-Glance

The Biological Weapons Anti-Terrorism Act of 1989 imposes fines and prison sentences on anyone who "knowingly develops, produces, stockpiles, transfers, acquires, retains, or possesses any biological agent, toxin, or delivery system for use as a weapon."

The problem we face today is that our federal government has been captured by forces that seek to destroy the U.S. from within. As such, we cannot trust the federal judiciary to prosecute and hold those responsible for the pandemic and the toxic COVID shots accountable

To circumvent the corrupted federal judiciary, we need to focus on locally elected prosecutors instead. Depending on the state, they may go by titles such as district attorney, states attorney, prosecuting attorney, or county attorney.

Organize locally to find people willing, as a group, to call on your local, elected district attorney to convene a grand jury and indict the individuals suspected of being involved in the creation of SARS-CoV-2, and those responsible for the COVID shots.

The charge that applies is "murder and conspiracy to commit murder." For starters, 15 researchers listed on a key paper can be indicted, plus those who funded the research. Those to be indicted in relation to the COVID shots include the chief executive officers, chief operating officers, and chief scientific officers of Pfizer, BioNTech, Moderna, and Johnson & Johnson.

Dr. Joseph Mercola: Welcome, everyone, this is Dr. Mercola, helping you take control of your health; and today we are pleased to have a repeat guest, Francis Boyle, who has been on twice previously—most notably at the beginning of all this craziness, when we interviewed him for insights on the origins of the SARS-CoV-2 virus and the fact that it was likely not derived from nature but was engineered in a lab. At the time, any mention of that would get you thrown in jail—at least social media jail—or de-platformed, and of course since earlier this year, that has become known as the reality of what has happened, and perhaps Dr. Boyle's investigations have been vindicated. So he's back with us to explore some of the ways and the strategies he's come up with, with respect to how to prosecute these individuals for what they're doing, because they're in complete, direct violation of legislation or treaties that he's written, actually, probably close to 50 years ago now or 40 years ago. So he's going to enlighten us and give us more information about the details of that process. So, welcome, and thank you for joining us today.

FAB: Well, thank you very much for having me on, Dr. Mercola. And yes—

Dr. Joseph Mercola: Oh, if I can interrupt. I'm sorry, I forgot to give your credentials. You're an attorney who graduated magna cum laude from Harvard Law School, went to the University of Chicago in my neck of the woods when I was around there at that time, and now are back at the University of Illinois where you're a full professor of law and have been for quite a number of decades. And obviously, a pioneer in exposing the fraud of the origin of the coronavirus. So I'm sorry for the interruption, but I forgot to enlighten people.

FAB: No, that's fine, and not to toot my own horn, but yes, I did draft the U.S. domestic implementing legislation for the Biological Weapons Convention, known as the Biological Weapons Anti-Terrorism Act of 1989, that was passed unanimously by both Houses of the United States Congress and signed into law by President George Bush Sr. with the approval of the United States Department of Justice. And I did want to thank you profoundly for being one of the first media people to let me appear on your program to point out that COVID-19 was in fact an offensive biological warfare weapon with gain-of-function properties that was existentially dangerous when, as you know, the entire scientific establishment here in America was discounting that and saying that that was nothing more than a conspiracy theory and fake news. So I want to thank you for that. I thought it was a public service, the two previous interviews we did.

Dr. Joseph Mercola: Yeah, well, and this is taking it a step further because obviously there are enormous crimes against humanity that have been committed that will likely exceed the atrocities of World War II because of what's—

FAB: You're right about that. Yes.

Dr. Joseph Mercola: —what's been implemented.

FAB: We can go through that in more detail as the interview progresses, yes.

Dr. Joseph Mercola: OK. So I think in September, you gave a presentation to some group and outlined a process where a strategy, not so much a process, but a strategy that could be implemented to get the treaty that you wrote enforced, because there is no way in this world that the federal authorities will ever, ever seek to enforce that treaty, because they are totally captured. So you have a strategy that focuses more on local attorney generals, state [attorney] generals. So can you summarize what that plan is?

FAB: Right. And you are correct, all federal authorities are in the tank here with Biden and what I call these "Frankenshots." There's no other word for them. Years ago when I did work with the Council for Responsible Genetics, they were against biological weapons. I handled that, and they had another key campaign against genetically modified organisms for foods, which everyone called "Frankenfoods." So I thought it would be appropriate to call these Frankenshots and not dignify them with the word *vaccines*, wherever you stand on vaccines. But you're right—all the federal authorities are in the tank here for the Frankenshots. In my opinion, that would also include federal judges. They are part of the federal system. I've been appearing before federal judges since 1982 on matters of courage, integrity, and principles. I can only think of one federal judge who gave us a fair trial. So we can't rely upon federal judges to pull our chestnuts out of the fire.

And that then gets me to the Tenth Amendment to the United States Constitution: "The powers not delegated to the United States by the Constitution, nor prohibited by it to the States, are reserved to the States respectively, or to the people." So we, in my opinion, cannot rely on federal judges to pull our chestnuts out of the fire, they're not going to do it. So we have to do this ourselves. So my proposal is this: that we have to—the American people at a state, local, community basis—have to go to our local prosecutors, that is, states attorneys, district attorneys, county attorneys, attorneys general, any local prosecutor. And the last I read, there were well over 400 of these in the country. These local prosecutors are not part of the federal system. They have been empowered by the Tenth Amendment to the United States Constitution.

They are democratically elected by the people of their community. Federal judges are not elected by anyone. They're appointed by the president, and once they're on their bench with life tenure and they can only be removed by impeachment, which is almost impossible, and their salaries cannot be reduced, they're like God Almighty up there sitting on these federal benches. Not so state and local prosecutors—they're accountable to the people of the community. So what I am recommending is two steps: one, on the Frankenshots, and another on the COVID pandemic. And let me start with the COVID pandemic first, the origins of the COVID pandemic.

I would recommend that people organize together in your community and go to all of your local prosecutors—you know who they are, you voted for them—and demand that they convene a grand jury to seek the indictment for murder, and conspiracy to commit murder, for those people who were responsible for COVID-19.

Now, Doctor, we've discussed this before, that article "SARS-like Cluster of Circulating Bat Coronavirus Pose Threat for Human Emergence," and that is the smoking gun on who is behind COVID-19. Who's on that contract? [Vineet] Menachery from the University of North Carolina, their BSL-3, other people there from the University of North Carolina, including [Ralph] Baric. We also know that [Peter] Daszak was working with Baric on this entire project. A person from the Food and Drug Administration. Let me repeat that, Doctor. A person from the Food and Drug Administration was involved in the research, development, and testing of COVID-19. These are the exact same people, the Food and Drug Administration, who are authorizing all of these Frankenshots, including last week for kids from 5 to 12. Trick or treat on America's youth.

So they developed this biological warfare weapon, and now they're approving all the Frankenshots. This is a one-two punch here against the American people. I'm not going to go through the foreign institutes involved in this, but it also says on this exact same project, the Harvard Medical School. I repeat that, the Harvard Medical School. Well, I'm a triple alumnus of Harvard; and Harvard Medical School is involved in the research, development, and testing of COVID-19 as an offensive biological warfare weapon. We also know that Harvard was a sponsoring institution of the Wuhan BSL-4. That Wuhan BSL-4 is China's Fort Detrick. There's no doubt about it in my mind. OK?

And who is the current director of the CDC? Biden's director of the CDC? [Rochelle] Walensky. She is from the Harvard Medical School. You can't believe anything the CDC is telling you or Walensky is telling you—they're bald-faced liars, and they always have been. Indeed, the CDC has been involved in the research, development, and testing of offensive biological warfare weapons, at least as I've been able to determine from official government documents, from the early 1980s. And they then—the CDC and Walensky—have recently ratified the FDA approval of the Frankenshots. Then, in addition, of course, on the SARS project here is Shi Zhengli, the Bat Queen from the Wuhan Institute of Virology, the Chinese Fort Detrick. It says it right on there. They're all working in cahoots with each other.

And also, then, if you read the footnotes of this article, they are working with our own Fort Detrick, OK? So they're all in cahoots. You have Chinese Fort Detrick, you have our Fort Detrick, you have the UNC [University of North Carolina] BSL-3, Harvard Medical School, all working together to research, develop, and test—also with the Wuhan BSL-4—COVID-19. Who has funded all this? The contract makes it quite clear that it was funded by the National Institutes of Health, then directed by Francis Collins. He knew full well what was going on here. He was over there cooperating with China and the Wuhan BSL-4. And also NIAID, the National Institutes for Allergy and Infectious Diseases, Tony Fauci. He's on here too. They were involved in this.

Indeed, it was the Reagan Administration that first got involved in the abuse of DNA genetic engineering for biological warfare weapons purposes that first compelled the Council for Responsible Genetics and me to draft and lobby through Congress my Biological Weapons Anti-Terrorism Act of 1989, approved unanimously by both Houses of Congress and signed into law by Bush Sr. with the approval of the Department of Justice. And right at that time, Reagan, under the influence of his neoconservatives who believed in biological warfare and ethnic-specific biological warfare, put Tony Fauci in charge of this entire Nazi program. And about 95% of all this Nazi-type biological warfare research has been done by, and under the auspices of, Tony Fauci.

So what I am recommending here, then, is for everyone to go to their local prosecutors, have them convene a grand jury, and present the case for murder and conspiracy to commit murder for everyone on this contract, including Daszak, as it's been reported that he's been working in cahoots with all of them on this. Now I was originally hired here in 1978 to teach Criminal Law, and I taught Criminal Law for seven or eight years until I moved over to teach International Human Rights Law, but I still do criminal work, both prosecution and defense. And Anglo-American common law has a definition for murder that is applicable in all states of the United States except Louisiana that has the Napoleonic Civil Code, and I haven't studied that. But all the other states have the Anglo-American common-law definition of murder, and that definition is the unlawful killing of a human being with malice aforethought.

All right, let's parse that down. Unlawful, all right—all these individuals I just mentioned here on this contract, including Daszak, were involved in the research, development, testing, and stockpiling of biological warfare weapons in clear-cut violation of my Biological Weapons Anti-Terrorism Act of 1989. Killing of human beings: Doctor, you're free to disagree with me in good faith—we've had good-faith disagreements before—but I think the number of Americans who have been killed, murdered by COVID-19, is well over a million. This is just a substantial undercount, as far as I can tell.

Dr. Joseph Mercola: If I could just jump in.

FAB: Yes, go ahead.

Dr. Joseph Mercola: I do think it's over a million, but that would be if you included those who have been killed by what you call Frankenshots, but I think Vladimir Zelenko [a Ukrainian-American family physician and author known for promoting a three-drug combination for COVID-19] more accurately calls it the "kill shot," making it simpler and easier to remember because the kill shots clearly—200-, 300-, 400-, even 500,000 people have died from it in the United States alone. The reason that you have to be careful about the COVID-19 deaths calculated by the CDC is that they've perverted the definition of a death. So you could have a positive PCR test, and have terminal cancer, die in a motorcycle accident and you'd still be counted as a COVID death, which is not true. You died *with* COVID, not *from* it. So anyway, it's a moot issue.

FAB: Well, I was dealing with figures compiled and reported by the *Financial Times* on excess deaths from COVID, but—

Dr. Joseph Mercola: Isn't the *Financial Times* U.K.?

FAB: U.K. I subscribe to them to get a foreign perspective.

Dr. Joseph Mercola: They have stats on—

FAB: Let me—we can disagree about the numbers, but in any—

Dr. Joseph Mercola: Well, it's a moot issue. It's still over a million.

FAB: It's a moot issue, right.

Dr. Joseph Mercola: Yeah.

FAB: And then with malice aforethought. *Malice aforethought* is a legal term of art. It would take me three, four, five different class sessions to go through it all, and I'm not going to do that here. But one element of malice aforethought is reckless endangerment of human beings, and clearly they knew, if you read the contracts and the studies, they knew—all these people that I mentioned to you, including Fauci and Collins, who by the way just resigned because the proverbial *merde* was about to hit the fan on Collins. Pardon my French. But they knew that this gain-of-function work was existentially dangerous, and they did it anyway. And clearly that constitutes reckless endangerment of human beings, malice aforethought.

And so you have all the elements there for murder, and then conspiracy to commit murder. In common law, conspiracy is two people getting together to agree to do an unlawful act, violation of my statute, or a lawful act by illegal means. So I think we have all these people at least for murder, and conspiracy to commit murder; and my advice is that if you have lost a loved one or a friend living in the territorial jurisdiction of any of these local prosecutors, they would have jurisdiction to convene a grand jury and seek indictments for murder and conspiracy to commit murder against all of these people. Now let me move on to the Frankenshots.

Dr. Joseph Mercola: Well, before you move on—

FAB: I'm sorry. Yes. Go ahead.

Dr. Joseph Mercola: Who would you target as the result of the grand jury indictments? Would it be Fauci, for sure, Peter Daszak, probably Francis Collins, but are there any other specifics? Because you can't just generically have this indictment. It has to be the specific individuals.

FAB: That's correct, and they've got 12 different people listed by name on this contract at the UNC BSL-3. You are correct.

Dr. Joseph Mercola: OK, so Ralph Baric.

FAB: So I would go after all of them, including the Bat Queen, for murder and conspiracy.

Dr. Joseph Mercola: But she's a Chinese citizen.

FAB: Right. That's correct, but she did this here in the United States, so we would have jurisdiction over her. Remember, they had her working at the UNC BSL-3 along with Fort Detrick. Now, there are no names for Fort Detrick, so I can't really say who that would be, but you have all these names listed on the—

Dr. Joseph Mercola: OK, so whoever's listed on that contract.

FAB: That's right. And Francis Collins and Tony Fauci and Peter Daszak, right? Those would be the people I'd go after to start.

Dr. Joseph Mercola: OK. All right, good.

FAB: Now, let's get on to the Frankenshots, and again, with all due respect, I prefer Frankenshots because they're using DNA genetic engineering of the messenger RNA, et cetera. But call them what you want. Yes, they are kill shots.

Dr. Joseph Mercola: It's the end result.

FAB: Analogize it. People are aware of what Frankenfoods are.

Dr. Joseph Mercola: Yeah.

FAB: And we were opposed to Frankenfoods. I did not handle that legal work for the Council of Responsible Genetics because I was busy doing biological warfare work, but I was fully aware of all the work, and I'm sure you were.

Dr. Joseph Mercola: Yeah, and for those who don't know, you were real ahead of the game, because that work that you refer to was the absolute very first effort to put a halt and a block on this effort. That was the first professional effort.

FAB: That's correct.

Dr. Joseph Mercola: Nothing was done before that. That was in the '80s.

FAB: That's correct.

Dr. Joseph Mercola: I mean, the real work to get done—

FAB: Starting 1983, Doctor. Yes.

Dr. Joseph Mercola: Yeah. They were the absolute first group.

FAB: Back then, they were called the Committee.

Dr. Joseph Mercola: They were the pioneers.

FAB: And I point out, they had some of the top life scientists in the world involved in the Council—Harvard, MIT, Sloan Kettering, elsewhere. They lined up some of the top people in the world to oppose GMO food. They did the pioneering work. I'm sure you have probably in your library our newsletter called *GeneWatch*, and so I would read that to find out what they were doing there, as well as any biological warfare work that I was doing as well. Sure.

Dr. Joseph Mercola: Mm-hmm {affirmative}.

FAB: All right, now to deal with the Frankenshots. Unlawful killing of human beings with malice aforethought. OK, unlawful. Here we have a blatant, obvious violation of the Nuremberg Code on Medical Experimentation, which is a Nuremberg Crime that the United States government prosecuted Nazi doctors at Nuremberg and executed some of them. Indeed, you can read all of this in the Nuremberg *Medical/Doctor's* Judgment.

Indeed, I heard from some doctor saying, "Well, this really destroys your credibility to say that the United States government actually executed doctors." And I said, "You know, you never studied the Nuremberg *Medical/Doctor's* case; the list of executed doctors is right there at the end." That's correct. And what we're seeing now with these Frankenshots for children, this is Dr. Mengele at Auschwitz all over again. That's where this Nuremberg Code on Medical Experimentation came from.

Second, unlawful killing of human beings is the Nuremberg Charter, Judgment, and Principles. The Charter, 1945; the Judgment, 1946; and the Principles of 1950, defining a crime against humanity. You pointed this out, a crime against humanity—yes, that is correct. In the Nuremberg Charter, Judgment, and Principles, a crime against humanity is defined in part as "murder, extermination . . . or other inhumane acts committed against a civilian population." That's what's going on right now against the American population. And, Doctor, I should point out that provision in there, crime against humanity, was put in there to deal with precisely and exactly the Nazi persecution of German-Jewish citizens, OK?

That's exactly what the Biden Administration today is doing to all American citizens, a crime against humanity as defined by the Nuremberg Charter, Judgment, and Principles. And again, we executed Nazi leaders at Nuremberg for committing crimes against humanity in conjunction with either crimes against peace or war crimes. But since that time, the connection there, that they have to actually be in war, has been eliminated. So crimes against humanity stand on their own. You can also read this in the Rome Statute for the International Criminal Court. Now, the United States government is not a party to the Rome Statute, but it simply reflects customary international criminal law today. All right, killing—I'm sorry, go ahead, you had a question.

Dr. Joseph Mercola: Yeah, before we go on, I just want to wrap this point up because I'm curious. To the best of your knowledge, have any individuals ever been prosecuted or even convicted under the Nuremberg Charter, even the Helsinki Act or Accord?

FAB: I did defend Captain Dr. Yolanda Hewitt-Vaughn, who refused to give the Frankenshots in Gulf War I for anthrax and botulin. And I came to her defense in February 1991; she was court-martialed for this, facing five years. And I helped defend her. I was part of the team, and the expert on the Nuremberg Code of Medical Experimentation. And we argued that quite extensively in her court-martial at Fort Leonard Wood, in which I appeared before two satellite dishes saying that Bush Sr.; Dick Cheney, the secretary of defense, Colin Powell, who's now been adulated all over the country; and Norman Schwarzkopf, General Norman Schwarzkopf, have perpetrated a Nuremberg Crime on our own troops for violating the Nuremberg Code on Medical Experimentation.

I was told that went out nationwide, made it all the way to the White House by a lawyer who was there, and they were all shaken up. Later on, Senator Jay Rockefeller held hearings on this, and he also accused Bush and the rest of them of committing a Nuremberg Crime on our own troops. Now, at the time we didn't know what the consequences would be, but within the next two years, it came to my attention that the Gulf War Sickness—and the Pentagon still lies about these figures—out of about 500,000 U.S. troops inoculated with these two Frankenshots, 11,000 were killed and 100,000 were disabled, and those were healthy young men and women in the U.S. Armed Forces.

Well, you can extrapolate from there, Doctor, what's going to happen with these current Frankenshots. They're even more dangerous than the Frankenshots during Gulf War I. The figures are mind-blowing if you just sit down, and that is a floor, it is not a ceiling, because the current Frankenshots are far more dangerous.

Dr. Joseph Mercola: That's a whole separate discussion, but just to clear it up, I guess you used this as part of your defense for that soldier who was being prosecuted, the Nuremberg Code—

FAB: She was a medical doctor.

Dr. Joseph Mercola: I get that, but from the best of your knowledge, that was more of a defense, but no one's been specifically prosecuted under Nuremberg or Helsinki since those treaties were enacted, subsequent to the actual Nuremberg Trial itself.

FAB: Not that I'm aware of, but they are still valid and binding and on the books.

Dr. Joseph Mercola: Yeah, I know, but it's just curious. Seventy years later, no one's been prosecuted under this treaty, no one.

FAB: Not that I am aware of.

Dr. Joseph Mercola: Yeah, that's just—

FAB: But in the Captain Doctor Hewitt-Vaughn case, it is one case I know where these arguments were made. There was another case I was not involved in preventing mandatory anthrax shots on U.S. troops, and a federal district judge did stop that, but that's about it, that I am aware of. No one's been prosecuted. But let me go back, then, to the Frankenshots, the third element, malice aforethought. All right, and here one other element of malice aforethought is an intention to inflict death or grievous bodily harm. Well, let's give these people the benefit of the doubt and say, "Well, we didn't intend to kill anyone with our Frankenshots." Well, okay, but you did intend to inflict grievous bodily harm on human beings, and it killed human beings, large numbers of them.

Again, we do not have an exact estimate, and it could be, as you said, several hundred thousand, we just don't know. But they clearly intended and knew that this would inflict grievous bodily harm on human beings. Just look at what they've already conceded and reported that the adverse effects would be—the list is astounding. So they knew this, and they did it anyway. So my position here, then, would be, if you believe you have lost a loved one or a friend as a result of the Frankenshots, again, go into your local prosecutor and ask your local prosecutor to pursue before a grand jury indictments for murder, and conspiracy to commit murder, against the chief executive officer, chief operating officer, chief scientific officer for Pfizer, BioNTech, Moderna, and Johnson & Johnson.

By the way, J&J are the same people who gave us the opioid epidemic, killing about 500,000 Americans, and also gave us talcum in baby powder.

Dr. Joseph Mercola: Asbestos. Asbestos.

FAB: That was giving women cancer of the ovaries. So my advice again, seek these indictments for murder, and conspiracy to commit murder, at least against those three individuals at the top of these four companies whose Frankenshots are now in circulation here in the United States.

Dr. Joseph Mercola: So if this strategy is to be effective, it would be wise to empower the people who are doing this request to go with resources. So I've heard you mention in previous interviews that there's a paper you have written that summarizes this strategy, but there's also a recent book that goes into great detail and with many references. Is it the—

FAB: Yeah, let me get that book.

Dr. Joseph Mercola: —*Search for the Origin of COVID-19* book?

FAB: Well, the one I just read, Markson, *What Really Happened in Wuhan.*

Dr. Joseph Mercola: Okay, *What Really Happened.* OK, there are a few of them out there.

FAB: I think there's another book coming out. I haven't read it yet, but I read through this book, and I think she's got it all there. She didn't deal with the Frankenshots, but she has, I think, a valid summary of all the evidence that has been compiled so far involving all these individuals. For the first set of indictments I called for, yes. As for the second, I think Robert Kennedy Jr., his Children's Health Defense—and you've done good work on this too—have compiled—

Dr. Joseph Mercola: Well, Robert Kennedy—

FAB: —this information the best they can.

Dr. Joseph Mercola: Yeah, and he's written a new book that will be released after our interview gets aired, and that is—

FAB: That's correct. I listened to his podcast on the book.

Dr. Joseph Mercola: Oh my gosh.

FAB: And it seems to me, he's—

Dr. Joseph Mercola: I've read the entire book.

FAB: I haven't read the book yet.

Dr. Joseph Mercola: Yeah, well, it was only given to about a half a dozen people prerelease, so I was fortunate to get it, and it's beyond outstanding and is an indictment for Anthony Fauci, and it is hard to imagine how he will survive this exposure and not result in a resignation. You could tell, Rand Paul interviewed him yesterday, the day before this interview, in Congress, and you could just listen to his voice. But even more important, you can view the hundreds and thousands of comments that were posted on this YouTube video, and it was shocking because I didn't see one, not one, that didn't agree that Fauci was a villain. And that he should be—

FAB: He should be indicted for murder, and conspiracy to commit murder.

Dr. Joseph Mercola: Absolutely.

FAB: Just speaking as a law professor, right.

Dr. Joseph Mercola: Yeah, he's a sociopath, and I mean, he's just—

FAB: He clearly is, yes.

Dr. Joseph Mercola: So anyway, I think his days are numbered.

FAB: And I don't have the book yet. I've ordered it, and I did listen to RFK Jr.'s podcast on it, but it seems to me there's going to be a lot more evidence, from what you're telling me and what he is saying is in there.

Dr. Joseph Mercola: Oh, there are thousands of references.

FAB: That will support what I've been saying here, yes.

Dr. Joseph Mercola: Yeah.

FAB: And it can be used to take to your state or local prosecutor to seek the indictments that I have recommended here today for murder, and conspiracy to commit murder. Likewise, I also want to point out this: as we know, Bill Gates is an investor in BioNTech.

Dr. Joseph Mercola: Mm-hmm [affirmative].

FAB: Right now, he's been very careful to stand back and stay out of this, but with the development of more information as to what Gates was involved in, we very well might be able to pursue an indictment for conspiracy to commit murder. But right now, I'm just throwing that out here. Right now, I don't have all that evidence, and when the prosecutors convene grand juries, they can subpoena these people and subpoena *duces tecum*—not only show up themselves, but bring whatever evidence they have. Their office files, their emails, et cetera, sure, that can be done. So I'd think Gates needs to be considered. I'm not recommending he be indicted at this time because I haven't seen enough evidence there implicating him, but since he is a well-known investor in BioNTech, sure.

Dr. Joseph Mercola: Well, Bobby Kennedy goes into detail, great detail, in the book with Gates.

FAB: Right, that's my understanding.

Dr. Joseph Mercola: Even an extension to Rockefeller, whose strategy he followed and implemented almost a century later because they had similar paths, and they were both vilified massively by the public and had incredibly poor public images until they shifted to philanthropy.

FAB: Well, as we know, the Rockefeller Foundation always supported eugenics.

Dr. Joseph Mercola: Yes.

FAB: And they were working in cahoots with the Nazis. And, Doctor, I know the American people are probably going to find this hard to understand, but I've been studying the Nazis not only in Harvard Law School, but I have a PhD in political science from the Harvard Graduate School of Arts and Sciences, where Harvard produced future professors of political science. I'm afraid what we're seeing here is just this Nazi mentality. It's that simple. You said sociopath, I think it's clearly a Nazi mentality at work here among the highest-level officials of this country. And it's really going to be up to the American people to stop this and bring them down at a state and local basis.

FAB: I think that if we can even get one out of 400 local prosecutors to convene a grand jury and return indictments for murder, and conspiracy to commit murder, this whole house of cards will collapse.

Dr. Joseph Mercola: OK, I've got a question with respect to previous strategies that have been implemented successfully, and the one that comes out as a glaring example would be the process used to essentially decimate the tobacco industry, which—

FAB: Which industry? Oh, tobacco. Yeah.

Dr. Joseph Mercola: Tobacco. So I mean, they were successfully able to lie to the public on a consistent basis, and I can remember and I'm sure you well do, when they had the five CEOs of the major tobacco companies testifying before Congress, and every one of them denied that (a), tobacco was addictive, and then (b), tobacco caused lung cancer. It was just shocking that they would do that. But nevertheless, there was a strategy that was deployed where there was a coalition of a large number of state attorney generals who got together and sued the tobacco companies, and that's what took them down. They literally were able to levy tens of billions of dollars of fines against them and implement warnings that are to this day on every package of cigarettes. So the reason I'm mentioning that—and I'm sure you're more familiar with the legal details than I am—but is this a similar process that you're suggesting?

FAB: Oh, not at all. First, I think, as you know, that took years to bring down tobacco and fine— we also know now today, yes, many state attorney generals are filing lawsuits, which is a good thing, fine. But the problem is, they're filing these lawsuits in federal court, and as I told you—

Dr. Joseph Mercola: Oh, that's the problem.

FAB: The federal judiciary, my experience as a licensed attorney and having appeared in federal court since 1982, it's going to be a long time coming, if ever, before we can stop what's going on here, and especially stop these Frankenshots from—

Dr. Joseph Mercola: OK.

FAB: Their objective is to poison everyone in America with these things.

Dr. Joseph Mercola: This is a very, very important detail that literally escaped me, so I'm sure it escaped most other people, so can you help everyone understand the different processes they're employing. So the regular state attorney generals who are filing these lawsuits, they're filing them in federal courts, and as we—at the beginning of this interview, we both agreed widely or conclusively that that's not going to be effective because they've been captured. They've been captured completely by the industry, so it's got to go outside of the system. So how does the local prosecutor do this? He just files it in his state or his local jurisdiction where they're filing these indictments of the grand juries?

FAB: Even in his or her own county, right.

Dr. Joseph Mercola: Okay.

FAB: That's it.

Dr. Joseph Mercola: All right, so that's outside the federal system.

FAB: And please understand, I'm not criticizing any state attorney generals who are filing these lawsuits, but it's going to take time, and regretfully, Doctor, it will end up that these lawsuits will end up in the United States Supreme Court.

Dr. Joseph Mercola: Mm-hmm [affirmative].

FAB: And given the current constituency of justices up there, I'm afraid they're going to uphold these things, except from the few decisions that have come down, and will permit religious exemptions and medical exemptions. But at the end of the day, I don't see them stopping the Frankenshots, so that is the dilemma. I applaud the state attorney generals who are now filing these lawsuits, that's great. I guess your governor down there in Florida is involved in this.

Dr. Joseph Mercola: Mm-hmm [affirmative].

FAB: But I'm saying, we cannot rely on the federal courts—including the United States Supreme Court, the American people cannot—to pull our chestnuts out of the fire, because I don't think they're going to do it at the end of the day. Look at these articles, these exposés in the *Wall Street Journal* where you found out well over 130 federal judges were unethically ruling on cases where they had investments involved. OK? So I don't really trust the federal judiciary at all to do the right thing here. I don't think the American people should. And you certainly can't trust the current U.S. Supreme Court. As I said, I think they will give a religion exemption and a medical exemption, but all the rest of us will get screwed there at the U.S. Supreme Court.

Dr. Joseph Mercola: OK. Well, thank you for that clarification, because it's really an important distinction. So I have another question with respect to the funding of the SARS-CoV-2 genetically engineered virus that's been inflicted upon the population, the global population. So you make very compelling evidence that the United States has supported research, and indeed they have. I don't think anyone who is rational could refute that, but the other component is a position that I've come to appreciate from interviewing a Chinese MD/PhD virologist, Li-Meng Yan, and she really had some interesting components because she grew up in that system, and she was directly involved with that research. And she actually defected to the United States out of Hong Kong, and they've been trying to, she refers to it, "disappear" her ever since for stating her beliefs.

Dr. Joseph Mercola: But her position is that the Chinese were the primary funders of this, that their intention and their desire was to wipe out the United States, and the collateral damage to the rest of the world is fine, but their primary target was the United States. And it appears that the United States—because the United States contribution to the funding was relatively small to what the Chinese input is—so I'm wondering if you looked deeply into that and offer any opinions on it.

FAB: I've read her paper, yes. And let me say this, clearly China was researching, developing, testing, and stockpiling existentially dangerous biological warfare weapons, and the Wuhan BSL-4 was their first Fort Detrick. And, by the way, the Bat Queen went to our BSL-4 at Galveston, which I've condemned before, to get training on how to run their BSL-4, their own Fort Detrick. So, yes, what happened, Doctor, was this: when the Reagan Administration heavily got into DNA genetically engineering biological warfare weapons, it set off an offensive biological warfare weapons race around the world. I've never worked for the United States government, I've never had a security clearance, I've never had access to classified information. Everything you needed to know was all out there in the public record if you looked at it.

And so what happened here, I believe under President Xi, was that he wanted his own Fort Detrick. He wanted to play with the big boys, so they put large amounts of money into the research, development, and testing of offensive biological warfare weapons, without a doubt, and COVID-19 was one of them. That's correct. Now I, again, Doctor, disagree with this Chinese scientist. So far I have not seen the evidence that China deliberately unleashed this; I still go along with our original discussion. I believe that this was a leak out of Wuhan BSL-4, the Wuhan complex. All of these BSL-4s leak, every one of them.

Dr. Joseph Mercola: Mm-hmm [affirmative].

FAB: Including our own Fort Detrick, and indeed, if you are interested, Doctor, there is a video available online, a documentary by Coen and Nadler called *Anthrax War*, going through the existential dangers of BSL-3s and BSL-4s. I believe this was 2009. I served as a consultant to them on this, it won awards, and I was in there, and I conclude on the last shot in there, saying, "This is a catastrophe waiting to happen." OK? The BSL-3s and the BSL-4s are what I was referring to, that they were all involved in the research, development, and testing of biological warfare weapons. Well, it happened in China. What can I say? So I still have not seen the evidence that China deliberately unleashed this.

Dr. Joseph Mercola: Well—

FAB: But I'm keeping my mind open, but I haven't seen it, so right now, I'm dealing with the theory that, yes, they were involved. And this was—

Dr. Joseph Mercola: The crux of the question wasn't so much if they intentionally released it, that's sort of not relevant to the central issue, which was the primary funder of the research.

FAB: That's correct.

Dr. Joseph Mercola: Her contention was that the Chinese—that China contributed far more than the United States did because it was their intention. Now in my interview, I don't recall really discussing the intentional release versus an accidental lab leak.

FAB: Well, I did read her paper on this, and that's the only part I disagree with.

Dr. Joseph Mercola: OK, 100% of it, but she seemed really sincere with very limited reason to—

FAB: I accepted the rest of her argument, yes.

Dr. Joseph Mercola: Yeah. All right, so that's interesting, then. So from your perspective and hers, China really had this designed. It wasn't like the U.S. came in there and said, "Let's design this." They were already going for it, and they just participated in this research.

FAB: They did.

Dr. Joseph Mercola: Yeah.

FAB: As a matter of fact, the Bat Queen took this synthetic biological warfare agent with synthetic biology over to the UNC BSL-3 to give it gain-of-function property, so you're right. But of course, Doctor, we do the exact same thing here at Fort Detrick.

Dr. Joseph Mercola: Yeah. Yeah.

FAB: The Chinese, and the British do it at Porton Down, and the Israelis do it, and the French do it, and the Germans do it. The major military powers are all heavily into developing an offensive biological warfare weapons industry. If you read what has happened here in the United States, it's very similar to what we had before the Biological Weapons Convention. Seymour Martin Hersh had a book around 1968 exposing everyone involved in the U.S. biological warfare weapons industry at that time when technically it was not illegal. That industry has been reestablished here in the United States—the British have it, the French have it, the Germans have it, the Israelis have it. The Israelis are not a party of the Biological Weapons Convention, and China has followed in lockstep with it, sure.

Dr. Joseph Mercola: OK, so let's get back to your central thesis and argument, which is your proposal to catalyze a movement to convince a number of the local elected attorney generals and district attorneys to file or make a motion for a grand jury to indict these criminals for the millions of people they killed or will kill. So in my view, it seems best not to do that by yourself, but to find a few friends in your local community, because they can understand that there's a number of people in their community who are interested in this, and they'll not just dismiss you as a local crackpot, especially if they're somebody who's bought the media propaganda on this topic.

So once you find a few people in your area and identify the attorney who is going to be responsible for doing this filing, what process or strategy would you recommend or endorse? How do they even go about finding the responsible individual, because I guess there are several levels—you can do it at the local, the county, and if there's a level above that, the state of course to identify these individuals? And how would they go about beginning the communication and putting together a formal proposal or plan of action?

FAB: Sure. They're on your ballots when you vote. All you have to do is look at who's running for—

Dr. Joseph Mercola: We don't keep our ballots, right? We look at them briefly and forget about them.

FAB: Right, but you can just call that up on the internet.

Dr. Joseph Mercola: OK.

FAB: The old ballot, the recent ballot, who you were voting for, that's the beauty of this that you elected these people, and they are accountable to you, and you pay their salaries, and you can dis-elect them if they don't do what you want them to do. So you need a core of people in that community to go in and personally—emails don't do it, between you and me, I'm a lawyer, I pay attention to emails—but anything serious I expect to talk face-to-face, person to person. So you set up a meeting, you go in, you talk to this person, you can bring in the book, you can bring in my lecture that I sent you, you can bring in this video, and say, "We want you to convene a grand jury and present this evidence."

And, of course, it will be for the grand jury to decide whether or not to return an indictment for murder, and conspiracy to commit murder, against anyone. Fine. If the grand jury doesn't return an indictment, well, they don't. But the old saying goes that a prosecutor can get a grand jury to indict a ham sandwich if the prosecutor wants to. So I think the prosecutor then at that point will say, "OK, I'll look into this," they've got a staff, they can get together the evidence, and convene the grand jury. Indeed, if you are interested, Doctor, I'm a political independent. I have been for my entire career because I figured that's the only way I could do this work. The House Minority Intelligence Committee recently produced a report on this, and I read through this report, and they have everything in there on the origins of COVID-19, so that is another source.

Now, maybe a Democratic prosecutor will reject that, but there are a lot of Republican prosecutors around the country who I think would pay attention to this latest House Minority Intelligence Report on the origins of COVID-19, and they have a staff and go out there and dig up the evidence that is clearly out there in the public record, sure. And we'll now have Bobby Kennedy Jr.'s book as well.

Dr. Joseph Mercola: Yeah, you bring up a good point, because while this clearly is not a partisan issue, it would seem that the likelihood of success is far higher for those who are—if the attorney they're seeking to convince is a

Republican versus a Democrat, or more generically someone who's bought the propaganda, but the percentages of people who bought the propaganda are much higher in the Democratic party than the Republican. I mean, it's very clear. So if you're just going by odds, it seems like you're more likely to be successful in a red district than a blue.

FAB: I think you're right on that, yes.

Dr. Joseph Mercola: Yeah, so—

FAB: I mean, our local district attorney here, she's a Democrat, so I don't think she'd really be doing—

Dr. Joseph Mercola: Yeah, well you're in a strong blue community with Illinois.

FAB: Well, I regret to say, our Governor Pritzker, he's gone full Nazi here.

Dr. Joseph Mercola: Yeah. And the Chicago mayor is probably even worse.

FAB: Frankenshots. Right, but you now have—just read the *New York Times* and *Wall Street Journal*, there's an Associated Press report this morning where I read about all the attorney generals of the states now filing lawsuits in federal court against this. Well, I'm saying fine, those are states that you should also go to your local prosecutors. I don't really see it happening here in my district.

Dr. Joseph Mercola: Well, let me just walk this back a step, because I think it may be effective because you've already got a number of states—I don't know the exact number, but I believe it's more than 20, if not it's very close to 20—that have filed these lawsuits in a federal court. Wouldn't it make sense to parallel process and multitask and also file it in their own jurisdiction outside of the federal bureaucracy?

FAB: Doctor, that could be done too, but I think if you're going to do something at a state and local basis, it should be to go for the indictments for murder, and conspiracy to commit murder.

Dr. Joseph Mercola: Yeah, I agree, but—

FAB: That will really get everyone's attention.

Dr. Joseph Mercola: Wouldn't it make more sense to hit the state attorney generals who are already convinced to also apply this strategy and do it locally with the understanding that it's highly likely they're going to be roadblocked by the federal system?

FAB: Well, the problem here is that the OSHA [Occupational Safety and Health Administration] regulations that Biden just put out, they're taking the position that federal law will supersede state law in this whole area, and that is a problem you have under the Sixth Amendment to the Constitution, suing—

Dr. Joseph Mercola: Well, that's for the mandates, but it doesn't apply to the grand jury indictments for murder.

FAB: No, of course not. So that's what I'm saying at the state and local level, I think the best thing—

Dr. Joseph Mercola: Yeah, I agree. But that's what I'm saying, that the attorney generals who are filing these lawsuits in the federal judiciary, in the federal law system, shouldn't they concurrently file in their own state these indictments or the—

FAB: They should pursue. You don't—

Dr. Joseph Mercola: Yeah, that would be a no-brainer, because they're already on board.

FAB: —file indictments. Right. Technically you don't—I misunderstood what you were saying. Technically you don't file indictments; you seek an indictment from a grand jury. Yes.

Dr. Joseph Mercola: Right.

FAB: They should do that, yes. They all should.

Dr. Joseph Mercola: OK. So it would seem to me, if you're in one of those lucky states where the state attorney general has filed the lawsuit for the mandate, then that attorney general is ripe for harvesting and to convince him to call a grand jury to indict these criminals for murder.

FAB: That's right, but I don't live in one of those states, unfortunately.

Dr. Joseph Mercola: Yeah, but a lot of our viewers do.

FAB: They do, and that would be my advice, yes.

Dr. Joseph Mercola: That could be a ticket, because you've already got 20 high-level state attorneys or maybe more, I just don't know the number, I can't recall, that they're on board with this. But these are the guys who would be up for convening a grand jury in their own state.

FAB: That's correct.

Dr. Joseph Mercola: Outside the system. Yes! That is a winning strategy.

FAB: Yes.

Dr. Joseph Mercola: All right, I'm glad we solved this problem.

FAB: Well, we've started to solve it. What can I say?

Dr. Joseph Mercola: Yeah, I know, but it's just—

FAB: But I think—

Dr. Joseph Mercola: —you've got to work out the details because the implementation is so important, and if you have someone in a strongly Democratic jurisdiction and they're trying to get their local county district attorney to file something, it ain't going to happen.

FAB: Right. I don't think so.

Dr. Joseph Mercola: So you've got to be—you've got to limit, everyone has limited resources, time being the most significant, but you've got essentially an opportunity, it's a massive opportunity, and we'll identify the specific states when we write this article so it'll be in there.

FAB: Right.

Dr. Joseph Mercola: And give people and encourage people in those states to catalyze this process, because I think it's really important.

FAB: Right. That's why I'm appearing here today with you, I guess for the past hour, to articulate this in language that common, ordinary, everyday Americans can understand. I've tried to stay out of a lot of legalese or anything like that. And I have had to use a few legal terms, but I think it all could be understood.

Dr. Joseph Mercola: I'm suspicious that you would be open and willing to serve as a consultant to those who are willing, or not willing, but are successful in engaging with the state attorney generals to file or to issue these calls for convening the grand juries if they need it.

FAB: Right, I've been asked for help on this matter ever since I first blew the whistle on January 24, 2020, that COVID-19 was an offensive biological warfare weapon leaked out of that Wuhan BSL-4. And all BSL-3s and BSL-4s around the world need to be immediately shut down. You'll see, Doctor, they're already talking about the next pandemic, right?

Dr. Joseph Mercola: I'm sure.

FAB: Where's the next pandemic going to come from? Their own BSL-3s, and their BSL-4s, and their offensive biological warfare programs that have been in operation under Fauci and Reagan. That's how far back, that's where the next pandemic is coming from, and we have to shut down all these BSL-3s and BSL-4s immediately. Yes.

Dr. Joseph Mercola: Yeah, that is a big step. We've got some other bigger ones, I think, before then, though, like stopping the killing of the majority of the United States population.

FAB: I agree with you on that too.

Dr. Joseph Mercola: Yeah, because it's like a one-two punch. I mean, we're going to be—even if it doesn't kill you, it's permanently impairing your immune response, making you far more susceptible to future exposures to these pernicious lab-engineered viruses. So they're weakening your system.

FAB: As I told you on the Gulf War Frankenshots, one-fifth disability, and they were far less dangerous than what we're dealing with here. That's correct.

Dr. Joseph Mercola: Yeah. Well, so it's—I think it's encouraging. There is a reasonable, rational strategy that I don't think would require a lot of time and effort, certainly some to go forward and meet with these—I mean, you provided the outline for it, but really another important component is to meet with these attorneys in person.

FAB: Right.

Dr. Joseph Mercola: This is not an email campaign, folks.

FAB: No.

Dr. Joseph Mercola: You need to connect with them personally and hopefully identify individuals in your local community who are very eloquent, articulate, and knowledgeable about the facts, because otherwise they're going to dismiss you easily, even though you're right.

FAB: Right.

Dr. Joseph Mercola: So you need to have an eloquent communicator on your team—

FAB: Right.

Dr. Joseph Mercola: —who can engage in the dialogue. So I think this is a reasonably good strategy, and I thank you for coming up with it. But it takes guys like you to figure this thing out.

FAB: Well, thank you very much for having me on. My best to your audience here.

Dr. Joseph Mercola: OK. Any other words of wisdom you'd like to share with us?

FAB: Well, I think I've given everything I can, except we have to act immediately, as soon as possible, to stop this Nazi insanity that is being imposed on the American people by the Biden administration.

Dr. Joseph Mercola: Yeah.

FAB: And they know what they're doing there. Biden's chief of staff, Ron Klain, was behind me at Harvard Law School and he was President Obama's Ebola Czar; and Obama, too, was behind me at Harvard Law School. All right, and Klain personally handled the cover-up of the fact that the Black West African Ebola pandemic started out by the testing of experimental Ebola vaccines in violation of the Nuremberg Code of Medical Experimentation that came out of the United States government's own BSL-4 at Kenema, Sierra Leone. And Klain covered all that up for Obama, and he is now Biden's chief of staff, so that is a very dangerous situation. This guy knows exactly what he is doing; he has done it before.

Dr. Joseph Mercola: Yes, indeed. Challenging times for sure, but they present an opportunity for individuals to really come up into the forefront and make a dent. There's plenty of opportunity up there.

FAB: Right.

Dr. Joseph Mercola: So thank you for helping provide a rational practical strategy that seems to have great potential for making a dent in the craziness that we're going through.

FAB: Well, thanks, and please keep up your good work, especially now having me on three times to try to explain to the American people what is really going on here.

Dr. Joseph Mercola: Well, you did successfully the first time. This is one of the first major interviews that got out there exposing the fraud. I mean, literally it was one of the first. I know you had been on other shows before, but we have a bigger reach. I mean, we go to like 30 million people a month, so that's a pretty significant penetration.

FAB: Right.

Dr. Joseph Mercola: So a lot of people are going to hear this message, I can assure you.

FAB: Good.

Dr. Joseph Mercola: All right. Well, thanks for all your efforts.

FAB: All right, thank you, Doctor, you keep up the good work too.

Dr. Joseph Mercola: All right, thanks.

FAB: Bye-bye.

Following this interview, Boyle gave several others in which he pointed out that the "Frankenshot" mandates are a Nuremberg Crime against Humanity.

He told me, "Now, with the booster campaign, I can only conclude that we are seeing Frankenshot genocide against the American people." The Polish lawyer Raphael Lemkin is known for having coined the term *genocide*, which refers not only to the physical killing of a people but also includes the slow, intentional destruction of a nation or ethnic group.

As explained by Lemkin: "Generally speaking, genocide does not necessarily mean the immediate destruction of a nation, except when accomplished by mass killings of all members of a nation.

"It is intended rather to signify a coordinated plan of different actions aiming at the destruction of essential foundations of the life of national groups, with the aim of annihilating the groups themselves.

"The objectives of such a plan would be the disintegration of the political and social institutions, of culture, language, national feelings, religion, and the economic existence of national groups; and the destruction of the personal security, liberty, health, dignity, and even the lives of the individuals belonging to such groups.

"Genocide is directed against the national group as an entity, and the actions involved are directed against individuals, not in their individual capacity, but as members of the national group."

CONCLUSION

As this book goes to print, all humanity is facing the existential crises presented by the worldwide COVID-19 pandemic and its related Nazi COVID-19 Frankenshots. Today, the human race is now fighting World War III against the offensive biological warfare weapon known as COVID-19 and its related Nazi COVID-19 Frankenshots. At this preliminary stage of World War III, I cannot predict what the consequences will be for all humanity. But as of now, they are shaping up to be existentially catastrophic.

We human beings are in the fight of our lives against the worldwide COVID-19 pandemic and its related Nazi COVID-19 Frankenshots. COVID-19 and its related Nazi COVID-19 Frankenshots could very well prove to be an exterminationist event for the human race, even worse than the so-called Spanish flu virus pandemic of 1918. If both are not stopped immediately and effectively, the human toll could very well rival the Black Death Bubonic Plague pandemic of the late Middle Ages.

In the meantime, while we are fighting this World War III against the worldwide COVID-19 pandemic and its related Nazi COVID-19 Frankenshots, the rules of domestic and international law as well as the principles of international human-rights law will provide us with basic guidance and direction about how to conduct this battle. I cannot at this time anticipate all the circumstances that will arise during this mortal struggle for the future of humanity. However, our foremost lodestars of domestic laws and international laws as well as principles of international human-rights law for dealing with all the problems, crises, and dilemmas that will confront us against the worldwide COVID-19 pandemic and its related Nazi COVID Frankenshots are the United States Constitution and especially its Bill of Rights; the domestic constitutions and bills of rights of all states around the world; the United Nations Charter; the Biological Weapons Convention of 1972 and its U.S. domestic implementing legislation, my Biological Weapons Anti-Terrorism Act of

1989, as well as the domestic implementing legislations for the BWC in other states around the world; the Nuremberg Code on Medical Experimentation; the Nuremberg Charter of 1945, the Nuremberg Judgment of 1946 and the Nuremberg Principles of 1950; the Rome Statute for the International Criminal Court and its required domestic implementing legislation for the contracting parties thereto; the International Covenant on Civil and Political Rights; the International Covenant on Economic, Social, and Cultural Rights; the International Convention on the Elimination of All Forms of Racial Discrimination; the International Convention on the Elimination of All Forms of Discrimination Against Women; the International Convention on the Rights of the Child; the 1948 Genocide Convention; and the Universal Declaration of Human Rights, inter alia.

I teach three different and long-standing courses to American law students and foreign lawyers on International Law and International Human Rights Law and The Constitutional Law of U.S. Foreign Affairs. I have written somewhere in the area of about 23 books. There is no point summing up here my scholarly work in these fields since I began teaching these subjects to undergraduates at Harvard in September 1976, and then moving on here to teach law students and foreign lawyers continually starting in August 1978 in order to bring them all to bear upon fighting World War III against the COVID-19 pandemic and its related Nazi COVID-19 Frankenshots. But for these purposes, the one book directly on point is *Protesting Power: War, Resistance, and Law* [Rowman & Littlefield Publishers Inc.: 2008]. I wrote that book expressly for the purpose of explaining how to use international law, international human-rights law, the laws of war, the principles of Anglo-American criminal law, and U.S. constitutional law against criminal policies and practices being pursued by the United States government around the world, and for that matter, by any government in the world.

That is exactly what is going on here all over the world with the COVID-19 pandemic and its related Nazi COVID-19 Frankenshots: Nazi Nuremberg Crimes against Humanity. And the people perpetrating them are modern-day Nazis; 75 years after World War II, the Nazis have won! We have met the enemy, and he is us!

All that you, the reader, needs to do is take the arguments and facts presented in this current book and then plug them into the template and framework of *Protesting Power* in order to develop the arguments and strategies needed to resist against any government's Nazi criminal maladministration of the COVID-19 pandemic and its related Nazi COVID-19 Frankenshots around the world. *Protesting Power* also explains the justification and rationale and strategy for establishing a Worldwide Grassroots Human Rights Civil Resistance Campaign against the COVID-19 pandemic and its related Nazi COVID-19 Frankenshots. It has already begun!

It is We the People of the world who are going to have to stop the COVID-19 pandemic and its related Nazi COVID-19 Frankenshots. Nobody else is going to pull our chestnuts out of this Nazi COVID-19 fire for us. Government officials around the world are operating in accordance with the principle of "herd immunity," which is, in reality, a euphemism for the Nazi philosophy of "useless eaters," which was soundly condemned by the Nuremberg Judgment in 1946. The world's Scientific Establishments have been bought off, corrupted, and perverted into this Nazi philosophy, and practices of useless eaters by the lure of filthy lucre.

The world's Medical Establishments have been bought off, corrupted, and perverted into this Nazi philosophy and practices of useless eaters by Big Pharma, which is literally making a "killing" from the sale of their Nazi COVID Frankenshots at the expense of our lives and our bodily integrity. The proof of these propositions is that they are all purveying, advocating, promoting, and enforcing Nazis COVID-19 Frankenshots in gross violation of the well-known and well-established Nuremberg Code on Medical Experimentation that was used by the United States, Britain, France, and the Soviet Union to prosecute and convict Nazi doctors at Nuremberg. Q.E.D.

Civil resistance by the peoples of the world against these modern-day Nazis and their Nazi COVID-19 Frankenshots is critical for preserving the future of our shared humanity. Every person around the world possesses the basic human right to terminate these internationally criminal Nazi COVID-19 policies and practices by their respective government officials, Scientific Establishments, Medical Establishments, and Big Pharma companies, because of their specter of inflicting biological extinction for the human race. Thus, all human beings possess the basic right under international law to engage in civil-resistance activities for the purpose of preventing, impeding, thwarting, or terminating the ongoing commission of these Nazi COVID-19 Crimes against Humanity by these modern-day Nazis. Every citizen of the world community has both the right and the duty to oppose these modern-day Nazis and their Nazi COVID-19 crimes against humanity by whatever nonviolent means are at his or her and your and our disposal. The time for preventive action is now! Civil resistance is the way to go!

Toward that end, this book has been written. Good luck!

FAB
January 24, 2022
COVID Year 3

ACKNOWLEDGMENT

The dedication at the beginning of the book is in memory of my friend Dick Lewontin. There are many funny Dick Lewontin stories I could tell, but this one stands out. Shortly after Dick had moved from the University of Chicago to Harvard in 1973, I sent him a letter suggesting that we get together for lunch and dropped it into the Campus Mail addressed to his new lab at the Museum of Comparative Zoology (MCZ). These digs were a lot fancier than those he had at the University of Chicago, where he was the Block Professor of Biology and the number-one-rated population biologist in the world, as ranked by his academic peers, with the number-one-rated Population Biology Department in the world, also as ranked by his academic peers.

About two weeks went by and I hadn't heard back from Dick, so I called him up at his MCZ lab and asked him if he'd gotten my letter. He asked me how I'd sent the letter, and I told him that I'd sent it through the campus mail service. Dick told me that he doesn't read campus mail, saying that if a sender wasn't willing to pay for a postage stamp on an envelope, it wasn't worth reading. Only Dick Lewontin could afford to throw out his campus mail unopened! The rest of us mortal professors at least have to open our campus mail and then glance through it before throwing it out. And the same with campus emails.

While I was a junior at the University of Chicago in the fall of 1970, I asked Dick if he would write me a letter of recommendation so I could apply to law school. He told me that this was the first time a student had asked him to write such a letter of recommendation. He also told me that he would have liked for me to continue working with him. I told him that Nixon had just invaded Cambodia, and I had to do something about it. Hence, law school.

Dick certainly understood, and he wrote the letter of recommendation. I got admitted to Harvard Law School about six weeks later, during the first week of February 1971—13 months after I'd first started studying Population Biology with Dick. I was 20.

And so, this book.

R.I.P., Dick

—FAB

ABOUT THE AUTHOR

Francis A. Boyle is a professor of law at the University of Illinois College of Law, and also a professor in the Unit for Criticism and Interpretive Theory in the College of Liberal Arts and Sciences at the University of Illinois at Urbana-Champaign. He was the Parhad Lecturer at the Faculty of Medicine for the University of Calgary in Canada in 2001, and was the Bertrand Russell Peace Lecturer at McMaster University in Canada in 2007.

He drafted the U.S. domestic implementing legislation for the Biological Weapons Convention of 1972, known as the Biological Weapons Anti-Terrorism Act of 1989, which was passed unanimously by both Houses of the U.S. Congress and signed into law by President George Bush Sr. with the approval of the U.S. Department of Justice.

Dr. Boyle served on the Board of Directors of Amnesty International USA from 1988 to 1992. He served as legal adviser to Chairman Yasser Arafat and the Palestine Liberation Organization on the Palestinian Declaration of Independence of November 15, 1988, and its creation of the State of Palestine, which is now a United Nations Observer State. From 1991 to 1993, he served as legal adviser to the Palestinian Delegation to the Middle East Peace Negotiations and its chair, Dr. Haidar Abdul Shaffi, who instructed him to draft the Palestinian counteroffer to the now-defunct Oslo Agreement.

In 1993, he represented the Republic of Bosnia and Herzegovina before the International Court of Justice, where he won two World Court Orders overwhelmingly in favor of Bosnia against Yugoslavia to cease and desist from committing all acts of genocide in violation of the 1948 Genocide Convention. He also represented the Republic of Bosnia and Herzegovina at the Owen-Stoltenberg Negotiations in Geneva in 1993, where he prevented Bosnia's destruction as a state, saved Bosnia's membership in the United Nations Organization, and stopped the ethnic cleansing of 1.5 to 2 million *more* Bosnians. He was Attorney of Record for the Mothers of Srebrenica and Podrina before the International

Criminal Tribunal for the Former Yugoslavia and secured the indictment of Yugoslav president Slobodan Milosevic for almost every crime in the ICTY statute, including two counts of genocide: one for Srebrenica and the second for Bosnia in general. He started the Divestment/Disinvestment Campaign against Israel in 2000, and at the request of Palestinian Civil Society, joined with them in 2005 to form the Palestinian Boycott, *Divestment*, and Sanctions (BDS) campaign. He is D in the Palestinian BDS campaign.

Francis A. Boyle (far left) on the floor of the International Court of Justice on April 1, 1993, squaring off against his adversary Shabtai Rosenne from Israel (far right) representing Yugoslavia, just before he argued and then won the first of his two World Court Orders overwhelmingly in favor of the Republic of Bosnia and Herzegovina against Yugoslavia to cease and desist from committing all acts of genocide in violation of the 1948 Genocide Convention on April 8, 1993, and then again on September 13, 1993. This was the first time that any government or lawyer had ever won two such Orders in one case since the World Court was founded in 1921. On August 5, 1993, he also won an Article 74(4) Order from the World Court to the same effect. Under Article 74(4) of the Statute of the International Court of Justice, when the Full Court is not in Session, the President of the Court exercises the Full Powers of the Court and can issue an Order that is binding upon the states' parties in a case.

CPSIA information can be obtained
at www.ICGtesting.com
Printed in the USA
LVHW081942100822
725649LV00001B/37

9 781957 807126